Tim Wallace-Murphy was bor studied medicine at University College, Dublin. His first book, *The Mark of the Beast* (Sphere, 1990), was written in collaboration with Trevor Ravenscroft. He is the author of *An Illustrated Guidebook to Rosslyn Chapel* (1993) and *The Templar Legacy and the Masonic Inheritance Within Rosslyn Chapel* (1994), both published by The Friends of Rosslyn. A popular and fluent speaker, he lectures on the Knights Templar, Rosslyn Chapel and the Sinclairs (founders of Rosslyn).

Marilyn Hopkins was born in Totnes, England. Gifted with a natural dowsing ability, she has a deep interest in complementary medicine. She spent ten years studying various forms of Christianity and esoteric spirituality. She has contributed to seminars, talks and lectures including the recent Ecological seminar at Rosslyn organized by the Scottish Ecological Design Association.

also by Tim Wallace-Murphy

The Mark of the Beast (with Trevor Ravenscroft)

An Illustrated Guidebook to Rosslyn Chapel

*The Templar Legacy and the Masonic
Inheritance Within Rosslyn Chapel*

ROSSLYN

*Guardian of the Secrets
of the Holy Grail*

**Tim Wallace-Murphy
and
Marilyn Hopkins**

ELEMENT

Shaftesbury, Dorset • Boston, Massachusetts • Melbourne, Victoria

© Element Books Limited 2000
Text © Tim Wallace-Murphy and Marilyn Hopkins 2000

First published in Hardback in 1999 by
Element Books Limited

This edition first published in the UK in 2000 by
Element Books Limited
Shaftesbury, Dorset SP7 8BP

Published in the USA in 2000 by
Element Books, Inc.
160 North Washington Street
Boston, MA 02114

Published in Australia in 2000 by
Element Books and distributed
by Penguin Australia Limited
487 Maroondah Highway, Ringwood,
Victoria 3134

Tim Wallace-Murphy and Marilyn Hopkins
have asserted their rights under the
Copyright, Designs and Patents Act, 1988
to be identified as the authors of this work.

All rights reserved.
No part of this book may be reproduced or utilized
in any form or by any means, electronic or mechanical,
without prior permission in writing from the Publisher.

Cover photograph © Scotland in Focus/M. Moar
Cover design by Mark Slader
Illustrated by Countryside Illustrations
Design by Pete Welford
Typeset by WestKey Limited, Falmouth, Cornwall
Printed and bound in Great Britain by
Creative Print and Design Wales, Ebbw Vale

British Library Cataloguing in Publication
data available

Library of Congress Cataloging in Publication
data available

ISBN 1 86204 742 1

CONTENTS

Acknowledgements   ix

INTRODUCTION The Genesis of the Project   xi

PART I The Mystical Chapel of Rosslyn   1
1 First Impressions   5
2 Our Investigations Begin   20

PART II The Development of the Western Esoteric Tradition   27
3 The Spirit of the Place   31
4 The Sophisticated Celts   39
5 Gnosticism and Faith   53
6 The Unholy Alliance   71
7 Underground Streams of Spirituality   82
8 The Knights Templar   93
9 The Rise of the Gothic   108

PART III The Pilgrimage of Initiation   123
10 Rosslyn Chapel and Spiritual Fulfilment   127
11 Our Own Pilgrimage   141
12 The Cathedrals of Chartres, Paris and Amiens   159
13 The King of The Holy Grail   180
14 The St Clairs of Roslin   197

Notes   214

Selected Bibliography   229

Index   235

ILLUSTRATIONS

Text Illustrations

1 Plan of Rosslyn Chapel	9
2 Routes to Compostela – 12–14th centuries	129
3 The Seven Oracular Sites of Pilgrimage	134
4 Plan of Santiago de Compostela	146
5 Plan of Notre-Dame de Chartres	161
6 Labyrinth at Notre-Dame de Chartres	167
7 Plan of Notre-Dame de Paris	171
8 Cross-section of Rosslyn Chapel	198

Plate Illustrations

Colour plates

1   The Retro Choir, Rosslyn Chapel
2   The Virgin of the Pillar, Chartres Cathedral
3   Alchymical symbol, Amiens Cathedral
4   The West front of Notre-Dame de Paris
5   Statue of St John the Baptist, Orleans Cathedral
6   Figure of Mercury [Hermes] overlooking the site of
    the temple, Toulouse
7   Statue of St James the Just, Compostela

Black and white plates

8   Ruined Templar church at Balantradoch
9   Engrailed cross of the St Clair family showing the Templar
    cross at the junction, Rosslyn Chapel
10 The Apprentice Pillar, Rosslyn Chapel
11 Green Man carving, Rosslyn Chapel
12 Carving of the head of the 'murdered apprentice', Rosslyn Chapel
13 Central rose, Retro Choir, with Madonna and Child, Rosslyn Chapel
14 Lintel with reference to the Book of Esdas and Zerubabel's temple at
    Jerusalem, Rosslyn Chapel
15 Carving of Ladislaus Leslyn and the future Queen Margaret of
    Scotland carrying the Holy Rood, Rosslyn Chapel

Picture Credits

The authors would like to thank the following for permission to use their illustration: 1 © Antonia Reeve/Rosslyn Chapel; 4 © Carlos Friere/Hutchinson Library. All the other plate illustrations are © Tim Wallace-Murphy.

*This book is dedicated
to the memory of our
good friend and Templar scholar
Michael Bentine,
a truly remarkable man,
whose courage, compassion and humour
sustained all who knew him.
Michael's insight reached far beyond
the boundaries of family or friendship,
when he taught so many to open
'The Door Marked Summer'*

ACKNOWLEDGEMENTS

From inception to completion, this work has undergone many changes. No authors can produce a book of this complexity unaided, and we would, therefore, like to express our gratitude to all those companies and individuals whose ideas, information and assistance made this venture possible.

Firstly we would like to pay tribute to Trevor Ravenscroft, whose insight and thinking pervades our own. We also express our thanks to the late Anthony Tancred whose idea it was to write this work, and also to Michael Bentine, who was such a source of inspiration and encouragement.

We are grateful to Oneworld Publications of Oxford for permission to quote from Evelyn Underhill's book, *Mysticism* and to Shiel Land and Co for permission to quote the well-known lines by Louise M Haskins.

So many people have helped in both the planning and writing of this book that we can only mention those who assisted us during its three-year gestation period: Gerard and Jocelyn Bacquet of Auxi le Chateau; Yves Bacquet of Bargemon; Stuart Beattie and the Rosslyn Chapel Trust; Nicole Dawe of Spreyton; Guy Jordan of Bargemon; Frederic Lionel of Paris; David Nelson of Lorgues; and David Pykitt of Burton on Trent, who has shared the fruits of his research so generously. We also wish to thank Michael Mann of Element Books; John Baldock, his editorial consultant, who has been a constant source of strength; and Florence Hamilton, our editor.

On the basis of keeping the best wine until last, we wish to pay tribute to two very special friends: Pat Sibille, who made this work possible and contributed heavily to the research, and Niven Sinclair, our guide, mentor and spiritual brother.

INTRODUCTION
The Genesis of the Project

The English mystic William Blake claimed that 'Prisons are built with the stones of the Law, brothels with the bricks of Religion'.[1] Karl Marx was even more scathing when he described religion as 'the opium of the masses'.[2] In the name of religion magnificent buildings have been constructed, great works of art executed, and acts of selfless courage carried out on the one hand, and wars, brutality and genocide on the other. The religious and scientific communities of today seem set on a collision course in their efforts to describe the origins of the universe and the future of mankind. How then did I, a typical product of the twentieth-century scientific educational system, become involved in a search for mystical reality that started at Rosslyn Chapel, a little-known ecclesiastical building in Scotland?

Since the early 1970s there has been a worldwide upsurge in interest in esoteric spirituality, sustained by a flood of books such as *The Holy Blood and the Holy Grail*,[3] *The Temple and the Lodge*,[4] *The Sword and the Grail*[5] and *The Hiram Key*.[6] Each of these focuses on one or another of the fascinating enigmas within Rosslyn Chapel.

One well-respected spiritual principle states that 'When the pupil is ready, the Master will appear!' That was certainly true for me, for my interest in Rosslyn arose from my collaboration with Trevor Ravenscroft, author of the controversial work *The Spear of Destiny*. We first met in 1986 when Trevor sought my professional help on his return to England from America, and we soon became close friends. Trevor was a gentle near genius with an unbounded enthusiasm for all matters esoteric. The teacher rapidly became the pupil, and *I* was the one who truly began to learn. Trevor knew how to turn his soul into a mirror, which he used to reflect the warmth of God's love onto all who knew him. He set my feet firmly on the spiritual pathway that I now follow.

In 1988 we completed the sequel to *The Spear of Destiny*, which was published after Trevor's death as *The Mark of the Beast*.[7] One theme in the book was Trevor's intuitive study of the group of magnificent buildings known as 'the apocalyptic configuration in stone': seven sacred sites (*see* page 21), bounded by twin carved pillars at Rosslyn Chapel in Scotland and Cintra in Portugal; a series of magnificent medieval ecclesiastical buildings with Templar connections, all built on sites which were of spiritual significance in Druidic, pre-Christian times. Trevor posed an intriguing question: 'Did the alignment of these specially sited and uniquely constructed cathedrals hide a secret configuration built to represent the Earth as "The Temple of God" as it is described in Revelation?'[8] He also suggested that the alignment had prophetic significance, possibly forecasting a time of cataclysmic change for the Earth.

After Trevor's death in 1989, I felt compelled to continue his research. One place above all others came to represent the physical embodiment of this mysterious spiritual impulse; a small, half-hidden chapel that has exerted a mystical appeal to generations of pilgrims and visitors of every denomination, religion and form of belief for over five centuries. Lying 7 miles south of Edinburgh, Rosslyn Chapel is a temple to the spirituality and mysticism that transcends all of the great religions and yet pervades each one of them. The name Rosslyn recurred again and again as I researched the Knights Templar, the Rosicrucians and the Freemasons; direct references to it were particularly abundant when studying the history of the Templars in Scotland.

My own curiosity about this chapel, which first developed while writing *The Mark of the Beast*, became obsessional. Inseparably entwined with this fascination for a building I had yet to see were two other, related strands of interest: the mysterious history of the Knights Templar, and the intriguing story of the St Clair, or Sinclair, family, whose roots are to be found at Roslin in Scotland, in Norway, and at St Claire-sur-Epte in Normandy, and who played a vital role in Templar history.[9]

The St Clairs, in the person of Henri de St Clair of Roslin, were involved in the first crusade which led, ultimately, to the capture of Jerusalem and the formation of the Knights Templar. Their name also occurs among those visited by the founders of that mysterious order immediately after their return to Europe, when the St Clairs of Roslin granted them the land on which they built their headquarters in Scotland at Ballantrodoch, later renamed Temple.

The Mark of the Beast was published in July 1990 and in late December of that year I was approached by Anthony Tancred, a TV presenter, who suggested making a mini-series based on the part of that work describing the so-called apocalyptic configuration in stone. After some discussion it was agreed that this could form the basis for a vivid and highly pictorial project to submit to independent producers. The theme of the proposed series was that the builders of these great cathedrals had deliberately erected them on Druidic sites dedicated to planetary oracles, in order to draw attention to their ancient mystical significance. This would only be revealed to the initiated when the planetary and prophetic nature of the alignment was fully understood. To grasp the full meaning inherent in this Christian celebration of pagan sacred sites it is necessary to employ not only a knowledge of astrology and astronomy but also the ancient esoteric and heretical principle of 'as above, so below'. According to Trevor, when the planets in the heavens mirrored the alignment of the planetary sites on Earth, this would be an omen of potential world disaster or massive planetary change. A new and expanded book needed to be published as a substantive basis for such a series, as there was insufficient material included *The Mark of the Beast*.

I made various attempts to raise the funding to pursue the project, but met with little success. Some months later, however, the friend who had financed the writing of *The Mark of the Beast* sent me an article from *The Sunday Times* which disclosed the fascination of businessman Niven Sinclair with the history of both Rosslyn Chapel and the St Clair family. Niven and I were soon in contact. When I received a cheque for £500 in payment for a French project, my photographer and good friend Mike Green suggested that we could make a start on the one site that was accessible. With Niven's generous help a visit to Rosslyn Chapel was arranged. And so nearly four years after my interest had first been aroused, we set out on the journey from Totnes in Devon to Rosslyn near Edinburgh. The long search had begun at last.

> Do what you like, destiny has the last word in human affairs.
> There's real tyranny for you.
> According to all the principles of Progress
> destiny should have been abolished long ago.[10]

Destiny had indeed taken a hand in my affairs; it soon became apparent that I was totally and irrevocably committed. I still wished to pursue the wider project suggested by Anthony Tancred, but for the moment at least the ancient chapel at Rosslyn had me under its mystical spell. I had embarked on an enterprise that would lead me along paths that I had not even dared to dream of.

PART I

ᛒᚾᛋ

The Mystical Chapel of Rosslyn

A little over 7 miles from Edinburgh, in a small and otherwise insignificant village, stands a building that is the very antithesis of the worldly achievements of the Scottish people: Rosslyn Chapel, where, according to local tradition, one is nearer to heaven and hell than anywhere else on earth, and which is a temple to mysticism and spirituality. It is a memorial to the heretical order of the Knights Templar, which lies cheek-by-jowl with churches of the very different Calvinistic fundamentalist Protestant tradition. Rosslyn Chapel is an enigmatic, arcane library of secrets, sculpted in stone and shrouded in mystery.

The powerful impact of the chapel on the local populace was celebrated by one native of Roslin who emigrated to the far west of America during the last century. Many years later he returned in what he described as a pilgrimage and recorded his thoughts:

> I stood in breathless rapture gazing at the beauteous building, from the windows of which streamed a rich amber light, for the interior was filled by the glory of the setting sun, and the windows being opposite each other, a magnificent effect was produced by the tinted glass . . .
>
> Think of what has come and gone in the world since this building was erected – of the mighty procession of humanity which has passed from the cradle to the grave – from mystery

to mystery – from God to God – of the wars and revolutions which have taken place in State and Church – of the Kingdoms and Empires that have risen, flourished and fallen – of the progress of civilization – the advance in art, science and literature. While the epochs thus marked have opened and closed, while the silent wheel of history has evolved these mighty events, the Chapel of Roslin has stood unmoved on this height . . .[1]

He was far from alone in expressing his awe. We found the following passage in one early guidebook to Scotland:

It is in some respects the most remarkable piece of architecture in Scotland . . . when looked at from a strictly architectural point of view, the design may be considered faulty in many respects, much of the detail being extremely rude and debased, while as to construction, many of the principles wrought out during the development of Gothic architecture are ignored. But, notwithstanding these faults the profusion of design, so abundantly shown everywhere, and the exuberant fancy of the architect strike the visitor who sees Rosslyn for the first time with an astonishment which no familiarity ever effaces.[2]

Another commentator, from the seventeenth century, also recorded his impressions:

Two Miles Further on we saw Roslen Chapel, a very pretty design, but was never finished, the choir only and a little Vault. The roof is all stone, with good imagery work; there is a better man at exact description of the stories than he at Westminster

Abbey: this story is told us, that the Master builder went abroad to see good patterns, but before his return his apprentice had built one pillar which exceeded all that ever he could do, or had seen, therefore he slew him; and he showed us the head of the apprentice on the wall with a gash in his forehead and his master's head opposite him.[3]

1

First Impressions

Imbued with a deep sense of wonder, I was hardly in a mood conducive to dispassionate analysis when I arrived with photographer Mike Green in Roslin village for the very first time on a damp November night in 1992. We tried to visit the chapel as soon as we arrived, but the building was wrapped in the dusk of evening and hidden behind high walls, with just the tips of turreted buttresses visible, starkly outlined against the night sky. Disappointed, we had to bide our time until the following day.

Roslin Glen

In the early morning light, an hour before our appointment with Judy Fiskin, the curator, Mike and I began to explore the valley of the river Esk, that wends its way beside and below the chapel. We found ourselves standing at the side of a narrow, hawthorn-lined track, silent except for the occasional cry of a wild bird. Rising before us was a steep hillside covered with trees, leafless yet suffused with subtle, pastel shades of colour; woodland that had teemed with deer and other wildlife at the time of the chapel's foundation in 1446, and that had inspired poets such as Burns, Wordsworth, Byron and Sir Walter Scott. Halfway up the hillside, resting on an outcrop and masked by trees and mist were the ruins of Roslin Castle. Gradually the autumn sun cleared the mist, and warmed the sandstone of the ruined keep. There was a slate-roofed house set solidly within the fragmented castle walls.

The St Clairs built their first castle at Roslin in the eleventh century on College Hill, the site of the present chapel, and it was rebuilt on its present site during the time of an earlier Sir William St Clair. Sir William returned from the battle of Roslin Moor in 1302 accompanied by an Englishman captured during the day's engagement. The prisoner, 'a man of no small estimation'[1], was generously entertained and kept in some splendour by the Scottish lord. As an act of gratitude he advised Sir William on the defensive qualities of the land, and suggested that the castle would be better placed on a nearby promontory which was surrounded on three sides by the river Esk. Within a short time the new castle was built on the site it occupies today.

The glistening grey sky, the cry of birds flying overhead, and the almost tangible atmosphere of that magical valley kept us in companionable silence as we surveyed the hillside. Mike spied it first. High above and tucked neatly under the lee of the ridge that separated us from the village lay the chapel. Even at this great distance we could see the flying buttresses and feel the presence of this dark, solid building; short, squat, truncated and unfinished, yet lying naturally on the upper ridge almost as if it grew there. Unobtrusive, yet clearly visible silhouetted in the gleaming morning light, Rosslyn Chapel lay before us for the very first time.

Rosslyn Chapel

The wide, unmetalled and distinctly muddy track that leads towards the chapel gate gives little indication of what lies beyond. Secure and safe behind its walls the chapel is almost completely hidden from the sight of any casual passer-by. Yet despite its private ownership and seclusion it is still what it was intended to be – a place of worship which caters for the spiritual needs of a local congregation.

To our delight Judy Fiskin possessed great knowledge of the chapel and her graphic exposition of its history, interwoven with the fascinating story of the St Clair family proved a godsend. Standing or strolling quietly, looking and listening, questioning or just absorbing the peace and serenity of this mystical place, we both began to appreciate something of the history of the noble family who bear the name of Roslin.

The chapel was founded by Sir William St Clair, third and last St Clair Earl of Orkney, who lived in the middle of the fifteenth century. Not only Earl of Orkney and Lord of Roslin, he also rejoiced in the somewhat odd title of the 'Knight of the Cockle and Golden Fleece'.[2] This indicates his membership of two distinctly different orders, The Order of the Knights of Santiago[3] – represented by the Cockle – and the Order of the Golden Fleece, an exclusive order founded by the Duke of Burgundy. Sir William was also described as 'one of the Illuminati, a nobleman with singular talents' and 'as a man of exceptional talents much given to policy, such as buildings of Castles, Palaces and Churches'.[4] So far as it can be established, Rosslyn was the only church he founded, and that in the later part of his life.

According to Trevor he was the patron of craftmasonry throughout Europe, a Grand Master and an adept of the highest degree.[5] Records later confirmed that Sir William was appointed not only hereditary Grand Master of the Craftmasons but also of all the hard and soft guilds in Scotland,[6] such as the shipwrights, paper makers, tanners and foresters.[7]

The foundations for the large collegiate church, of which the present chapel was to be the choir, were begun in 1446 and took over four years to complete. The chapel itself took considerably longer. Masons from all over Europe were employed in its construction, and Roslin village, which was given its royal charter in 1456 by King James II, was built to house them. Due to the intricate designs used in the carvings, and the manner in which Earl William exercised personal control of the whole operation, the building work proceeded at a slow and measured pace. The four walls and the carved interior were complete and the designs for the roof had been approved when Earl William died, in 1484. He was succeeded by his son Oliver, who finished the roof according to his father's design, but left the building incomplete.

At first sight the chapel appears small, and even somewhat grotesque, with its strangely curved roof flanked by lines of buttresses, each topped by square and conical towers. Even the most inexperienced eye can tell instantly that the building is unfinished and that only the choir has been completed. This stands on thirteen pillars which form an arcade of twelve pointed arches which Trevor believed were built to represent the twelve constellations of the Zodiac.[8] A fourteenth pillar between the penultimate pair at the east end of the chapel form a three-pillared division between the nave and the Lady Chapel which extends for the whole width of the building.

The roof is barrel-vaulted in stone and powdered in diaper work with a profusion of stars, lilies and roses – medieval symbolism which may contain some clues to the real significance of Rosslyn as part of the apocalyptic configuration, as well as to the specific spiritual intent of its founder. Five-pointed stars and roses were the traditional decoration of the temples dedicated to the goddess Ishtar and her resurrecting son, Tammuz, in Babylonia circa 2,500 BC.[9] The stars were also held to signify

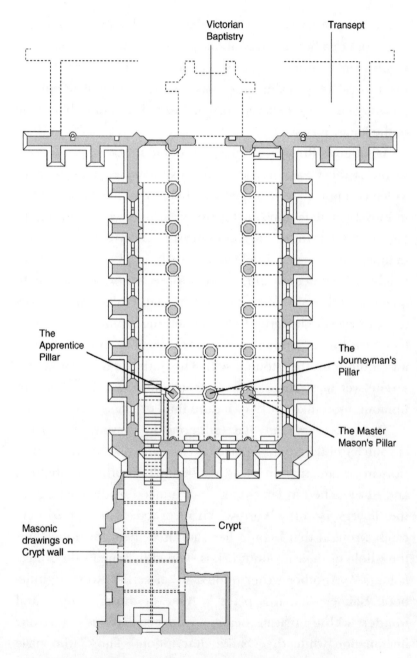

Victorian
Baptistry

Transept

The
Apprentice
Pillar

The
Journeyman's
Pillar

The Master
Mason's Pillar

Masonic
drawings on
Crypt wall

Crypt

Ground plan of Rosslyn Chapel – only the choir was completed.

those of the Milky Way which arched across the whole configuration, bounded by the two symbolic pillars of Boaz and Joachin, in Rosslyn and Cintra respectively. The lilies had been carved above the two pillars guarding the portal of the original temple in Jerusalem and are believed to signify the descending bloodline of the kings of Israel.

What gives Rosslyn Chapel its reputation today as a unique shrine is the variety, candour and exuberance of its carvings which certainly have no equal anywhere else in Britain, and few in Europe. The feelings that arose within me while standing in the chapel had more in common with a spiritual experience than with any formal, intellectual conclusion I could ever have reached. I felt deep within me that there is more to the innate quality of this quiet place of worship than craftsman's competence or even architectural skill. Something infinitely more than mere art, for something spiritual, yet tangible and intelligible, was built into the stone itself. The individual carvings are serene, yet masterly and, apart from the occasional touch of humour, more like works of nature than of man.

Over the years many have admired the carvings. One early chronicler of this strange place had a view similar to my own: 'It riots in ornamentation of an exuberance unprovoked before, and not reached in later days'.[10] Entranced by the carvings of the flowers, Dorothy Wordsworth recorded, 'They are so delicately wrought that I could have admired them for hours, and the whole of their groundwork is stained by time in the softest colours.'[11] Another writer quoted in an earlier Rosslyn guidebook claimed that this place is 'One of those Architectural wonders whose intricate beauties and peculiarities extort our imagination while they baffle description.' Those who have direct experience of the chapel will agree.

The harmony of design to be found here is the result of two simple factors coming together: an inspired plan originated by a remarkable and supremely gifted man who exerted absolute control over design, quality and construction, and a steady rate of build which left no time for contamination of the original conception from outside influences. Trevor's simplistic reverence was more perceptive than even he had thought when he expressed the view that 'The sculptures in Rosslyn are magnificent manifestations of spiritual insight or vision, given substance in stone.' An article published by Douglas Sutherland in 1982 described the chapel thus: 'A medieval masterpiece of masonry, containing some of the most exquisite carvings ever fashioned in stone, Rosslyn Chapel may now be half-forgotten but it is still very memorable.'[12]

Mystery, Myth and Legend

As a source of mystery, myth and legend Rosslyn stands unequalled even in the annals of a Celtic culture justly famous for its wealth of magical and spiritual fantasy. It has been a focus of attention for poets, artists and story-tellers for centuries. It is perhaps because of this that it has until recently failed to attract the attention of serious historians. Records are scanty; few family archives have survived the violent and dramatic history of Roslin Castle in their entirety, and the sculptures themselves have not been studied in depth.

Studied with precision and detachment the building and its contents tell a very different story. The myths and legends themselves can provide a starting point for archival research that reaches far beyond present levels of factual knowledge.

Interpreted with care, and in conjunction with archaeological evidence and expert opinion, myth can play a vital role in stimulating reasoned and proper speculation. The truth that is being revealed by the many investigators adopting a rational approach to the enigmas of Rosslyn are already proving far more intriguing than some of the incredible stories published in the past.[13]

The fascinating and complex character of Earl William St Clair has a strong bearing on any analysis of the meaning of the spiritual and artistic content of the carvings within the chapel. Considered in isolation they remain mysterious and capable of misinterpretation, for they celebrate nearly every spiritual influence that prevailed in the centuries before Rosslyn was built. For example, the carving of the head of Hermes Trismegistus, who is reputed to be the author of the Hermetic texts, the foundation of many ancient Greek schools of initiation. Hermes was identified by the Greeks as a composite figure combining the attributes of the Egyptian deity Thoth, the god of knowledge, with those of the Greek deity Mercury, who was both the god of wisdom and the messenger of the gods.[14] Such an effigy taken on its own could be very misleading, but there are many others, all referring directly or obliquely to the mystery cults of both Christian and pre-Christian times. Within this supposed Christian church are artistic references not only to the religions of Ishtar and Tammuz from Babylonia, but also pagan Norse beliefs, Greek and Egyptian mystery schools and Hebraic mysticism, as well as the gnostic streams from within the Christian tradition, such as the Knights Templar.

Carvings of the Green Man abound. This figure is, of course, well represented in other medieval church buildings such as

Chartres Cathedral, but over a hundred appear in Rosslyn Chapel. Even the Celtic influences one would expect in Scotland seem an inadequate explanation for this massive profusion of what many describe as pagan fertility symbols in a place of Christian worship. Do they constitute a series of coded references to Cybele, Demeter or Gaia, but in Celtic guise? Or is this one of the direct linkages of the Grail impulse with its original Celtic roots in the legendary exploits of Cuchullin?[15] Why is it that so many commentators, mainly from the ranks of Freemasonry and Rosicrucianism, believe that a strong prophetic element is at work here, apparently foretelling the advent of later spiritual brotherhoods, springing from some divinely inspired common root? Are these prophetic carvings simply the accidental by-products of men of pious imagination, or are they deliberate?

We must remember that in the minds of the medieval Craftmasons *Ars sina scienta nihil est* – Art without knowledge is nothing – and, in this context, the knowledge to which they refer is 'gnosis', spiritual knowledge or mystical insight. Even the name Roslin translated into Gaelic hints at this: 'Ancient knowledge handed down through the generations.'[16]

Of all the mysteries and legends that envelop Rosslyn Chapel few can be so well known as that surrounding one of its most puzzling and beautiful artistic gems, the so-called Apprentice Pillar. The legend of the murdered apprentice with its overt references to the initiation rituals of the ancient guild of craftmasons and its parallels to the legend of Hiram Abif[17] has immense, emotional overtones for the worldwide brotherhood of Freemasonry. Close examination of the carving of the apprentice himself discloses that it once had a beard that has been chiselled off; apprentices were not allowed beards in that era. Was this carving and that of the bearded master mason facing him a representation of the heretical concept of the Holy Twins, namely Jesus and his supposed twin brother Thomas Didymus? Trevor discerned an even stranger symbolism in the carving of the head of the murdered apprentice; he believed that this strange tale marked the watershed that separated atavistic, medieval man from our present-day, materialistic, Cartesian level of consciousness. Trevor posed another fascinating question: had Earl William St Clair gained the spiritual ability to look backwards and forwards through time and foresee the dramatic change in human consciousness, when human thinking would gain a new objective: to gain mastery over nature itself?[18]

The legend of the murdered apprentice has been recounted in every guidebook written about the chapel.

> The master mason having received from his patron the model of a pillar of exquisite workmanship and design, hesitated to carry it out until he had been to Rome or some such foreign part, and seen the original. He went abroad, and in his absence, an apprentice, having dreamed the finished pillar, at once set to work and carried out the design as it now stands, a perfect marvel of workmanship. The master mason on his return was so stung with envy that he asked who had dared to do it in his absence. On being told it was his own apprentice, he was so inflamed with rage and passion, that he struck him with his mallet, killed him on the spot, and paid the penalty for his rash and cruel act.[19]

Some apparent credence is given to this bizarre story by the oral tradition that the chapel was re-consecrated just before its completion. Another, somewhat plausible, indication of the possible truth of this tale comes from another source:

> The tradition has come down in almost unaltered form for over two hundred and twenty years. Mr Thompson finds, moreover, that the bishop of St Andrews – whose diocese included Rosslyn – being in Rome at about the time when the chapel was approaching completion, obtained from the Pope a dispensation to 'reconcile Rosslyn' that is, to cleanse it from the pollution of some deed of violence committed within its precincts.[20]

According to the Rev Mr Thompson, a minister who served at Rosslyn, precise details of the circumstances that made it necessary to 'reconcile' Rosslyn are not given, but it seems likely that it may have been the event so faithfully preserved by means of the legend for over 300 years.

Certain questions inevitably arise from this mysterious legend. Did a murder take place? Could it have been what we would now call manslaughter rather than murder, which occurred when a ritual initiation of the newly qualified apprentice went tragically wrong? Did some innocent bystander who had inadvertently witnessed a Masonic rite misunderstand what he saw? Or, perhaps more likely, was the legend deliberately created to hide something deeper and far more important, some great secret hidden within the structure of the chapel? There is another possible explanation. The carvings and the legend surrounding them may simply be a vehicle to act as legitimization of heretical Templar symbolism, such as the grieving Widow. Ever since the days of ancient Egypt, initiates of the mysteries were known as 'the Sons of the Widow'[21]; even today, the internationally recognized cry for help among Freemasons is 'Who will come to the aid of a son of the widow?'

To discover the 'right' answers to these intriguing questions may not be as difficult as it seems. If a violent death had occurred, whether by accident or by design, a trial or an inquest would have taken place and records which verify this may exist. If a dispensation 'to reconcile Rosslyn' were even applied for, some trace of it may be found in the Vatican archives. The third question may lead us to a more mundane explanation, but that can only be deemed valid if the documentary trails are unproductive and the archives for that period are complete. The last is the most intriguing question. Is there some hidden secret within the chapel? Has some enormous deception been perpetrated upon us all? There is some physical evidence in the chapel to support this theory.

The carved head of the murdered apprentice has for centuries looked down not on the pillar of his own creation but, surprisingly, on the subtly designed pillar carved by the allegedly murderous master mason himself. Above that very pillar, looking outward into the main body of the chapel, there is a carving of the master's head, said by some to be contorted in the manner of one recently hung by the neck. Closer examination of the carving through a telescopic lens tells quite a different story: the master is clearly laughing most immoderately.

There is also a coded sign on the wall of the crypt wherein the masons plied their creative craft. Beneath an outline of an arch, sketched on the wall as a design for some part of the construction, is an almost circular mark which is the focus of a strange legend told by Judy Fiskin. When we were discussing the working drawings, she drew my attention to this small and unobtrusive piece of medieval graffiti which, she claimed, was reputed to indicate the presence of some hidden secret. Apparently she had first heard the story from her predecessor, and it had been confirmed several times by visiting Freemasons and Rosicrucians. However, she had no clear idea as to the nature of this 'hidden secret'. She ventured several suggestions that she had heard over the years, ranging from hidden documents and religious artefacts, with a Black Madonna being mentioned most frequently, to the old legend that is inevitably associated with such a place, that of enormous treasure.

Some things are beyond all doubt, however, such as the innate quality of the Apprentice Pillar itself, which surpasses all the other carvings in the chapel. This supremely beautiful pillar represents a transformation of an ancient pagan conception, the Yggdrasil tree of Norse mythology, the world Ash which binds together heaven, earth and hell, into the Christian Tree of Life. The crown of this tree comprises the twelve constellations of the Zodiac; the spiralling branches symbolize the planets, and the roots dig deeply into the elements of the Earth. At the bottom of the pillar the dragons of Neifelheim can be seen gnawing at the roots to rob the tree of its fruitfulness.

Thus we have to add Norse influences to the curious admixture of Celtic, Greek and medieval Christian spiritual references. The dragon is also said to symbolize evil in the mythology of the eastern Mediterranean; good is represented in this context by the orb of the sun, a carving of which lies high above the nave, seemingly hidden among a myriad of stars in the diaper work of the high, stone-vaulted roof.

The parallels between the story of the murder of the apprentice and the rituals of Craftmasonry commemorating the murder of Hiram Abif are so obvious that their deeper meanings are usually overlooked. Was this legend created to enshrine in the public mind a perpetual reverence for the secrets of the craft? Is the Apprentice Pillar an embodiment of the ideal level of knowledge that may be attained at the end of the apprenticeship of a novice of suitable humility, diligence and insight? Time alone will tell.

There is yet another persistent yet unexplained legend about Rosslyn. No one has been able to reason why pilgrims who had made the long and arduous trek to the ancient shrine of St James of Compostela should journey to Rosslyn and there deposit their treasured scallop shells, the only visible evidence of their pilgrimage. In the brief period between the opening of Rosslyn Chapel and the Reformation, so many pilgrims passed this way that the stone steps leading down into the crypt are worn almost beyond belief.

Was there some sacred relic here of which the records are lost, or which were deliberately kept secret for fear of persecution – a Black Madonna perhaps? Was there an apparition, condemned and discredited by the prelates of 'Holy Mother the Church'? Was this a reaffirmation of some pre-Christian cult that occupied the site in earlier times? All these strange and mysterious puzzles are but parts of the larger enigma of Rosslyn Chapel itself.

The situation is made more complex still by the fact that the mysterious and much-maligned Order of the Templars have left their indelible mark within the chapel confines, not once, but many times. Clearly recognizable Templar symbolism abounds, half-hidden except to the initiated. In the vault of each bay in the main chapel and arching across the vault of the crypt are carvings of the engrailed cross of the St Clairs. At the junction of the arms of every cross, subtly but clearly delineated, is the simple, distinctive, splayed cross of the Templars. From the time of the chapel's foundation until the present it has been used, not merely by the St Clairs of Roslin, but also as a meeting place for the leading families in Scotland who were intimately involved with the suppressed Templar Order. This small Scottish chapel is still used for initiatory purposes by members of the worldwide modern Templar Order.

Other sculptures within Rosslyn Chapel refer to the little-known colonization of part of North America by Earl William's grandfather, Prince Henry St Clair, who led an expedition which over-wintered on the north-eastern coast of that continent over 100 years before Columbus supposedly discovered it. There are carvings of aloe and maize, a crop unknown until the discovery of the New World.

In any account of the 'spiritual insight' that runs through the history of the St Clair family, it is important to remember that the founder of Rosslyn Chapel was described as 'one of the Illuminati'. What else are the qualities of 'the enlightened ones' in this context, save those of deep and abiding spiritual knowledge and perception? They were the possessors of the same knowledge that was the true spiritual treasure of the Knights Templar, and which is encoded within the carvings of Rosslyn Chapel.

No wonder Mike and I could identify with the comments of the knight Parzival on Good Friday when he said: 'I have hardly taken a step, yet I feel I have gone far'.

2

Our Investigations Begin

The past is a very strange place; people behaved differently there. Our perception even of recent history is often distorted by our inability to try and understand the thinking patterns and basic attitudes that were taken for granted at another time.

We are all products of the modern scientific age and have great difficulty in accepting, much less understanding, the thinking of those who hold a very different world view to ourselves, even in our own time. When we try and understand the early history of mankind we are inevitably beset by problems which arise from our own consciousness and complex levels of understanding. However, interpreted with care, evidence from an archaeological site can provide us with indications of the truth we are seeking.

In our attempt to understand the cultural influences inherent in all seven of the sacred sites in the configuration, our starting point must be the physical buildings that remain. Our investigation would therefore be founded on the evidence provided by tangible artefacts, starting with the building and carvings of Rosslyn Chapel. We would evaluate these with the aid of insights provided by historical scholars and mystics of far greater wisdom and experience than ourselves, and incorporate our own knowledge and experience moderated by the mythology which enfolds these mysterious places. Wherever possible, personal experience and hands-on contact would be used to test any evidence that would tend to support or deny the underlying concepts linking the structures of the apocalyptic configuration.

Much of the interpretation of the evidence even from medieval times has been made without allowing for the inevitable distortion we introduce by projecting our own subjective consciousness backwards in time onto our own early, and distinctly different, ancestors. If we are to come to terms with the reality of these spiritually inspired structures we need to understand the very beliefs they celebrate. But surely the medieval cathedrals are a celebration of Christian belief, a system which we can study at first hand today? As we were about to learn, nothing could be further from the truth!

The apocalyptic configuration in stone comprises seven Christian buildings erected on the alleged sites of ancient Druidic planetary oracles. These are the chapel at Rosslyn; the cathedrals of Chartres, Amiens, Notre-Dame de Paris and Orléans; the church at Toulouse, and the Cathedral of St James of Compostela.[1] All were, to some extent, the fruits of heretical belief structures that lay hidden beneath the apparently seamless façade of orthodox, medieval Christianity. History, as we have all been taught it, is the record compiled by the victors, not the vanquished. The victors in this case were the Church/State establishment, a very powerful and oppressive regime in the Middle Ages. Those who were foolish enough to disagree openly with the official views of Holy Mother the Church were persecuted out of existence.

However, from the viewpoint of the spiritual historian, the general sweep of history is often described as being guided by 'Schools of Initiation'. Even from the perspective of the more academic historian, there is evidence that reinforces the belief that behind the 'official' view of the historical process lies another, the so-called 'hidden hand' of history which is recorded in the secret traditions handed down over centuries by folklore, poetry, esoteric academies and secret societies such as the Freemasons and Rosicrucians.[2] Cautious acceptance of this is steadily growing. One such esoteric academy, the medieval mystery school at Chartres, was dedicated to the same gnostic beliefs that later inspired Earl William St Clair to create Rosslyn Chapel.

The secrets hidden in the symbolism of the carvings at Rosslyn have fascinated the worldwide brotherhood of Freemasons for centuries, and members come from all over the world to study them in depth. Some Freemasons, such as Robert Lomas and Chris Knight, have written books about them that have enjoyed a very wide circulation.[3] The chapel attracts Rosicrucians, modern-day 'new age' spiritual seekers after truth, anthroposophists and theosophists in their thousands. In the late 1930s several leading members of the Nazi party visited the chapel, for they were obsessed by the legends surrounding the Holy Grail. Rosslyn was not the only site of this nature to interest them: Montségur in the south-west of France exerted the same attraction. The daring commando leader, Otto Skorzeny, led a raiding party that abseiled down the cliffs of this Cathar stronghold, explored the caves and took away several lorry-loads of loot. The precise nature or extent of their finds has never been disclosed.

Some aspects of Rosslyn are far from secret, however, and have been studied and written about. The art and skill of Templar sacred geometry, brought to perfection in the construction of Chartres, can clearly be seen in the construction of the chapel to the extent that it has been commented upon in the proceedings of 'The Society of Antiquaries of Scotland'.[4]

Rosslyn Chapel is almost limitless in the effect of its mystical power. It was here that I began to consolidate the foundation for my spiritual quest. Despite the barriers that had prevented the initial full exploration and investigation of the apocalyptic configuration in stone, frequent visits to Rosslyn provided the means to expand my knowledge and understanding. I spent over three years attempting to discern and understand the esoteric message that lies hidden in its mysterious carvings.

Rosslyn is absurdly and wildly generous to those who come to its spiritual or material aid. It has exerted its beneficial and ecumenical blessing upon a wide variety of people from all cultures and walks of life. Thupton Tushi, the Dalai Lama's archivist, described his visit there as 'a truly spiritual experience'. The Roman Catholic Cardinal Gray, who participated in an ecumenical service held at Rosslyn Chapel, an Episcopalian church, said of that occasion: 'It was the most enjoyable ecumenical service of my life.'[5] Professor Thomas Lin Yun, the leader of the Buddhist Black Tantric sect, claims that Rosslyn is one of the most powerful sites he has ever visited and one that will play an important role in the move towards world peace.[6]

The Team Assembles

Within an hour of our arrival at the chapel the mystery of Rosslyn had Mike well and truly hooked. He believes that every time we seem to find an answer to a small part of the many-layered enigma that is Rosslyn Chapel, we discover at least three more puzzles. Also many coincidences, all beneficial, have occurred since we became involved with Rosslyn, and Mike became rather worried, but I pointed out to him that if the coincidences stopped, then I would stop too. The chapel, as always, played its central catalytic role, for towards the end of the third year of my work at Rosslyn I cemented the relationship with my present life partner and collaborator, Marilyn Hopkins, so that the *I* became *we*.

The third member of our present creative triumvirate came to us as a direct result of a visit he made to Rosslyn. Pat Sibille from Louisiana was already well-versed in esoteric lore when he first visited the chapel, where he happened to purchase a copy of *The Mark of the Beast*. When he had read the book he telephoned me and expressed a keen interest in the section describing the apocalyptic configuration in stone. After exchanging a couple of letters and phone calls, the decision was made to start this work. The three of us would investigate Trevor's theories to the point of destruction, and Marilyn and I would describe precisely what we found or experienced.

We were well aware of the potential difficulties, but as though inspired we knew that they could be overcome. The Christian habit of adopting pre-existing pagan sites to their own use is well known, but Celtic use of the sites of the so-called seven planetary oracles would be virtually impossible to prove directly because of the oral nature of the Druidic tradition. Other pre-Christian use of these sacred sites is, however, a different matter. Thanks to the Roman habit of religious absorption, we knew that we could find hard evidence of the type of worship in vogue before the Roman occupation. The Romans, above all, ruled by logic and continuity. They tended not to impose their gods to the exclusion of native deities, but usually re-dedicated a sacred site to the Latin equivalent of the native god who had been worshipped there since time immemorial.

The visual, artistic and spiritual connection between the various Christian structures upon these particular sites would need to be investigated in depth. The hidden symbolism inherent in much of the artwork within the buildings would need intense study in order to discern the various strands of belief they represented. Despite the seemingly unified and inviolable doctrine of Catholicism that held sway during the Middle Ages, various strange undercurrents of belief exerted a profound, yet secret, influence that was completely contrary to the outward expression of dogmatic Christianity. One such underground current was that of gnostic dualism. Were there any dualistic beliefs linking the Benedictines, Cistercians, Knights Templar and Craftmasons, all of whom were involved, in some way, in our quest? Due to the authoritarian regime of the Church, the heretical nature of gnostic dualism meant that any evidence would be of an esoteric or hidden kind.

To follow Trevor's theory of prophetic alignment, the sites of the Christian buildings representing the planetary oracles would have to be plotted with absolute precision. When the relative positions of the sites had been firmly established we would need to discover if, or when, the planets in the heavens come into a similar spatial relationship. Our results would then be compared to the actual planetary positions using a computer model of star and planetary movements.

We were obviously in for an exciting time. We would have to visit some of the most beautiful buildings in Europe and investigate interesting if somewhat troubled times. This creative era was punctuated by the crusades and haunted by repression, torture and the *auto-da-fé*, yet it produced some of the most inspiring buildings and artwork in the history of Europe. We would study the master craftsmen, masons, glass makers and sculptors on the one hand, and the dreaded Inquisition on the other.

Whatever the result, we knew that the investigation could alter our own spiritual perspectives in such a dramatic manner that it might well cast us across the threshold of the spiritual world into another level of consciousness. Perhaps this journey might even prove to be an essential part of some initiatory process. What was certain was that if we were to fully understand the complex issues before us we needed to look at the origins and development of the Western esoteric tradition which, in many respects, played a major role in the evolving consciousness of Western man.

PART II

―――――――― ⚜ ――――――――

The Development of the Western Esoteric Tradition

The little-known yet powerful Western esoteric tradition is the major influence underpinning many of the significant events that contributed to the development of European culture and civilization. Despite, or perhaps because of, its hidden nature, it exerted a seminal influence on the thinking of the builders of the great cathedrals, on leading teachers in ecclesiastical schools, on philosophers, playwrights and poets such as Shakespeare, Goethe, Blake and W B Yeats, on artists and Renaissance giants such as Leonardo da Vinci and Michelangelo, and indirectly on every generation of European Christendom up to and including today.[1] Nearly all the founding fathers of the Royal Society, when it was inaugurated in 1660, were members of one or another of the hidden streams of spirituality which fed off and contributed to this secretive yet dynamic[2] tradition dedicated to that ancient way of knowing which recognized the indivisibility of the spiritual and temporal worlds.

It has been claimed that this formative, spiritual influence on European culture has its origins in the teachings of Zoroaster.[3] It certainly owes an incalculable debt to the initiatory traditions of Babylonia, ancient Egypt and early Mosaic Judaism. One strand of this tradition came into European consciousness through the Greek Hermetic schools, another through the somewhat confused early history of Christianity. The esoteric tradition has never been a static body of sterile dogma, but has always manifested itself as a vibrant, creative entity. Today it is carried on by students both inside and outside formal institutions.

This development was continuous in Europe from the early years of Christianity and on up to the late medieval era and the early Renaissance, when Christian Hermeticists synthesized a Christianized version of the Jewish Kabbala. This probably derived originally from Syrian–Egyptian gnosis, although in the Middle Ages it was thought to be part of the Law as given to Moses. For this reason it was called tradition, or kabbala. The *Sefer-ha-Zohar* or Book of Splendour expressed its principal aspects, which were mainly Jewish gnosticism tinged with Sufi mysticism, recently synthesized neoplatonism and magic.[4] It was written about 1280 and spread into Christian Europe from the Rabbinical schools in Moorish Spain. It shared with Catharism a belief in the doctrine of reincarnation or rebirth, which is the most common recurring theme in religious traditions worldwide. Life itself offers the opportunity for improvement, and rebirth came to be seen as a fresh chance for the individual soul not merely to make up for previous failures but also to take a conscious and active part in the aim of spiritual self-perfection. The soul itself was deemed to possess free will, and, thereby, could exercise choice in matters of morality.[5] The ultimate purpose of the whole process was the reunification of the divine and human wills.

The roots of the Western esoteric tradition that link it with the ancient civilizations of Babylonia, biblical Israel, Egypt and Greece are widely recognized by many scholars. What is not so often clearly appreciated are the other roots which are to be found in Europe. These started to develop in the period we call prehistory, in the neolithic age. The wandering tribes of the Celtic peoples who came considerably later and colonized most of Western Europe also played an important role in the development of this hidden tradition that is the foundation for much of our culture; evidence of their influence can be seen in some of the carvings in Rosslyn Chapel (*see* page 41).

3

The Spirit of the Place

The Western European landscape is punctuated by many thousands of megalithic structures of great antiquity: stone circles, solar temples, dolmens and long barrows. Ancient stones of varying size point heavenwards in silent testimony to mysterious forms of belief and ritual that predate the art of writing by a thousand years or more. These sacred sites are imbued with a mystical power which, even today, attracts tourists by the thousands. Is it simply the size of the structures that amazes the visitor, or is it something entirely different – something spiritual, perhaps? Is it, as the Romans used to describe it, the *genius loci*, the mysterious spirit of the place itself, which we felt so strongly at Rosslyn Chapel?

This puzzle is complicated further by the vast range of megalithic structures found throughout the world, constructed by people who left no written records. Their compelling allure arises both from the immense size of the stones used, and the mystery as to how and why they were built. Some, such as the long barrows and dolmens, are quite obviously burial places, but the exact function of many of the others is still beyond all understanding. It is obvious from the very difficulties inherent in their construction that their location was deliberate. All the sites so far investigated are situated on sites of telluric power, a form of terrestrial energy that can be located by dowsing.

Telluric Power and Alignment

In the early 1920s came the suggestion that there was a complex network of straight tracks – 'ley lines' – linking a wide variety of ancient sites. Water divining had been practised for centuries, and was accepted as a God-given means of finding water.[1] Now a new use was found for divining, or dowsing – the location of lines of natural Earth energy which connect the sites with amazing precision. These lines of energy, or *chi*, have been recognized by Chinese feng shui experts for millennia, but the ability to detect and use them in the Western world appears to have been lost for many centuries.[2]

Another intriguing puzzle arises from the precise alignment between so many monuments and the planetary bodies and stars. Many neolithic sacred sites are orientated to receive light and energy from heavenly bodies. Stonehenge and Avebury are probably the best-known examples in Britain. In Newgrange in Ireland there is another strange alignment, especially so as this site is clearly a passage grave and not a temple. This structure dates from about 3200 BC, predating both Stonehenge and Avebury and, according to the accepted chronology of ancient Egypt, is several centuries older than the Pyramids of Giza. In 1963 excavations revealed that a roof box immediately over the entrance was deliberately constructed in such a manner that on mid-winter's day the first rays of the morning sun shine down the passageway and fall upon the burial chamber at the far end.[3] This is not unique; Maeshowe, on one of the Orkney islands off the north coast of Scotland, is smaller but has a similar construction to Newgrange, with an almost identical alignment of startling precision which operates on the winter solstice.

How did our 'primitive' and illiterate ancestors know how to do this? They must have possessed a phenomenally high degree of astronomical knowledge. The study of ancient Egyptian buildings of later eras clearly shows that this level of expertise was not an isolated phenomenon and persisted well into the era of civilization.

Perhaps the best-known man-made constructions are those once listed by Philo of Byzantium as the seven wonders of the ancient world: the Colossus of Rhodes; the Lighthouse at Alexandria; the Gardens of Semiramis at Babylon; the statue of Zeus at Olympia; the Temple of Artemis at Ephesus; the Mausoleum at Helicarnasus; and, above all, the Pyramids of Egypt, the only one to survive.

The seven-stepped Pyramid of Zoser at Saqqara is the oldest masonry building in the world. Its designer was a genius of a priest-architect, Imhotep, High Priest of Annu and the astronomer general to the Pharaoh Zoser.[4] The Greeks of the later classical era equated Imhotep to their god of medicine, Asclepius. His wisdom, knowledge, insight, and healing powers were qualities particularly prized and revered in ancient Egypt.

The Pyramid Texts

The Pyramid Texts, the key to the essentially spiritual nature of the levels of skill and technology needed to construct the Pyramid of Zoser, were discovered nearby in pyramids of a later dynasty.[5] They take the form of over 4,000 lines of hymns and formulae, in the form of hieroglyphic inscriptions, incised into the limestone walls, and decorated with a most exquisite gold and turquoise colouring. According to the Egyptologist

Masparo, most of them were first formulated during the prehistoric period in Egypt. Thus the texts and the astrological knowledge they embody predate the writing of the Old Testament by at least two millennia, and the writing of the New Testament by nearly 3,400 years. They are, like most early religious texts, such as the Bible, the written recordings of a much older oral tradition.

The Pyramid Texts are the earliest known collection of sacred knowledge, or esoteric wisdom, yet discovered anywhere in the world. They are the written expression of a secret tradition handed down from master to pupil among Egyptian priestly initiates. The modern translation describes a complex and well-developed stellar cult, one within which the dead pharaoh would ascend heavenwards and be reunited with the stars.

There are repeated references to the 'first time', a mythological era when Egypt was supposedly ruled directly by the gods, especially Thoth who, according to legend, gave the Egyptians the sacred gift of knowledge. Although there is no archaeological or archival evidence to indicate when, or even what, the first time was, many believe it may be a reference to an earlier Babylonian or Sumerian civilization. There are obvious parallels between the Osiris legends and the worship of the Babylonian goddess Ishtar and her resurrecting consort, or son, Tammuz, to support this. Many modern fantasists equate the first time to the lost civilization of Atlantis, or more fancifully to an era when beings from outer space supposedly walked the Earth.

What is certain is that the Pyramid Texts disclose a highly complex and uncannily accurate knowledge of astronomy which, in such an esoteric context, is inseparable from the cosmic ideology that reflects the idea of 'as above, so below'; a concept that is also celebrated in the Hermetic texts of classical Greek gnosticism, and echoed again by the phrase in the Lord's prayer 'In earth as it is in Heaven'. In ancient Egypt, as above, so below carried great force for the stellar cult that held sway when the Pyramid Texts were first inscribed. The physical features of the Egyptian landscape, as viewed from the Nile valley, were seen to match the stars in the heavens. The Pyramids of Giza, for example, were deliberately built to relate, with uncanny accuracy, to the constellation known as the Belt of Orion.[6]

The Power of Myth

Egypt was not the only civilization to possess such esoteric wisdom. Other centres that developed elsewhere and at different times all revered a similar body of knowledge that disclosed the 'divine' origin of the gifts of agriculture that enabled the process of civilization. It may seem bizarre to talk of the divine origin of anything in this modern age, but our main guideline in any reasoned attempt to understand our own early development is the mythology that has been handed down over the ages.

The value placed on myth as an indication of historical truth has undergone a profound change. Interpreted with discretion and used in conjunction with archaeological evidence, mythology can provide the keys to understanding our own origins. Professor Joseph Campbell, who until his death was the world's foremost authority on mythology, claimed that '. . . mythology is the penultimate truth – penultimate because the ultimate cannot be put into words.'[7]

There are many mythologies which tell of the divine origin for agriculture and handicrafts.[8] Professor Campbell has written prolifically about the mythology of the North American Indians and the Polynesian peoples of the Pacific who both claimed, quite clearly, to have received agricultural knowledge as a God-given gift. Although there is no evidence for any cultural contact between these races, there is a unanimity between their myths which is truly startling. This is in harmony with the ancient traditions of all peoples who invariably speak of a divine origin for their practical skills. In Persia the prophet Zoroaster, founder of Zorastrianism, learned the art of agriculture from the sun god, Ahuro Mazda; Osiris, the Egyptian deity who was ruler and judge in the underworld and described as both the brother and consort of Isis, the goddess of fertility, taught the Egyptians the art of growing corn; Dionysos, the Greek god of wine and fertility, travelled the lands to impart the knowledge of the vine; Moses received the Table of the Law from Jehovah on Mount Sinai; Khammurabi, the King of Babylon from 1792–50 BC who collated the laws of his people and the Sumerians, was personally instructed by the god Shamash; the goddess Egaria inspired Numa Pompilius, the second legendary King of Rome, to instigate nearly all the ancient Roman religious institutions and rituals.[9]

In each of the early civilizations an élite corps guarded and interpreted a body of sacred knowledge and magic which was then used to the benefit of the entire community. This body of rulers, priests and kings acted as stewards of the gods. The knowledge that they held was the very foundation of the sacred texts and rituals of the state religion and influenced the way of life of the entire people. This was as true for the civilization of ancient Egypt, as for that of the Chinese, Mesopotamian and

Mayan peoples. In each instance this gnosis had its roots deeply embedded in the mysterious era of the prehistory of the civilization that recorded it. Its early origins and development can only be guessed at, but by the time each civilization had evolved to the point of literacy, the knowledge itself had already developed a complexity that is far beyond our present understanding. The astounding levels of comprehension and knowledge of these early civilizations is baffling, and it was all built upon foundations laid down by our neolithic ancestors. The well-preserved neolithic village at Skara Brae on Orkney clearly demonstrates that neolithic people led domestic lives of considerable sophistication, and left us their only records in the form of ritual sites, aligned with the stars with incredible precision; alignments that modern man can barely accept, much less understand.

The problems of the interpretation of the history of early ancestors are compounded by our own previous reluctance to concede that man himself is an integral part of the evolutionary process, a process which is not simply a biological one, but also one of intellect and consciousness. Also, we must recognize that phenomena are always changing; they are all processes, or parts of processes. Scientific research now clearly demonstrates that the universe as a whole, the planet Earth and our own individual lives are all parts of one gigantic evolutionary continuum. The brilliant and perceptive Jesuit, Pierre Teilhard de Chardin, described in vivid terms the process of the gradual evolution of the mind and of mental properties. This continuous development of intellect and the thinking which derive from it are the twin keys to our understanding of both the past development of human culture and also of what is to come in the future.

The American psychologist, Julian Jaynes, claims that in neolithic times human consciousness was united with the divine to such an extent that early man responded to divine commands that he 'heard' in much the same way as a schizophrenic hears voices. Jaynes developed his theory on the early stages of human development and the origins of this early knowledge by describing the process of the evolution of consciousness as a descent of consciousness from this state of divine union, step by step, to our present level of independent, complex scientific thinking.[10]

Whatever the true origins of this high level of knowledge may have been we, in our arrogance, have the temerity to describe the people who used it as 'primitive'. Our more recent ancestors, the Celts, have been equally misunderstood. Celtic Christianity, in its turn, was a profound influence on the thinking which inspired the creation of Rosslyn Chapel.

4

The Sophisticated Celts

Any student delving into the misty realms of life in pre-Roman Britain faces the difficulty of stripping away the accretions of 'official' opinion that have tainted our thinking for the last 2,000 years. History tends to be taught as a form of distorted mythology used to buttress the complex aims of the Church/State establishment, an account of past events written by the victors in any conflict of ideas, ideology or religious belief. Happily, since the 1960s radical historians have been working to challenge dominant views.

The received account of the Roman invasion of Britain carries an implicit, and sometimes explicit, message that their sole purpose was to bring the benefits of civilization, law and the Pax Romana to a barbaric tribal people riven by constant warfare. Nothing could be further from the truth.[1] The general thrust of our history has derived from Latin sources, either from the Roman Empire or the Roman Catholic Church, with the main objective being to instill the belief that we owed all progress and civilizing influence to Rome.

It comes as something of a revelation to learn that prior to the Roman invasion the Celtic peoples of Britain were among the most highly educated and cultured in the then known world.[2] The fact that their creative abilities were matched by skills in healing and science which surpassed even the standards reached in classical Greece and Rome, is attested to by Strabo[3] and Pomponius Mela.[4] Rome actively sought to learn the highly prized skills, such as enamelling[5] and glass making, that were common among these 'primitive' Celts.[6] The early development of many of Britain's modern roads is wrongly attributed to the

Roman invaders; their origin lies with the Celts, who were renowned for their long straight highways.[7] Julius Caesar commented on the fact that Britain was surprisingly well populated; over fifty cities of considerable size were known to exist prior to the Roman invasion. The large and vibrant rural and urban population was sustained by international trade and a wide variety of local industries, trades and crafts.

The Phoenicians had been trading with Britain for tin for many centuries before the Roman invasion;[8] mining for copper, iron, lead and silver was widespread and profitable; gold was mined in large quantities in Wales and Ireland and was used to supply the highly skilled native craftsmen who were renowned throughout Europe.[9] The Celts were justly famous for their metalworking skills, not only in the manufacture of intricate jewellery, but also in iron, and especially as makers of agricultural machinery and war chariots.[10] Agriculture flourished, producing a large surplus, and many ships were employed to export corn to Western Europe. Britain's pastures were lush and fertile and sheep and cattle grazed in abundance. British wool and cloth were highly prized by the Romans, Greeks and, perhaps surprisingly, by the people of biblical Israel. A recent exhibition at the British Museum displayed finds from the archaeological excavations of Masada, which included evidence of Celtic cloth.

Centuries before the Romans gained a foothold in Britain, Celtic culture had attained a phenomenal degree of complexity and sophistication.[11] The Celts were famous for their tolerance, renowned for their hospitality, and were as skilled in arms as they were in learning. Celtic tribal society had become a highly complex organic entity governed by well-established customs and institutions, all deeply imbued with religious reverence.[12]

The forty Celtic tribes of Britain were bound together by a body of oral law comparable to that of any great civilization that Europe has seen before or since. The Celtic system of jurisprudence, the Brehon Laws, has been deemed by many authorities to be far superior even to the laws of Rome.[13]

The Celtic peoples were characterized by an adventurous, questing nature that had led them to migrate across almost the entire breadth of the known world from the Far East, across Asia Minor and Europe, before settling in Gaul, Spain, Scandinavia, Britain and Germany. A vast array of artifacts and incisions of Ogham script, an ancient Celtic alphabet, have also been found in the north-eastern and Atlantic states of North America, which prove beyond all doubt that there was prolonged contact with the Celts over several centuries, between 800 BC and 100 BC.[14] Ogham script can also be found in Roslin Glen near the chapel, alongside a primitive carving known as the Diva, demonstrating Celtic usage of the site for some religious purpose. What do we know about the origins of the Celts, and what influence did their constant migrations have upon their belief systems and the institutions that gave them their sense of identity?

Celtic and Druidic Origins and Beliefs

It is thought that the Celts migrated across Europe from India or the Middle East, but their exact place of origin is a matter of dispute. Some historians suggest that they emerged from Indo-European migrant tribes, as a racial group, around the middle of the second millennium BC; others that they were recognizably Celtic and reached Western Europe as early as 1300 BC, and that the Druids' educational system can be traced back to at least

1800 BC, when Hu Gadarn Hysicion (Isaacson) led the first wave of Celts from Asia Minor to the British Isles.[15] A number of tribes are known to have occupied Galatia in Asia Minor for several centuries; their descendants were the Galatians, to whom St Paul wrote several epistles. The name of Drunmeton in Galatia, now Anatolia in Turkey, has been translated as 'the sacred grove of the Druids'.[16] Many Celtic tribes settled for some time in the region of Lake Balaton in what is now modern Hungary. They moved out in many directions from this base and finally settled permanently in Britain and Ireland about 400 BC.

Druidism, shamanism and the Brahmanism of the Hindus have all been described as close variants on the same theme.[17] From very early times the Druids were given parity of esteem with these religions originating in such diverse places as India, Persia and Babylon. One classical scholar from the third century AD, Diogenes Laertius, equated the Druids with the Persian cult of the Magi,[18] the group which spawned the three 'wise men' who were said to have attended the birth of Jesus; in later Celtic hagiology they were constantly referred to by this title. What was it that Druidism shared with these other religions?

The first three centres of civilization, Egypt, Sumer and India, arose completely independent of one another. The other two, China and Central America, came much later but followed the same pattern. They all derived their strength and stability from a spiritually inspired, gnostic and theocratic base, where god was regarded as the supreme ruler, and all temporal power lay in the hands of a priestly caste who claimed divine sanction for all their pronouncements. It has been suggested that this caste had deliberately created rituals which enhanced their innate abilities to maintain the earlier links between the human and divine consciousness.

The ancient initiates guided their peoples as priest-kings, mediating between mankind and the gods to the benefit of all. The Egyptian pharaohs are the best-known examples, but there were many others: Melchizedek, Moses, Elijah and Solomon in the Old Testament; Numa Pompilius and Virgil in Rome; Pythagoras, Plato, Socrates and Aristotle in Athens; the Druids amongst the Celts; the respected sages, such as Confucius, or K'ung fu-tzu, among the Chinese; and the witch-doctors and shamans among the tribal peoples.

Novices were selected with care and trained by a hierophant, or teacher, who was himself an initiate. At the end of their novitiate, these spiritually gifted students underwent trials to test their fortitude, motivation and humility. In ancient Egypt the final ceremony was known as the 'three day Temple Sleep', where spiritual knowledge which was held to be beyond mere words was imparted. Sacred knowledge encompassed many subjects; religion, magic, astronomy, astrology, physics, healing, engineering, architecture and mathematics – the list is almost endless.

The beliefs, rituals and practices of the Druids have a great deal in common with those of the early Hebrew prophets and certain esoteric groups in biblical Israel. Some scholars imply not merely common practices, but common racial, religious and esoteric roots. Sir Norman Lockyer, the respected author and historian who worked in the early years of the twentieth century, states: 'I confess I am amazed at the similarities we have come across'.[19] The editor of the 1876 edition of Cory's *Ancient Fragments* observed that: 'We learn from an Assyrian inscription, translated by Surgon, that the correct pronunciation of the most sacred name of God among the Semitic people was Ya'u, or Yahu'; it is the same in Welsh. Another theory links the

Druids with a Near Eastern group known as the Kibeiri of Galatia, who were followers of Melchizedek and, therefore, the precursors of many esoteric groups in biblical Judaism such as the Zadokites, the Therapeutae and the Essenes. In order to prevent disrespect and dishonour to God, a Celtic bard was forbidden to name him except inwardly and in thought. This bears startling resemblance to Jewish custom, where the Tetragrammaton (the unutterable name of God) is never to be spoken aloud.

Posidonius, the classical Greek philosopher who was renowned as 'the most learned man of his time', stated that Abaris the Druid was one of the principal teachers of Pythagoras, the famous philosopher and mathematician who helped to shape the philosophies of Socrates, Plato and Aristotle. It was Robert Graves, the poet and mythologist, who described how Pythagoras, in his turn, influenced the Essenes. Thus Druidic knowledge, which may have derived, in part at least, from the teachings of Melchizedek, flowed back through the teaching of Abaris to Pythagoras and then to the Hebrew esoteric sect on the shores of the Dead Sea.

Scholarship, Healing and Law

All the available evidence stresses that Druidic culture was dedicated to the furtherance of peace, liberty and the rights of the individual. It was not just a religion; it was the source from which radiated the entire system of organized civil and religious knowledge and practice of the Celts.[20] The Druids, all drawn from the Celtic aristocracy, also had a political, judicial and philosophical function. The fact that they acknowledged the superiority of an Arch Druid and attended festivals such as those reported by Caesar at Chartres, shows that they had a national basis that was truly independent of inter-tribal strife.

There is a considerable body of circumstantial evidence testifying to Druidic abilities in water divining and hypnotism. Other indications of their mystical skills are to be found in their reputation as herbalists and healers who also showed surprising skill in surgery. Archaeological evidence of this can be seen in the Brighton Museum in an exhibit known as the Ovingdon skull. This artefact was discovered by chance when it was found in the net of fishermen working off the Sussex coast in January 1935. An inquest was held and evidence was called from medical experts and archaeologists. The skull was dated to the pre-Christian era, to the time of the Celts. The medical report indicated that there were two neat holes trephined into it over the brain which, according to the medical examiners, had been made on two separate occasions. The state of the bones indicates that the patient survived the first operation, but died of sepsis some weeks after the second. This demonstrates an incredibly advanced degree of medical knowledge among the Celts. Similar finds from the same period have been made in France and Ireland. Examination of Egyptian mummies also shows that complex brain surgery was common and survivable. Egyptian healing skills reached standards of subtlety not equalled in Western Europe until the twentieth century.

In ancient Egyptian and Babylonian cultures, medical science and astronomy were traditionally the preserve of initiates of high degree. The Druids' skill as astronomers aroused such awe among the scholars of classical Greece and Rome that it became the subject of much comment by Cicero,[21] Caesar,[22] Diodorus Siculus,[23] the Sicilian writer who was a contemporary of Heroditus, Pliny[24] and Tacitus.[25] Pomponius Mela wrote of the high regard in which the Druids were held, due to their ability to 'speculate by the stars'.[26] They were more than mere priests or astronomers, however; they were also the sacred custodians of their culture, teachers, lawgivers, judges, bards and interpreters of the divine who believed in cosmic justice and balance.

A twenty-year novitiate was necessary to master Druidic knowledge, which was passed down orally from teacher to novice. The range of such sacred knowledge was wide and included the study of natural philosophy, astronomy, mathematics, geometry, medicine, jurisprudence, poetry and oratory.[27] By the time Caesar first came to Britain there were at least forty Druidic centres of higher learning, equivalent to universities, situated at the capitals of the forty tribes of Britain; the students attending these colleges at that time have been estimated at about 60,000.[28]

Sacred knowledge was not the only subject for study; copies of the best Greek and Roman authors circulated widely among the literate aristocracy and were studied at the chief centres of Druidic learning. Cicero listened with profound respect to Divitiacus, a Druid who lived for some time in Rome.[29] He described the Druidic system to Caesar in such a manner that Caesar believed the centre of Druidism to be Britain. A more recent scholar, John Eliot Howard FRS, believes however that Druidism was not purely a British institution, for its resemblance to the other great priestly dynasties of Egypt, Chaldea and Persia was too great to allow the tradition of an independent origin to have much weight.

Thus far from being the uncultured barbarians who desperately needed the gentle civilizing hand of Rome, the

Celts of Britain were a highly cultured, deeply god-fearing, law-abiding and hospitable nation who had much in common with the people from whom Jesus sprang.

The Mosaic Law, which was of supreme importance to the Jews of biblical Israel, was given to Moses on Mount Sinai as the living embodiment of their *Berit* or Covenant with the One True God. In similar manner the Brehon Laws administered by the Druids were of the utmost importance to the Celtic inhabitants of Britain. They included the following:

> There are three tests of civil liberty; equality of rights; equality of taxation; freedom to come and go.
>
> Three things are indispensable to a true union of nations; sameness of laws, rights and language.
>
> There are three things free to all Britons; the forest, the unworked mine, the right of hunting.
>
> There are three property birthrights of every Briton: five British acres of land for a home, the right of suffrage in the enacting of the laws, the male at twenty-one, the female on her marriage.
>
> There are three things which every Briton may legally be compelled to attend; the worship of God, military service, the courts of law . . .
>
> There are three classes which are exempt from bearing arms; bards, judges, graduates in law or religion. These represent God and His peace, and no weapon must ever be found in their hands.
>
> There are three persons who have a right of public maintenance; the old, the babe, the foreigner who cannot speak the British tongue.[30]

Laertius summarized the three main principles promulgated by the Druids as: to abstain from evil, behave valiantly and reverence the deity.[31] Is that so remarkably different from 'Honour the Lord thy God and Love thy neighbour as thyself'?

Sacred Sites, Spirituality and Immortality

Druidic use of pre-existing megalithic sites was widespread and commonly reported in folklore. They used and revered the sacred sites of antiquity, for they recognized that these centres of telluric energy were made more potent by the structures sited upon them. They knew that the megaliths accentuated the natural Earth energies detected on these sites. These telluric forces were known to the Druids as the 'Wouivre'. The Sarsens, or standing stones, at Avebury, for example, have been described as acting like a series of giant resonators, amplifying the telluric forces and vibrating them heavenwards in order to fructify the surrounding terrain.

All known spiritual paths recognize that seven is a magical number, for it is a combination of two other numbers of particular significance: three, representing heaven, and four, representing earth. It is thereby a coded form of mathematical shorthand for the age-old spiritual principle of 'as above, so below'. Ancient initiates knew of the vital importance of the seven chakras, or energy centres, in the human body. Knowledge and insight into their working was an essential part of the mystery wisdom of the Druid, who knew that the awakening of the chakras was an essential first step on the long road to spiritual enlightenment. The Druids knew that similar chakras existed in the body of the Earth itself,[32] and so they founded the seven oracles on these powerful points, which were often grottoes amongst the sacred groves of oak, where they instructed their novices in the hidden secrets of the planetary mysteries. As in the human body, the pathway to illumination started with the awakening of the base chakra and moved on and upwards, step by step; until true enlightenment arose as a result of the awakening of the crown chakra. The sites of these oracles were also used for rituals of fertility, involving sacrifice, or to propitiate the gods.

The magic of seven is not the sole link between spiritual paths from different cultures. Fertility – and the rites and symbolism associated with it – is one that is far more common. The Druids, like most initiatory tribal cultures, worshipped the principle of the Eternal Feminine as the source of all fertility. Julius Caesar describes, in *de Bello Gallico*, the veneration accorded to a fire-blackened, female figurine which was worshipped at a Druidic sacred grotto at Carnutum, now the modern city of Chartres, situated between the rivers Loire and Eure – a fertility symbol he called Virgini Pariturae, the virgin about to give birth. In pre-Hellenic Greece this veneration of the eternal feminine took the form of the worship of Gaia as the Earth Mother. Other early cultures revered the same principle of fertility under the name of Sibille or, later, Artemis. With the rise of classical Greece this veneration of the feminine principle was transformed into the worship of Cybele and Demeter.

Ammianus Marcelinus, the Roman historian from the fourth century of the Christian era, described the Druids as men of great talent and members of the Pythagorean faith characterized by searching into secret and sublime things, who also believed in the immortality of the soul.[33] Even some early Christians, a group not renowned for their tolerance of other faiths, had a deep respect for the Druids. One of the most respected fathers of the early Church, Clement of Alexandria, wrote:

> Thus philosophy, a science of the highest utility, flourished in antiquity among the barbarians, shedding its light over nations. And afterwards it came to Greece. First in its ranks were the prophets of the Egyptians; and the Chaldeans among the Assyrians; and the Druids among the Gauls; and the Samanaeans among the Bactrians; and the philosophers of the Kelts; and the Magi of the Persians.[34]

Clement claimed that it was Pythagoras who accepted the Druid's doctrine of the immortality of the soul and not the other way around, citing Polyhistor, the Greek philosopher and historian, as his source. Origen, Clement's successor as head of the Christian school at Alexandria, was another of the most revered early theologians. He believed that the Druids were monotheistic, although Caesar had written that they:

> . . . worship the God Mercury; of him they have many images, him they consider the inventor of all arts, as the guide of ways and journeys . . . After him they worship Apollo, Mars, Jupiter and Minerva.[35]

Christianity and the Roman Invasion

The first evangelization of Britain – which, according to St Gildas, writing in 542 AD[36], and the early Christian historian

Freculpus,[37] took place only four years after the crucifixion – spawned a distinctive religion known as Celtic Christianity. In complete contradiction to the intolerance of mainstream Christianity, Druidism lasted for several centuries after the advent of the new faith in Britain. Celtic Christianity was far closer in belief to that of James the Just, the brother of Jesus and the first Bishop of Jerusalem. Many Druids even became priests of the new religion, while continuing in their privileged position as members of an intellectual class as their forefathers had done for a thousand years before.[38] One early Celtic Christian theologian, Pelagius, was convicted of heresy for attempting to revive the Druidic philosophy. In Britain, however, it was not the Christians who first attempted to destroy the Druids, but the normally tolerant Romans.

When Caesar conquered Gaul he brought with him all the benefits of the Pax Romana, a peace founded firmly on law, military might and a surprising degree of tolerance for traditional forms of religion, local tribal customs and beliefs. Rome's own religion was simply a matter of strict, outward observance of simple ritual duties for the benefit of the State, which posed no great burden of belief upon its adherents, who were allowed the freedom of choice to follow a second or third religion.

As well as religions of Roman origin, each subject tribe or people had their own gods. Knowledge of the different deities spread widely throughout the Empire, providing an often confusing multiplicity of religious ideas which intermingled and spawned new ones.

The respect accorded to education and Greek culture in the Roman Empire provided an ambience wherein religious ideas were magically transformed, but those religions that lasted had their roots firmly embedded in the more ancient cultures of

Babylon, Persia and Egypt. The only real interference with tribal religious practice was the hijacking of some sacred sites, and in this the Romans were simply following in the footsteps of the Druids themselves. Unfortunately this era of toleration and respect for the tribal gods was to be short-lived. The Romans vigorously persecuted the Druids, for they feared their potential as a unifying force among the warlike Celtic tribes.

Soon, however, another invader was to arrive, in the wake of a declining Empire; one which was tolerant neither of the religious beliefs nor of the traditions and mythologies of the tribal peoples; a religion that was to transform emergent Europe into a seemingly unified society. However, this apparent unity of belief was bought at a rather high price, as the Christian Church took firm hold of all the levers of power, both religious and temporal. Its claim to absolute, God-given authority allowed no room for dissent. The Church controlled kings, emperors and peasants alike and restricted access to education to its own servants. The centuries that followed would be remembered for all time as 'The Dark Ages.'

5

Gnosticism and Faith

Why do so many students of Church history have great difficulty understanding the complex roots of the bitter conflicts that have their origin in the period immediately after the death of Christ? Some are blinkered by their own sincere commitment to Christianity; even the dispassionate and objective students are tainted by 2,000 years of Christian tradition. These disputes developed into an era of vitriolic debate culminating in the Roman Church's suppression of all its rivals.

Apparently the beliefs of the gnostics were, for some peculiar reason, particularly unacceptable. Gnosis was a way of knowing that brought its initiates into intimate contact with divine reality, to the very feet of God. It was not just taught, but imparted through initiation, a form of revelation culminating in the profound and secret knowledge of the divine mysteries.[1] The life of the newly enlightened gnostic, his beliefs, associations and comportment, were totally transformed as his new spiritual insight became a vehicle for change, creating an outward lifestyle that was truly in harmony with nature and in tune with the divine. He was aware that he was empowered to do, feel and know that which was impossible with his own unaided strength and resources. He had not only been granted the sublime gift of sacred knowledge but a new state of consciousness and being. As a result he was set upon a path of constant endeavour and service to both the temporal and the spiritual world.

In contrast to the gnostic quest for sacred knowledge, being a Christian meant accepting a body of dogma and belief and following a prescribed way of life, in order to obtain forgiveness for sin and eternal reward. This complex dogma flowed from the minds of sincere, devout, yet fallible men. The Church ruled its credulous flock by fear and the deliberate inculcation of guilt, so that the poor sinner was engaged in a lifelong struggle to obtain absolution for his sins and, ultimately, his personal, eternal salvation. What constitutes a sin was, of course, defined by the Church, who was also the self-appointed lawmaker, judge, jury and executioner. Gnosis on the other hand did not require belief in dogma or even in God. The gnostic 'knew' the vibrant spiritual reality of truth and recognized the fallacies and distortions that are an integral part of any dogmatic belief system. His primary purpose was to use his spiritual knowledge for the benefit of all in the community; the illusion of mere personal salvation was not his concern. It was in this spirit that Rosslyn Chapel was created by the enlightened William St Clair, to act as a perpetual guide in stone to the path of gnosticism.

The early Church fought a bitter battle against all forms of Gnosticism and defeated it, not by the superior quality of its spirituality, dogma or beliefs, but by distortion, personal attack on its opponents[2] and the constant, vehement repetition of the validity of its doctrine. By the fifth century most forms of gnosticism appeared to have been suppressed and its documents and gospels destroyed; a situation more apparent than real leading, then as later, to the Gnostics becoming adept at dissembling and disguise.

The Church used many weapons to establish its authority over both sacred and secular matters. As the self-appointed guardians and definers of divinely revealed truth the ecclesiastical hierarchy took to itself the right to decide which scriptural works were of God and which were spurious. Those which could be interpreted as supporting Pauline theology were included in the approved canon; those which told the truth in a way which was irreconcilably different were declared heretical. Oral tradition, of which there was a great deal, was dealt with in a similar manner.[3] Stories that reinforced Church teaching were approved, others were suppressed.[4] Some simply appear to have been invented to bolster the shaky authority of Rome.

One such example is the legend that St Peter went to Rome and there suffered martyrdom. There is no confirmation of this in the Scriptures, but there is one contemporary record which does place his death elsewhere. The French mystical writer Robert Ambelain cites the writings of Flavius Josephus, the first-century Jewish historian, who states that Simon Peter was crucified upside-down, in Jerusalem at, or about, the same time as James the Just was executed.[5] This was the Roman punishment for insurrection, which was quite a plausible scenario bearing in mind the nationalistic nature of much of Jesus' teaching and the attitude of James the Just. The Dead Sea Scrolls' scholar, Robert Eisenman, gives a more accurate dating for this event than Ambelain, placing it in 62 AD.[6]

The early Church fathers played the same game with the tradition that St Paul was martyred in Rome, but there is no evidence that he was executed at all, much less in Rome. The Church has ever been ready to use any story, however dubious, to support its claims to power. At the Reformation, while many of the new Protestant sects rightly disputed Rome's authority, they all, without exception, took on a great deal of its dogma as a basis for their own teaching. This is still the case today, even among the most vehemently anti-Catholic sects.

In trying to understand the Church's attitude, there is one vital issue to be considered. The gnostic sects apparently had knowledge that refuted the version of events propagated by the Church; they could still rock the Christian Church to its foundations and destroy its hold over its congregation for ever.

That the teachings of Jesus the Nazarene could be regarded as the foundation for a new and distinctly different religion did not occur to him or his family, much less to the Apostles. Without exception they were, and always remained, strict, devout, fundamentalist and nationalistic Jews. The only distinction between them and their neighbours was their fanatical adherence to Jesus' interpretation of the Law, underpinned by their faith in the Messianic nature of his role. There was absolutely nothing in his teachings, as understood by them, to cause any breach with traditional Judaism. On the contrary, as the Priestly and Kingly Messiahs, John the Baptist and Jesus, both of whom were members of the Nazorean (or Nazarene) sect of the Essenes, were the fulfilment of Jewish religious thought and belief. Conflict did occur between many of the priestly and Saducean factions and the followers of Jesus, because those in a position of power and privilege felt that his teachings undermined their authority.

The 'divine' origin and nature of Jesus, which later became such a divisive and controversial issue, was not a problem among his disciples. They knew from their own firsthand experience that he was a man supernaturally endowed by God. None of them took his teachings as an indictment of Judaism, nor was the crucifixion regarded as a means of salvation. Jesus was a teacher of righteousness and his followers were Jesus people, not Christians as we now understand the term. Nothing in the words or actions of their master, in his teachings or in the scriptures – which they, as devout Jews of the time, especially the Essenes, knew intimately – gave them any cause to think otherwise. According to Aristides, one of the early apologists for the

Christian faith, the worship of the first Jerusalem 'Christians' was fundamentally more monotheistic than even that of the Jews. After all, Jesus' brother James the Just was a high priest who was still granted entrance to the Holy of Holies in the Temple. For, like their cousin John the Baptist, both Jesus and James were Levites through their mother's family line.

After the crucifixion, the mysterious figure of James took on the role of the Priestly Messiah which was previously held by John the Baptist until his execution by Herod. James exerted great power and authority for many years after the crucifixion of Jesus and was clearly acknowledged by all the Apostles, including Paul, as a much more significant figure than the later Christian Churches have ever dared to admit.

> He was of the lineage of David . . . and moreover we have found that he officiated after the manner of the ancient priesthood. Whereof also he was permitted once a year to enter the Holy of Holies [on the Day of Atonement], as the Law commanded the high priests, according to that which is written; for so many before us have told of him, both Eusabius and Clement and others. Furthermore he was empowered to wear on his head the high priestly diadem as the aforementioned trustworthy men have attested in their memoirs.[7]

The pre-eminence and importance of James is referred to many times in a variety of ancient documents. Church teaching about him, scanty though it is, has been deliberately left vague and inconclusive. Why has his role been minimized by the Church to such an extent that the laity and most of the clergy know little about it? Two characters called James are described: James the Great and James the Less. Were there two

James operating among the followers of Jesus at that time and, if so, who were they? Why have the actions and importance of James the Just been either suppressed or glossed over, and why was his importance diminished by being called James the Less?

The 'Virgin' and her Family

Church doctrine poses other equally fascinating problems. Trapped by its own distortions over the nature of Jesus and the alleged 'virginity' of his mother Mary, the early Church had painted itself into a corner from which there was no escape. How could one who was dogmatically declared to be 'ever-virgin' be described as having a large family? In the Gospel according to St Mark we read: 'Is not this the carpenter, the son of Mary, the brother of James, of Joses [or Joseph], and of Juda [or Judas] and Simon? and are not his sisters here with us?'[8] In St Matthew's Gospel, it says: 'Is not this the carpenter's son? Is not his mother's name Mary and his brethren, James, and Joses, and Simon and Judas?'[9]

The tactics used by the Church to cope with this anomaly were marginalization, omission and evasion. Patriarchal religions, such as Judaism and Christianity, always devalue the role of women. Mary's role was marginalized by, paradoxically, seeming to exalt her in her role as 'the Mother of God' to the exclusion of all else. Omission was used to overcome the Gospel statements that Jesus had siblings, by the denial of their existence. However, as doctrine developed and they were challenged on this point by the privileged few who were per-mitted to read the Scriptures, they evaded the issue by claiming that in this context, 'brothers and sisters' meant fellow believers or 'cousins'. Early in Church history, Clement of Alexandria referred to James as the brother of Our Lord, and bishop of bishops.[10] Much later in the Vulgate translation of the Bible, St Jerome used the Latin word *frater*, which translates unequivocally as brother, and never uses the Latin for cousin. The Vulgate was the translation of the Holy Scriptures that carries the imprimatur, or official seal of approval, of the Roman Catholic Church to this day.

There are repeated statements both in the Gospels and in the various lives of the saints that James and John were the sons of Zebedee. Who was their mother and was there any family relationship to Jesus? For answers to these questions we have one source which even the Church itself dare not question: the Holy Gospels.

One possible clue is contained in a verse also from the Gospel according to St Matthew: 'Among which was Mary Magdelene, Mary the mother of James, and Joses, and the mother of Zebedee's children.'[11] It appears that Mary may have married Zebedee after the death of Joseph and therefore the sons of Zebedee were also the sons of Mary, the supposedly ever-virgin mother of Jesus. Remarriage after the death of a spouse was common; how else was Mary to support her family? If this is so then James the Great and John, the sons of Zebedee, were half-brothers of Jesus, while James the Just, called by the Church James the Less, Simon and Joseph junior were his full brothers and sons of Joseph.

There was also another brother, whose relationship to Jesus the Church has suppressed: Didymus Judas Thomas. He is the Judas referred to in the passages quoted above. He is also the undoubted author of *The Gospel of Thomas*, one of the Gnostic Gospels. Thomas' role has been cleverly devalued in the canonical Gospels by referring to him as 'Doubting Thomas', so casting doubt not only upon his commitment and spiritual insight, but also upon his personal knowledge of Jesus. Why should this slander be cast upon one of the Apostles?

The Gospel of Thomas was an important document that circulated widely for the first three centuries of Christian history, supposedly written by the twin brother of Jesus. It was a serious rival to the canonical Gospels as a source of authority and gives us further proof as to why the Church was running scared about the importance of Thomas. Eventually suppressed by the Church, it disappeared from sight for nearly 1,500 years until it was rediscovered at Nag Hammadi in 1945. In it we find the following:

> The disciples said to Jesus:
> 'We know that you will depart from us.
> Who is to be our leader?'
> Jesus said to them:
> 'Wherever you are, you are to go to
> James the righteous,
> for whose sake heaven and earth
> came into being.'[12]

Do Jesus' words indicate that James' role as the Priestly Messiah was superior in some way to that of Jesus as the Kingly Messiah?

Another puzzle arises when we discover that no explanation is offered in the Acts of the Apostles or the Epistles as to why, or how, the new 'Christian' community formed in Jerusalem almost immediately after the crucifixion of Jesus. How could a handful of 'peasants and fishermen' create such an elaborate organization with such speed? The Acts of the Apostles claims that this seemingly *ad hoc* structure sustained a massive influx of Jewish adherents from throughout the Diaspora.

This complex and efficient system of governance was ruled by a triumvirate, which consisted of James the brother of Jesus and the Apostles Simon Peter and John, assisted by area supervisors and administrators, renamed by the Church as bishops and deacons. James was, indisputably, the leader of the new Jesus sect in Jerusalem. The three were called 'the pillars' by Paul: 'And when James, Cephas and John who seemed to be pillars, perceived that grace was given me, they gave to me and to Barnabas the right hand of friendship.'[13] These three religious leaders simply replicated the ruling trio of the Essene community from which they and Jesus sprang; and in all probability they were all brothers of Jesus. James the Just is described in the Scriptures as the Lord's brother. According to Robert Ambelain, Simon Peter and the Simon listed among Mary's children are one and the same.[14] It is also possible that the John referred to as 'one of the pillars' was not John the 'Disciple whom Jesus loved', but John the son of Zebedee, the half-brother of Jesus. There is another story which confirms this. The group known as the Ebionites, previously known as the Nazoreans, were the sect from which Jesus himself sprang. They continued to elect their bishops from among the family of Jesus until well into the second century of the Christian era.[15]

The Controversial 'Deification' of Jesus

To a world completely indoctrinated by the idea that Jesus is God, it is perhaps difficult at first to accept that Jesus himself never claimed divine status. He, like all his disciples, was an ultra-orthodox and devout Jew who was well-steeped in esoteric Hebraic gnosticism which could trace its roots back to the Egyptian Temple mysteries. The origin of the name Essene is held by many to mean 'those with the light within', and Jesus was an Essene initiate. In the Koran, our Muslim brethren call the man we know as Jesus by the name of Issa. The derivation of this name is also of interest, not only to students of mainstream Christianity, but also to scholars studying the beliefs of the Knights Templar. One translation of the name is 'an initiate of Isis'. The Egyptian mysteries pervaded the entire esoteric belief system of biblical Israel from the time of Moses onwards. Isis was undoubtedly an object of adoration by the later Knights Templar, who venerated her in the guise of the Black Madonna. Another translation of the name Issa that is often put forward is 'an initiate of Light'. Was Jesus not called the light of the World?

Jesus was undoubtedly referred to as 'a Son of God', a phrase which, to the Jews of biblical times, meant something very different indeed from that ascribed to it by Christians today. To the Jews this title ranked Jesus with the many other Sons of God mentioned in the Old Testament, such as Adam, Abraham, Moses and David. The status of Son of God was held to be attainable to all those who followed Jesus' teaching and who attained enlightenment. Jesus himself said as much, as reported in *The Gospel of Thomas*: 'He who will drink from my mouth will become like me. I myself shall become he, and the things that are hidden will be revealed to him.'[16]

The canonical Scriptures leave us in no doubt whatsoever that it was St Paul who was the first to preach the doctrine that Jesus was divine. According to the Scriptures Paul never met the living Jesus. His other major, fundamental and theologically important divergence from the beliefs of James and the Apostles is demonstrated by the phrase 'Christ died for us'. A vicarious human sacrifice of this nature would be viewed as outright blasphemy by devout Jews, as was the alleged 'divinity of Jesus', but both ideas were totally in keeping with the traditions of the Greeks and Romans to whom Paul was preaching, where a noble, sacrificial death would be extolled.

Paul referred to Jesus as God, yet St Peter who, according to Catholic teaching at least, was made the founder of the Church by Jesus himself, describes Jesus as a man: 'Ye men of Israel, hear these words; Jesus of Nazareth, a man approved of God among you by miracles and wonders and signs, which God did by him in the midst of you, as ye yourselves also know.'[17]

The complete change in the way Paul viewed the nature of Christ is echoed clearly in many of his later letters:

Here is a trustworthy saying that deserves full acceptance: Christ Jesus came into the world to save sinners – of whom I am the worst.

But for that very reason I was shown mercy so that in me, the worst of sinners, Christ Jesus might display his unlimited patience as an example for those who would believe on him and receive eternal life.

Now to the King eternal, immortal, invisible, the only God, be honour and glory for ever and ever. Amen.[18]

... while we wait for the blessed hope – the glorious appearing of our great God and Saviour, Jesus Christ.[19]

It was because of this type of teaching, among other reasons, that it has sometimes been suggested that Paul may have been 'the Wicked Priest' referred to in the Dead Sea Scrolls, or the man described as 'the Liar', 'the Scoffer' and 'the Spouter of Lies'. Many of those who knew Jesus personally would have agreed with that, for Paul was despised and disliked by James and most of the other disciples. As this view is in conflict with that of many Christians, is there any evidence to back it up?

There is at least one other document of similar age to the synoptic Gospels which was written in the early years after the crucifixion, when the effects of Paul's teaching had already become all too evident. This document, known as the *Kerygmata Petrou*, describes the 'Apostle' Paul, venerated by the Church as the 'Father of Christianity', as 'the hostile man who falsified the true ideas of Jesus'. It originated among the Ebionites or Nazoreans, the people who were closest to Jesus throughout his ministry and who possessed the deepest understanding of his teaching. They were brutally dismissive about the Church's elevation of Paul to the rank of Apostle. According to them this title was reserved solely for those who had accompanied Jesus during his ministry.

Iraneus, Bishop of Lyon during the late second century, claimed that Jesus – whom he believed was God – had been in error, practising 'the wrong religion'.[20] Now Jesus is defined as being divine, therefore supposedly incapable of error, and yet, according to a Pauline theologian, God had led his flock into the wrong religion. The mind boggles! Iraneus then condemned the Ebionites as heretics for claiming that Jesus was a man and not God, as defined by the new Pauline form of Christianity. He admitted that even then the Ebionites spurned the Pauline epistles, and rejected Paul himself as 'an apostate of the Law'. Eusebius, writing in the fourth century, records that the Ebionites '. . . had poor and mean opinions concerning Christ. They held him to be a plain and ordinary man who had achieved righteousness merely by the progress of his character and had been born naturally from Mary and her husband'.[21] He also stated that the Ebionites '. . . affirm that Christ was born of Joseph and Mary, and suppose Him to be a mere man'.[22]

The Heresy of Paul

Paul was far from popular with the original followers of Jesus in his own time. His new doctrine of the divinity of Jesus and his claim that gentile converts did not have to live according to Jewish Law was in conflict with what they knew to be the truth. The English historian Paul Johnson describes these events as occurring because Paul had created 'monstrous difficulties' by his divergence from the teachings of Jesus as understood by the original disciples.[23] These events were touched upon and glossed over in Acts in its account of the 'first council in Jerusalem'.[24] As a result Paul found himself involved in direct competition with evangelists personally accredited by James, who preached a very different message, and he began to lose ground steadily throughout the missionary field.[25] It is now apparent that certain long-known ancient documents, studied in conjunction with translations of the Dead Sea Scrolls, have revealed that Paul was so incensed with the actions of James the Just that he attacked him with murderous intent in the Temple in the 40s AD.[26] Paul's arrest as a result of a riot in Jerusalem over his 'blasphemous teaching', described in Acts,[27] may well have been for a very different reason. According to Robert Eisenman this was an act of protective custody to save Paul, a relative of the Herodian family[28] and a possible agent of Rome, from mob vengeance following his attack on James the Just.

Paul was certainly repeatedly criticized, both by the accredited evangelists and those who sent them, and was well aware of this. In his first Epistle to the Corinthians we find the following:

> Am I not free? Am I not an apostle? Have I not seen Jesus our
>   Lord?
> Are you not the result of my work in the Lord?
> Even though I may not be an apostle to others, surely I am to
>   you!
> For you are the seal of my apostleship in the Lord.
> This is my defence to those who sit in judgement on me.
> Don't we have the right to food and drink? Don't we have the
>   right to take a believing wife along with us, as do the other
>   apostles and the Lord's brothers and Cephas?
> Or is it only I and Barnabas who must work for a living?[29]

As this Epistle can be accurately dated, the criticisms could only have come from James and the Jerusalem Church.

It would seem from this, and from other comments that he makes later in the same letter, that not only is his apostleship being called into question, but also that he is being accused of taking some sort of financial advantage from it. In his first Epistle to Timothy he repeats his concept of the redemptive sacrifice at Golgotha and stresses the 'legitimacy' of his apostleship yet again:

> For there is one God and one mediator between God and men,
>   the man Christ Jesus, who gave himself as a ransom for all
>   men . . .
> . . . And for this purpose I was appointed a herald and an
>   apostle – I am telling the truth, I am not lying . . .[30]

Here Paul is obviously sensitive to a charge of lying as well as that which accuses him of being a 'false apostle'.

When one reads all the Epistles of St Paul in one go this self-pitying and defensive tone becomes ever more apparent; read them in sequence and you may well begin to perceive St Paul in a very different light. From the point of view of James the Just and his followers, Paul *was* a false prophet. Iraneus, the Bishop of Lyon, claims that the Ebionites described Paul as 'an apostate of the Law'.[31] But that is not all; the events on the road to Damascus and Paul's claim to have received spiritual teaching directly from Jesus himself were scornfully condemned in the ancient Ebionite document the Kerygmata Petrou as 'visions and illusions inspired by devils'. The Ebionites would not have recognized many of the teachings or events recounted in the Epistles, the Acts of the Apostles or even in the Gospels themselves.

The 'Truth' of the Gospels

The Gospels and the Acts of the Apostles are, in an academic sense at least, an extremely unreliable source. The Acts and at least three of the canonical Gospels were written long after the events they describe, by people who were not present at the time and who based their accounts on hearsay evidence arising from faith rather than fact. The Gospel of St John, on the other hand, despite its many later additions, may have been written by, or at the behest of, an eye-witness, which may explain some of the significant differences between it and the synoptic Gospels known to us as Matthew, Mark and Luke. These were based, to one degree or another, on a mysterious source document known in scholarly circles as 'Q', and which has never been traced. It is not the only one of importance to have vanished; Professor Morton Smith discovered in 1973 a letter from Clement of Alexandria which refers to a 'secret apocryphal Gospel of Mark'.[32] Clement's writings disclose a wide-ranging knowledge of early Christian documents, many of which have since been lost or suppressed. Of the secret Gospel of Mark, Clement was of the opinion that all knowledge of its existence should be denied, in spite of its authenticity, because certain gnostics had used this document to claim that Jesus had been personally involved in a baptismal cult, in contradiction to Church teaching.[32] Another Gospel which survived for many centuries and has also been lost is the controversial 'Gospel of Love' used by the Cathars. This is now accepted to have been a Gnostic variation upon the Gospel of St John.

In the accepted and 'official' chronology of the New Testament, the Epistles of St Paul are universally recognized as being of the earliest origin, having been written in the late 40s AD. The Gospels and the Acts of the Apostles came very much later; Mark during the 70s, Matthew in the 80s, John during the 90s with the Acts, and the Gospel according to Luke early in the second century. They were all written after the fall of Jerusalem, and originate in the era when James and the disciples in the Jerusalem Church had been killed or scattered, and Paul and his followers had the field to themselves.

The Gospels were not merely written much later than most lay-people realize, but they were all subjected to amendment, alteration and distortion in order to bring the divinely inspired word of God into a closer approximation with the teaching of St Paul and the developing doctrine of the Church. Insertions, some glaringly obvious, some not, are many and varied. Which books were accepted as part of the official canon was also a matter of debate, which was finally settled by a show of hands. Hardly what we would expect when we hear clergy of various denominations talking about scriptural authority and divine inspiration.

If we examine the four Gospels using the earliest manuscripts that have survived, we find that there is little unanimity regarding the factual content of the teaching of Jesus. Each Gospel in turn describes what was important to the chronicler, for they were not written in the manner adopted by impartial modern historians. They were written, long after the event, to evangelize according to a new belief structure that had arisen, not in Israel itself, but under Paul's guidance in the Gentile world. They record, therefore, a seemingly authoritative historical basis for beliefs largely founded on the teaching of Paul, not Jesus.

The Fall of Jerusalem

With the murder of James the Just in Jerusalem, the stage was set for disaster. The killing of the Priestly Messiah who had inherited the mantle of John the Baptist lit the fuse that eventually led to the explosive revolt of the Israelites against the hated Roman oppressors. If Jesus was of supreme importance among his people, why did his murder pass without public comment or civil commotion? Why did the killing of his brother provoke the complex chain of events that resulted in the destruction of the Temple and the dispersion of the Jews? One early church father, Origen, was in no doubt about the cause of the fall of Jerusalem, for he claimed that Josephus records: 'James was of such great Holiness and enjoyed so great a reputation among the people that the downfall of Jerusalem was believed to be on account of his death.'[33]

With the death of James and the scattering of the remaining Ebionites, Pauline teaching was virtually unopposed and rapidly became the foundation for all Christian theology. After the Church had grown and eventually become 'established' by the Edict of Milan in 312 AD, its Pauline theological base became the foundation for a sustained campaign directed against all of its rivals – pagan temples, local deities and the wide range of mystery cults and gnostic groups, Christian or otherwise.

With the apparent success of the Church in its suppression of Gnosticism in the sixth century, the surviving Gnostics had to go underground in order to survive. In a clandestine 'esoteric form' they continued to transmit their vital spiritual truths to their courageous and devout followers, with their teaching continuing to flourish secretly under the seemingly obedient mask of outward Christian conformity.

The new Church, after several periods of persecution, was transformed from a minority and marginal organization into the major player in the religious spectrum of Rome. It was finally accepted as the main religion of the Roman Empire due to the actions of one remarkable man who was not even a Christian: the Sun-worshipping Emperor, Constantine the Great.

6

The Unholy Alliance

With his decisive victory at the battle of the Milvian Bridge in 312 AD, Constantine the Great became the ruler of the Roman Empire. The night before the battle that decided the religious fate of Europe for the next 1,700 years, he had a strange vision of the Cross of Christ and the legend *In Hoc Signo Vinces* – 'In this sign you conquer'.[1] To commemorate this victory and to give thanks to the God who had inspired him, Constantine erected a triumphal arch in Rome inscribed with the cross of Christ and the words: 'By this saving sign, I have delivered your city from the tyrants and restored liberty to the senate and the people of Rome.'[2]

The Emperor's motives were far from altruistic. He wished to use the Christian religion as a form of social cement to unite the divided peoples of the Empire.[3] Later that year he passed the Edict of Milan which granted religious freedom to the previously persecuted Christians,[4] giving Christianity the power to influence and sometimes to completely control the governments of Europe. It also united the passive, loving Christian church with the activity of war – in complete contradiction to the teachings of Jesus. The long-term effects of this marriage of secular and political power are described by Matthew Fox, the modern author and one time Dominican theologian, in his book *The Coming of the Cosmic Christ*:

> . . . the patriarchal and dualistic theologian Augustine of Hippo put forward a theology that legitimized the . . . conscription of Christians into the military, 'just wars' in the name of Christ . . . and rendering women into shadows and

71

scapegoats. 'Man but not woman is made in the image and like-ness of God'[5] . . . Only today are we beginning to free ourselves from this abortion of the maternal in the womb of the church begun sixteen centuries ago.[6]

One inevitable and immediate result of the Edict of Milan was to increase the accumulation of wealth by the Church, which led, in its turn, to corruption. New bishops were soon being appointed on grounds of their high birth, personal wealth or administrative skills rather than their piety.[7]

The Road to Repression

The Church claimed to be based upon the redemptive sacrifice of the Risen Christ, the Divine Son of Almighty God who had died to redeem not merely all of mankind, but the very cosmos itself. Yet it was battling with the pervasive influence of earlier forms of Christian and pagan belief. The key to victory in this 'spiritual' struggle was provided by the enthusiastic adoption of the ancient Jewish conception of heresy. David Christie-Murray in his *History of Heresy* states that 'heresy, a cynic might say, is an opinion held by a minority of men which the majority declares unacceptable and is powerful enough to punish'.[8] He was not far wrong! However, the necessity for punishment created the need for a far tighter and more precise definition, which was provided by St Augustine (354–430), the Christian theologian who became Bishop of Hippo in 396 AD. He described women as 'vessels of excrement', although it is far from clear whether or not he included Mary the Mother of God in that category. Augustine's other doctrines of 'the just war' and 'compel them to come in' became the foundation for a vigorously repressive and persecuting society which grew steadily.[9] This saintly bastion of tolerance and faith redefined heresy as 'the distortion of a revealed truth by a believer or an unbeliever': 'revealed truth' was simply and clearly described, by the Church of course, as 'what the Church itself had declared to be revealed truth'. This useful definition, and St Augustine's other pronouncements on heresy, were used by the Church leaders to help them to establish a total monopoly on all access to the sacred.[10] The Church hierarchy has always believed that heresy exists where man exercises his God-given gift of free will in matters of faith. Even today Cardinal Ratzinger, who is in charge of the Congregation of the Doctrine of the Faith, the modern equivalent of the Inquisition, claims that 'the freedom of the act of faith cannot justify the right to dissent'.[11] The New Catholic Catechism, published in 1990, also states that 'the task of giving an authentic interpretation of the Word of God . . . has been entrusted to the living teaching office of the Church alone'.

The first laws against heresy were promulgated in the 380s[12] and by the time of Theodosius in the fifth century had multiplied until there were over 100 statutes aimed at heretics and heresies. In 383, Priscillian of Avila became the first person in the West to be burnt at the stake, on a charge of witchcraft and of suspected Manichaeism.[13] This dualistic, gnostic philosophy which was founded by the Persian prophet Mani in the third century of the Christian era, was a form of Christianity within which God and Satan were believed to reign as equals. St Augustine of Hippo had been a follower of the cult in his early years.

In 1022, fourteen of the higher clergy and more respectable laity of the city of Orléans were burnt at the stake for heresy on the orders of King Robert I of France.[14] The birth pangs of the repressive society founded in the name of Jesus were thus announced to the world with the cries of the victims. The repression grew until it produced the dubious benefits of the Index of proscribed books, the Holy Office of the Inquisition and perpetuated that most notorious manifestation of Divine Love – burning at the stake, which was carried on as a penalty for witchcraft well until the late seventeenth century.[15] It was in this atmosphere of intolerance and persecution that Earl William St Clair erected Rosslyn Chapel as a coded guide to gnostic teachings, for he knew only too well that not only books but their authors could be burnt.

The Church Tightens its Grip

The Church's very need to survive not only caused it to refute anything it viewed as heretical with increasing venom, but also led to the rise of dogmatic, supposedly agreed, statements of belief which papered over areas of dispute and disbelief with a dictatorial rigidity, that sprang not from God to whom it was ascribed, but from a power-hungry priesthood. The Roman Church swept away all knowledge of the spiritual world. It campaigned vigorously for the destruction or closure of all the temples and centres of worship of rival faiths, hijacking these sacred sites wherever possible for its own use. The great Greek mystery temples were rendered defunct and the oracles silenced for all time.[16] The idea of reincarnation which had been an accepted part of both the Judaic and Hellenic roots of Christianity was declared heretical.[17] This was a distinct departure from the beliefs current at the time of Jesus. In the Gospel according to St John, the doctrine of reincarnation is obviously accepted; John the Baptist is questioned by his followers: 'They asked him, "Then who are you? Are you Elijah?" He said, "I am not." '[18] The idea that John the Baptist was the prophet Elijah come again passed without comment. The Greeks believed in the transmigration of souls, so it is no wonder that the early Christians who sprang from the classical world of Greece and Rome and who had adopted a new religion of Judaic origin also believed in reincarnation. This is obvious when one reads some of the works of respected theologians and early fathers of the Church.[19] St Gregory, the Bishop of Nyssa, wrote in or about 350 AD: 'It is absolutely necessary that the soul should be healed and purified and if this does not take place during its life on Earth, it must be accomplished in future lives.'[20]

The Church also became the major lawmaker in the declining Empire. Much of the customary law of the people of Europe was absorbed and codified into civil law by the clergy who were the final arbiters against whose decisions there was no appeal whatsoever. Being the sole literate guardians of history, the Church wrote down the oral legends, myths and stories of the various peoples, adding their own gloss, omitting all that was offensive to accepted doctrine, subtly changing the histories and forming the mould for a new, essentially Christian, culture. Tribal myths and legends were reduced to mere fiction, completely stripped of all power and validity. The Church distorted the histories of entire cultures, devaluing for all time any potential rivals in the field of religious beliefs. It increased its grip not only on the current reality of the tribes, but also on their past and on their ancient cultural heritage.[21] This escalating process was continued by the wholesale incorporation of pagan festivals into the new Christian calendar: the festival of Astarte, the Phoenician goddess of love and fertility, became Easter, and the summer equinox became the feast of St John the Baptist. The winter equinox was amalgamated with the birthday of Mithras, the Persian god of light. This pagan feast on 25 December became Christmas. Much of the mythology of Mithras himself was adopted. Legend recalls that at his birth shepherds were the first to adore him, and that after he had performed good deeds for his followers, he celebrated a last supper with them before returning to heaven. Mithras, the unconquerable sun, was to return to Earth at the end of time to judge the human race.[22] This may be disconcerting to many Christians indoctrinated with the belief that Christianity is unique.

Dogma Versus Spirituality

It was not only the doors that gave access to the spiritual and cultural heritage of the people that were slammed firmly shut by the Church. In its deliberate march towards absolute power and authority, it feared any access to the realms of either sacred or secular knowledge that it did not itself monopolize.[23] Education was thus restricted to the clergy. In this way the Church revealed its real objectives – total power and control over all people and territories, over this life and entrance to the next. All because the Church assumed unto itself the sole right to decide who would be saved and who would be eternally damned.

The fathers of the expanding Christian Church believed that they could legislate away all knowledge of the spiritual world, that they could persecute and terrorize all those who had knowledge of it and that they alone could control all access to spiritual powers. This delusion continued to influence the thinking of Church leaders and popes for many centuries. The only tangible evidence that has come down to us are the truly horrendous stories of the persistent and vicious persecutions that were the inevitable result of such an illusion.[24]

Legislation, dogmatism and keeping the laity in a state of perpetual ignorance undoubtedly bred a silent and fearful obedience to Holy Mother the Church, but it did not remove the Spirit from the world or knowledge of the Spirit from the folk memory of mankind as a whole. Whilst the Church tried to modify the outward attitude of the majority of people, there was no way that the dogmatic denial of spiritual reality could ever be 100 per cent effective.

Knowledge and beliefs that gave access to the Spirit continually invaded the sacrosanct domains of the growing and ever more powerful Church, sometimes from within its own ranks.[25] Early Celtic monasticism was characterized by its spiritual purity and simplicity. Priests in the Celtic Church were encouraged to marry and the priesthood was, like that in the early Jerusalem Church, an hereditary office.[26] No images of the crucifixion were allowed, and they also refused to practise infant baptism.[27] Unlike the emerging Roman Church, the Celtic Church resolutely rejected all the trappings and benefits of temporal power. This simplicity and humility posed a direct challenge to the pomp and circumstance of the comfortable and powerful priesthood in the rest of Europe. This situation was given force and point as a result of the enormous cultural dynamism possessed by the Celtic mystics and monks whose art work, scholarship and scriptural learning were exemplary. Nomadic by nature and intent, these inspired Celtic brethren evangelized much of Western Europe.[28] Thomas Fuller, the seventeenth-century historian, described the Celtic missionaries who traversed all of Europe, from Scandinavia in the north to Switzerland in the east, as the 'wandering scholars'. These peripatetic monks were as learned in the classics as they were in Holy Writ, another point that distinguishes them from their Roman Catholic counterparts. Such was the quality and range of their classical learning that Professor H Zimmer claims that 'it is almost a truism to state that whoever knew Greek on the continent of Europe in the days of Charles the Bald (10th century) was an Irishman or had been taught by an Irishman.'[29]

Rome had little alternative but to try and take over and change the Celtic Church. When Pope Gregory the Great sent St Augustine to evangelize Saxon England in 597 AD the island became host to two inimical strands of Christianity, and the stage was set for the opening rounds of the centuries-long battle between Celtic Christianity and the Roman Church. Despite the claims of the Celtic Church to both precedence and the true teaching that they had received directly from the disciples of Jesus himself, the leaders of the Roman Church were insistent that their way was superior in every respect. According to the received view of history that has come down to us, the differences between the two forms of Christianity were comparatively few and relatively simple: merely a matter of which tonsure was correct and who held the true date for Easter. These seemingly minor differences of opinion belie the many centuries of dispute and dissension that followed. It was supposed to be settled, once and for all, at the Synod of Whitby in 664 AD where, according to Bede, the eighth-century author of *A History of the English Church and People*, 'they signified their agreement and, abandoning their imperfect customs, hastened to adopt those they had learned to be better'.[30]

Officially that was the end of the dispute between the Celtic and Roman Churches. Why then, if that account is true, did it last for several centuries longer? Why was the Celtic Church condemned eventually as heretical, and why was William Rufus, the son of William the Conqueror, at first denied burial in consecrated ground because he had tried to reintroduce the 'heresy' of Celtic Christianity?

At the Council of Hereford, which took place only nine years after the Synod of Whitby, the Celtic Christians were condemned as 'non-Catholic'.[31] Despite being declared heretical by Rome, the Celtic Church struggled on as a separate entity for many centuries and became known, once again, by its original title of the Culdee Church. The Culdee Church was named after the 'culdich', or 'strangers from afar' who had brought Christianity to Britain a few years after the crucifixion. This form of belief survived in Ireland for several centuries after St Patrick, who was himself a Celtic Christian. In 1172 it was suppressed by the Roman Church which was aided by the English invader, King Henry II. In Scotland, Celtic Christianity survived until the eleventh century, when the Roman Church finally triumphed. It was at this time that William 'the Seemly' St Clair was granted the lands at Roslin. He was of the same family as William Rufus, the descendants of Rollo, first Duke of Normandy. Normandy was one of the strongholds of the Gallician Church, which sprang from the same Druidic and Culdee roots as the Celtic Church and was its French equivalent.

A E Waite, the Masonic historian who worked in the early years of the twentieth century, wrote *A New Encyclopedia of Freemasonry*, in which he cites an earlier author, Godfrey Higgins who, in his work *Celtic Druids*, described the Culdees as gnostics. This is undoubtedly true, as it is almost certain that the Culdees were gnostics as were the Druids before them. That would have been enough to justify charges of heresy, but there was far more to it than that. Firstly there was the British Church's claim for precedence as it had gained its original Gospel from the followers of James the Just, and not from Rome. Then there was the contentious matter of the claimed supremacy of the pope. Even as late as the sixth century, while the Celtic Church recognized that the Roman Pontiff was indeed the true successor to St Peter, they were also of the firm conviction that the Patriarch of Jerusalem, who ordained St David, the Apostle of Wales, was the true successor of Christ. This controversial view of the second-class ranking of the pope was shared by the Gallician Church in France.

Other gnostic and mystical beliefs that sustained this tendency to spiritual knowledge came from the atavistic insights of the newly Christianized Germanic tribes of the North. Despite vigorous, sustained and hideous persecution, the old gnosis of the Greeks and Egyptians continued to make inroads into the Christian world. Clergy reading the Pauline Epistles and the Revelation of St John stumbled across this ancient and inspiring knowledge in their devotional studies.

Humble and devout Christian mystics rediscovered it and, in their humble devotion to God made manifest in nature, experienced its transcendent beauty. The followers of a new form of Christianity, which expressed itself in the quest for the Holy Grail, strove steadfastly to explore the realities of the spirit, their secret search hidden behind the seemingly blind obedience that was the public face of clerical scholarship. In contrast to the Church of Rome, the form of Christianity that evolved in the old Eastern Empire was a vibrant and perpetual reminder of the eternal truth of man's ability to access and use the God-given gifts of the Spirit.

In seeking to monopolize all access to the sacred and claiming sole rights over all spiritual gifts, knowledge and insight, Holy Mother the Church had backed a loser, the terrible cost of which was centuries of persecution and the endless litany of names of the innocent victims of the dreaded Inquisition. Heretics, actual and potential, were sought, tortured, tried and burnt. Whole populations were put to the sword for heresy, the Cathar people of the Languedoc being the most notable. The Cathars were gnostic Christian dualists, who believed that Christ had come to reveal rather than to redeem. The spirituality, simple lifestyle and deportment of their priests, or perfecti, were in stark contrast to the pomp, comfort and pretensions of the Catholic priesthood. The Church was in the main corrupt, and its influence on intellectual and spiritual life was stultifying. Yet within this period were born some of the most deeply spiritual men and women seen on Earth; mystics and initiates who simply, humbly and wholeheartedly dedicated themselves to God, and who sought the Holy Spirit wherever they could.

7

Underground Streams of Spirituality

The medieval Church developed its dogmatic and legalistic structures under the delusion that it alone had absolute control over all forms of knowledge, education and divine revelation. It supported its repressive regime by a two-fold rule of fear – fear of persecution for heresy in the present buttressed by fear of eternal hell-fire and damnation in the life hereafter. This somewhat peculiar concept of Christian love spread its tentacles downwards from the pope through the hierarchy of bishops, priests and parishes to control emperors, kings, feudal lords and peasantry alike. All who openly ventured opinions or beliefs that contradicted those of the Church were persecuted, excommunicated, tortured or burnt at the stake. To make matters worse, in most countries, for the majority of the time at least, Church and State were effectively one. This Church/State alliance became *de facto* the establishment; all those of independent spirit were simply the oppressed.

The rise of the persecuting society was incremental and all-embracing.[1] A form of fearful stability ensued that did allow the development of complex social forms under the aegis of feudalism. By the early Middle Ages feudalism had developed a continuity that was to last in certain parts of Europe until well into the twentieth century. Alongside the feudal structures came the development of towns and cities and, in the eleventh and twelfth centuries, a second wave of monasticism.

The Church exerted a complete stranglehold over all forms of intellectual life and education from early on in its unholy alliance with Rome until the twelfth century. The respect for

1 The Retro Choir, Rosslyn Chapel

2 The Virgin of the Pillar,
Chartres Cathedral

3 (below) Alchymical symbol,
Amiens Cathedral

4 The West front of
Notre-Dame de Paris

5 Statue of St John the
Baptist, Orleans Cathedral

6 (left) Figure of Mercury (Hermes) overlooking the site of the temple, Toulouse

7 (right) Statue of St James the Just, Compostela

education that was one of the great distinguishing characteristics of the classical Roman Empire was swept away. The benefits of Greek learning, philosophy, mathematics and science were wiped from the memory of European man as if they had never existed.[2] The Holy Scriptures, a little Neoplatonism and a vast body of dogma and canon law were all that interested the ecclesiastical hierarchy. Apart from the efforts of the Celtic monks and their fellow scholars and heretics, the Nestorians, there was only one notable and ineffective attempt to bring the Greek classics back into European consciousness. This was when Boethius, the Roman philosopher who lived between 480 and 534 AD, wrote his *On the Consolation of Philosophy* while in prison on charges of heresy. He was later executed without trial.[3] With the scholastic revival of the Middle Ages this became one of the most influential accounts of classical thought.

In stark contrast, in Moorish Spain between 755 and 1492 learning was prized and respected. Art and architecture flourished, as did the centres of secular and religious education. The religious tolerance of the Islamic invaders allowed Christian, Muslim and Jew to live together in harmony. The Sufi mystery schools in Spain were one of the principal sources of mystical teaching in an otherwise barren continent. The Jewish rabbinical schools produced volumes of study devoted to the Kabbala, which later made their way slowly into Christian Europe. Needless to say it was from Spain that the classical learning of Greek civilization slowly permeated into Christian consciousness, a movement which gathered speed with the Scholastic revival in Paris in the thirteenth century.[4]

It was in translation from Arabic, not the original Greek, that knowledge of the Greek philosophers crept back into the mainstream of Christian thought and then slowly spread into the ranks of the aristocracy. It was not just the fruits of Greek civilization that came by this circuitous route; along with philosophy, mathematics and science came more recent advances in medicine, art and architecture. Many of the branches of knowledge we now take for granted would have withered away to nothing had they not been preserved and enhanced by our Arab brothers.[5]

An educated laity was not the only disruptive force that the Church now had to contend with. A strong strand of mysticism began to emerge in medieval Europe which posed particularly thorny problems for the religious authorities, for it challenged their claim to control all forms of spiritual experience. It seems paradoxical that a Church which placed such importance on the teaching of the mystics and prophets of the past should feel so uncomfortable with a mysticism that sprang directly from the spiritual experience of its own time.[6] The real reasons are not hard to find. The medieval mystics were by the very nature of their experience the divinely inspired messengers of peace, justice and the knowledge of God's presence in every part of creation. They, like the biblical prophets of old, were far from popular with those who reserved to themselves all power and authority over the sacred.

Medieval Mysticism

Mystical experience is the true foundation of all religious systems, and Holy Mother the Church was understandably terrified of the medieval mystics and their message of justice, harmony and hope which so blatantly contradicted papal teaching and dogma. It posed particular problems to the doctrine that 'outside the Church there is no salvation', for if the individual could access God by his or her own unaided efforts, what need had they of the Church? Mysticism also posed a direct challenge to the claim that the Church was the sole guardian of all revelation. The reaction to the teaching of the medieval mystics was predictable and extreme; when ignoring them failed to stem their influence, pressure and persecution were brought to bear on these devout servants of Almighty God.

One 12th-century medieval mystic honoured and revered today, Hildegarde of Bingen, was feared so much by the Church that she was excommunicated at the age of eighty-one along with her entire convent of nuns.[7] St Francis of Assisi, who was born in 1182 and lived until 1226 AD, had his order forcibly removed from his control. This provoked the manifestations of the stigmata and what we would now describe as a nervous breakdown. Hypocritically this physical identification with the wounds suffered by Jesus on the Cross, brought on by Church repression, was later used by the same organization (long after St Francis' death) as a divinely ordained sign of his true sanctity. The only time the religious hierarchy's attitude seemed successful was in its ultimate response to St Francis. After a period of impotent repression, they absorbed him whole, burying his creationist, pantheistic message beneath a mask of hagiography and the bland reinterpretation of his teaching. They drowned his message as completely as the ornate monstrosity of the basilica dedicated to him obscures the stark simplicity of his humble chapel contained within it. But perhaps nature has had the last word, as the basilica was irreparably damaged by a massive earthquake in 1997.

The premature death of St Thomas Aquinas in 1274 was hastened by his perpetual arguments with the Church authorities.

Faced with constant criticism of his teaching and brutal bullying
to bring him into line, this saintly scholar had a nervous breakdown of such severity in the last year of his life that he could
neither write nor speak.[8] Few of the clergy who venerate him
today are aware that he was condemned for heresy, not once but
three times, before his eventual canonization. Another mystic,
Mechtilde of Magdeberg, was driven relentlessly from town to
town because she criticized the clergy for their greed and indif-
ference to the plight of the poor, the young and the sick.
Persecution in life was not enough for these brutal, self-
appointed guardians of divinely revealed truth; they
condemned (and still do) Meister Eckhart, probably the great-
est mystic in Christian history, after his death in 1328.[9] The
English mystic, Julian of Norwich, was simply ignored, not only
during her lifetime but for more than two centuries after her
death. Despite unremitting pressure from the Church there was
no way that the medieval search for spiritual enlightenment
could be halted. The mystics of the Middle Ages were not alone
in their quest for truth and godliness. Many of the ancient and
well-tried paths to spiritual knowledge still flourished, albeit in
secret.

The Church persecuted all who were known to follow spiritual paths which resulted in direct mystical experience of God.
As we already know, prolonged persecution of such dissident
streams had produced a marked tendency towards secrecy, and
while the individual mystics and groups of gnostics remained
hidden for the most part, the fruits of their spiritual insights
became ever more apparent. This exerted a formative influence on the flowering of religious art and architecture, the
high point of symbolic expression of medieval culture. As we
shall see, one visible manifestation of this movement is to be

seen in Gothic architecture and the re-establishment of the Greek classics in European thought.

Mysticism and the traditional routes to gnosis were practised under the very eyes of the clergy in the guise of outward veneration of Church dogma. One centre of the true 'way' was established at Chartres, a site that had been used for these purposes since Druidic times.[10]

Chartres and the 'Eternal Feminine'

The Cathedral of Chartres had been rebuilt by Bishop Fulbertus after a fire had devastated the previous building and most of the town in the eleventh century.[11] Fulbertus' successor, Bernardus, founded what is now known as the Chartres mystery school which operated under the acceptable mask of a theological academy. When supposedly studying the seven liberal arts – grammar, dialectics, logic, music, mathematics, geometry and astronomy – the pupils of Bernardus were in fact developing the seven senses of the spirit, inwardly developing the spiritual capabilities that open the inner eye to a direct vision of the spiritual world.[12] After a prolonged and demanding period of probation the novices were progressively inducted into the seven degrees of initiation mirroring the pathways of the Egyptian mysteries: this same process is encoded in the carvings at Rosslyn Chapel.[13] The esoteric academy at Chartres lasted for over two centuries, including the years 1194 to 1240, during which the present cathedral was built after yet another fire.

The revelations of the ancient mysteries brought about a deep insight into the laws of all natural phenomena, revealing the very unity in nature which is the mainspring of creation, and the importance of the principle of the eternal feminine. To commemorate this heretical and pagan concept, they carved a replica of the Druidic statue 'Virgini Pariturae', the virgin about to give birth, which had been a focus of worship at Chartres in pre-Christian times.[14] To avoid persecution and to enable this powerful symbol to exert its influence the statue was carved in the guise of Mary the Mother of God with the infant Jesus seated on her lap. This symbolic representation of fertility and the archetypal feminine rests in the crypt of Chartres to this day. It is known as Notre-Dame de Sous-Terre – Our Lady Under the Earth.[15] A replica of this figurine was then carved in the place of honour above the main portal of the cathedral. After many years of theological dispute with the Orthodox Church in the East, Roman Catholicism had at long last stumbled across the perfect answer to the problems posed by the ambiguities inherent in the title 'Mother of God'. In emphasizing Mary's role, the Church was fulfilling a deep and long-felt need among its adherents by importing the pagan principle of the eternal feminine into the previously male-dominated and patriarchal realm of the Holy Trinity. Early Christians had taken up the theology of St Paul which described Jesus as the 'Second Adam'. They then fell into a theological trap by calling Mary the 'Second Eve', so reviving the old pagan concept of the divine son/spouse relationship as found in the Ishtar and Tammuz cult of ancient Babylonia and in the worship of Isis and Osiris in Pharaonic Egypt. This form of veneration also incorporated the concept of Sophia the goddess of Wisdom. The Church attempted to exert control over this Marian cult in its traditional manner by taking over pre-Christian forms of worship and sacred sites dedicated to various goddesses, renaming them in honour of the Holy Virgin. The symbolism, prayers and litanies associated with Demeter, Cybele, Ishtar and Isis were adopted and given a Christian veneer.

It is ironic that Mariolatry, one of the major and most pervasive aspects of modern Catholicism, should have been further strengthened by the spiritual understanding of hidden initiates in the Middle Ages. Even today the Church authorities fight a desperate rearguard action to hide this embarrassing fact. They refer to all accounts of the Chartres mystery school as 'the pretended mysteries of Chartres'.

Not all candidates for illumination had access to esoteric academies such as that at Chartres. Many other devout and mystical members of the Christian clergy in the Middle Ages found inspiration in what is, perhaps, the most bizarre book in the canonical scriptures, one which has fascinated, puzzled and sometimes appalled its readers for the last 2,000 years. This much misunderstood work of immense power and mystery is known as the Revelation of St John.

The Revelation and Sevenfoldedness

The mystery begins with the Revelation's reputed author, St John the Divine. John is believed to have played a leading role in the Jerusalem Church which, under the leadership of James the Just, was a group which extolled the sacred knowledge that Jesus had revealed to his followers. It is a matter of record, repeatedly referred to by many of the early Church fathers, that St John wrote prolifically, yet only the Gospel of St John, three letters and the Revelation have survived intact. No one knows how many of his works have simply vanished or, perhaps more likely, were suppressed by the Church. One work to which there are many references, *The Acts of John*, was condemned by the Council of Nicea, doubtless because its contents conflicted with the distorted body of dogma confected by the Church theologians.

The Gospel of St John, which is regarded by many scriptural scholars as an initiation document, was called 'the Spiritual Gospel' by Clement of Alexandria. This perception is completely in accord with the visionary nature of his other major work, the Revelation, a strange and compelling, apocalyptic book that has fascinated its readers for centuries. It is a bizarre blend of Essene apocalyptic tradition, Babylonian mythology and astrological fantasy derived from the Persian Magi and the Egyptian Temple mysteries. Its prophetic nature is incredibly puzzling, for it is written in a complex code for which we no longer have the key.

Trevor Ravenscroft believed that St John, as a result of his deep spiritual insight, foresaw the repressive regime of the Church and left this coded guide to true spiritual vision.[16] Walter Johannes Stein, the mystical writer and friend of Rudolf Steiner, believed that the symbolism and imagery of the Revelation of St John became for many later mystics a kind of magic mirror in which they could discern reflections of both the past and the future. He claimed that within it the pathway to divine truth and revelation can be discerned, which act as a form of spiritual antidote to the blatant distortions of Jesus' message enshrined in Church teaching.

We have mentioned earlier that seven is the magical number of all known spiritual paths. Even Christian theologians talk of the seven virtues and the seven deadly sins, so it is perhaps not surprising that in the mystical vision of St John, who sprang from the Essene tradition, this number once again acquires symbolic significance.

Sevenfoldedness is one of the most important and obvious keys to unravelling the complex coding inherent in the Revelation, as the whole work advances in repeating rhythms of seven. There are the seven stars; the seven golden candlesticks; the seven messages; the seven angels of the seven churches; the seven seals; the seven trumpet blasts and the seven vials of wrath. Seven was undoubtedly a number of supreme importance to the religions and initiatory systems of all the civilizations that preceded the time of Jesus, whatever their origins, as well as to the Christians that followed. In the Eastern world, the Buddhists speak of Nirvana – the seventh heaven. As children we learn of the seven wonders of the ancient world; the seven hills of Rome; the seven colours of the rainbow; lucky seven; and the superstitions surrounding the seventh son of a seventh son.

> The number seven symbolizes the movement of life in space and time.
> The seven days of the week, the seven colours of the spectrum, and the seven notes of the scale remind us that birth and death bear witness to eternal life in an eternal becoming.[17]

In our own search it recurs time and time again: the seven spirit senses, the seven chakras, the seven planetary oracles and the seven great cathedrals that stand on the planetary sites. Its symbolic influence can also be detected in the conditions to be fulfilled by a novice, and in the number of degrees of initiation sought by the Knights of the Temple of Solomon, otherwise known as the Templar Order.

As Christian Europe approached the end of the first millennium, a time that assumed immense significance to the superstitious and the devout, scholars and mystics found in the Revelation of St John the seven-fold key to a new Christian spiritual pathway which became known to history as the search for the Holy Grail. The origins of this mystical quest of medieval Christendom reached back into the far distant past. It was a spiritual search for enlightenment that owed much to its pagan ancestry in the religious traditions of Mesopotamia, Egypt and the Essenes.

It was the true teaching of Jesus given new and seemingly acceptable clothes in a repressive and intolerant era; a form of spiritual alchemy strongly influenced by the Sufi schools in Moorish Spain; a spiritual way of life enshrined forever in the mythology of Europe in the stories by Wolfram von Eschenbach, Chrétien de Troyes and the Arthurian legends known to every schoolchild. It was one of the principal objectives of an Order of Christian knights whose history is still shrouded in mystery 700 years after their brutal suppression by the Church: the brave and chivalrous Order of the Knights Templar.

8

The Knights Templar

Dr Walter Johannes Stein claimed that the first written references to the search for the Holy Grail date from as early as the ninth century.[1] When we try and understand the Grail quest in the light of the religious beliefs of the time, one question immediately comes to mind. What was so holy about the Grail? Relics of the various saints abounded in Europe; some were even believed to pertain to Jesus himself. Why should any devout Christian set out in search of the Holy Grail, when in every chapel he had immediate access to the most holy things of all? For in the act of communion, he or she could partake of the body and blood of the Lord Jesus himself.

But then the Grail quest is not what it seems. There is a hidden agenda, designed to conceal an heretical truth from the prying eyes of the clergy. The entire corpus of Grail literature is a coded guide to a form of initiation.[2]

The reality behind the Grail quest was hidden by an allegorical description of a search for a religious relic, which was a disguise for an individual, inner adventure in spiritual experience. Professor Joseph Campbell believed that 'The Grail represents the fulfilment of the highest spiritual potentialities of human consciousness.'[3] He quoted one saying of Jesus from the *Gospel of Thomas*, namely 'He who drinks from my mouth will become as I am, and I shall be he.'[4] In Campbell's view this was the ultimate form of enlightenment, which arose from a successful search for the Holy Grail. The Knights Templar, who sought the Holy Grail as Campbell defined it, were also involved in a very real search for holy treasure; and William St Clair of Roslin's shield carried an engrailled black cross on silver, clearly denoting

93

him as a Grail Knight – another twist in the mystery of Rosslyn Chapel.

An account by Guilliame of Tyre, written late in the 12th century, claims that the Order of the Poor Knights of Christ and the Temple of Solomon was founded in Jerusalem in 1118 by Hughes de Payne, André de Montbard and seven other knights. This new Order of nine knights, also known as 'la milice du Christ', was ostensibly created to fulfil the mammoth task of protecting the pilgrim routes within the Holy Land.[5] Both of the founding members of the new Order were vassals of the Count of Champagne. Hughes de Payne was married to Catherine de St Clair of Roslin and André de Montbard, who was a relative of the Duke of Burgundy, was also the uncle of Bernard de Fontaines,[6] perhaps the most powerful man in Europe in the early 12th century.

St Bernard of Clairvaux

Bernard de Fontaines (later canonized as St Bernard of Clairvaux) played a considerable, if somewhat mysterious, role in the foundation of the Knights Templar. He was the leading thinker of the Cistercian Order, a Benedictine offshoot founded to bring about a return to the spiritual and temporal austerity of the original Benedictine rule. After a period of struggle the Cistercians expanded rapidly and grew to phenomenal power and influence under the intellectual and spiritual guidance of this charismatic man.

The bizarre events within the noble family of Bernard de Fontaines at the time he joined the Order are mysterious. At that time the Order was relatively new, struggling and in imminent danger of collapse. Bernard's family were shocked when he announced his vocation, but their attitude was completely transformed for reasons that are far from clear. All opposition to his plans evaporated and, even stranger still, most of his male relatives and many of his friends chose to follow him into the new Cistercian Order; thirty-two of them became novices with him when he joined in 1112.[7]

No convincing explanation for this collective outburst of religious fervour has ever been offered by the Church. This massive influx of vocations included that of Bernard's elder brother, who was heir to the family estate, as well as his two younger brothers and his uncle, the Knight Gaudri of Touillon, and more than doubled the size of the struggling order.

Bernard soon rose to a position of incontestable leadership in the Church of his time. He became personal adviser to the pope and exerted great influence in purely temporal affairs, dealing with kings, emperors and nobility. His deep commitment to initiatory teaching is made clear by the 120 sermons he preached based on the Song of Songs by King Solomon.[8] He extended this teaching by enhancing the spiritual tradition of the branch of the Compagnonnage, or Craftmasons, known as the Children of Solomon.

Bernard was appointed to the position of abbot of the new Cistercian Abbey of Clairvaux soon after joining the order, when he was only twenty-four years of age. Shortly after the foundation of the Knights Templar he wrote a discourse on the Order which he addressed to Hughes de Payne, one of the co-founders of the Templars. In the last paragraph of this document we read:

Hail, land of promise, which, formerly flowing only with milk and honey for thy possessors, now stretchest forth the food of life, and the means of salvation to the entire world.[9]

What exactly did he mean by this? Had not the crucifixion of Christ brought about the salvation of mankind? Was he not sworn to uphold just that doctrine? It would appear that the means of salvation to which Bernard was referring was the discovery of sacred knowledge from some hiding place within Palestine. Knowledge whose location the new abbot was perhaps already aware of?

The discovery of the Dead Sea Scrolls provides a clue as to what the information may have been. One scroll discovered at Qumran lists the various sites where the treasures of the Temple were hidden.[10] It seems unlikely that the scroll found in 1948 was the only copy; did Bernard of Clairvaux have access to another? The first nine Templar knights in Jerusalem, where the Order was founded, spent several years excavating under the Temple Mount.[11] It would appear that they certainly knew exactly where to dig, for one of the most persistent esoteric traditions in Europe states that they found treasure, a variety of sacred documents and, according to some accounts, the Ark of the Covenant.[12] One modern royal author, HRH Prince Michael of Albany who is a direct descendant of Charles Edward Stuart (better known as Bonnie Prince Charlie), claims that the Templars discovered documentation which contained the fruits of thousands of years of knowledge. He also states that among the discoveries were documents which disproved the crucifixion and the resurrection of Jesus.[13]

The true motivation for the creation of this military Order is shrouded in mystery. It has been claimed that the Templars were founded to act as the front men for a far more secretive Order, the Priory of Sion, whose alleged list of Grand Masters includes several members of the St Clair family.[14] It is also claimed that this conspiracy involved St Bernard of Clairvaux and the Count of Champagne, who was related to both St Bernard and the St Clairs.[15] The Count was certainly involved in gnostic spirituality, for a kabbalistic school had existed at his court at Troyes since 1070 and it was he who donated land to the Cistercians for the Abbey of Clairvaux.[16] Bernard became prior of the new abbey and was joined there by the two brothers of André de Montbard, one of the founders of the Templar Order. Furthermore, the Templars were endorsed soon after their foundation by both St Bernard and the pope.[17] It is doubtful if Bernard personally attended the Council of Troyes, which formally gave the rule to the Knights Templar and increased the legitimacy of the new Order. It was, however, certainly dominated by his thinking.

The records of the foundation of the Order do nothing to clarify the alleged linkage with the Priory of Sion. In most respects they create more confusion; according to some documents the Templars were founded in 1119, while others suggest that this occurred at least nine years earlier, at or about the time that St Bernard and his influential family joined the Cistercian Order.[18] Another far more plausible, but little-known, legend speaks of a hidden, hereditary group of families who have exerted great influence over European life from before the time of Jesus to the present. They call themselves 'Rex Deus' and claim direct descent from the twenty-four priestly families of the Temple in Jerusalem and from Jesus himself.[19] Was information about the Temple treasure handed down through the oral traditions of these families? Were Hughes de Payne, the Count of

Champagne, the St Clairs of Roslin, André de Montbard and his nephew Bernard of Clairvaux all part of this secret group? It would certainly explain the strange events among Clairvaux's family when he joined the Cistercians, the efficiency with which the nine knights completed their excavations under the Temple Mount in Jerusalem and the intimate association of the St Clairs with the Templars.

The Knights of the Temple of Solomon

When the Templars had completed their excavations, their return to Europe was swift. All nine knights of the new Order escorted their finds back to their associates in France, and their founding members then visited both England and Roslin. It was at this time that the St Clairs of Roslin, relatives by marriage to Hughes de Payne, made the first grant of land to the Templars in Scotland for their headquarters at Ballantrodoch.[20] It has been argued that the story of the Priory of Sion, as told by Baigent, Leigh and Lincoln, was nothing more than a clever cover story designed to distract attention from the reality of the Rex Deus group. Time alone will answer these enigmas, but the Rex Deus hypothesis does clarify some of the otherwise inexplicable actions of many leading figures of that era and later.

Owing allegiance to neither king nor emperor, only to the pope himself, the wealth of the Knights Templar grew at a remarkable speed. In addition to the treasure they are said to have found in Jerusalem were numerous donations of land from the many noble families with which they were connected. This gave the Knights a power base which they used to create a multitude of enterprises, and Europe was soon adorned with a network of Templar holdings, many strategically situated near the most important trade and pilgrimage routes. There is evidence of these in place-names today: in England, Temple in Cornwall, Templecombe in Somerset, and the centre of the legal profession, the Temple in London; in Wales, Templeton and Temple Bar in the county of Dyfed. Scotland abounds with Templar names, such as Temple (previously Ballantrodoch) in Midlothian, Temple in Strathclyde, Templehall in Fife and Templand in Dumfries/Galloway. France, where the Order had most possessions, abounds with Templar names: Doncourt aux Templiers, Templehof et Colmar, Bure-les-Templiers, Moissy-le-Temple, Ivry-le-Temple.[21] Spain, Germany and other European countries also have their quota indicating Templar origins.

Their commercial interests were impressive and varied. Neither just simple soldiers nor idle aristocracy, these knights were experts in mining, quarrying, building, viniculture and farming in every climatic zone of Europe and the Holy Land. Furthermore their superb fleet enabled them to extend their trade routes to the very fringes of the known world. Their boats carried passengers, troops and horses, and they also had a number of highly manoeuvrable war galleys fitted with rams. Their ships plied the Mediterranean between Italy, France and Spain and their main base situated on the island of Majorca. Their principal port on the Atlantic coast of France was La Rochelle from where, it is alleged, they conducted trade with Greenland, the North American mainland and Mexico.

In effect the Knights Templar became the medieval precursors of modern multinational 'conglomerates', richer than any kingdom in Europe. By ensuring the security of all major trade routes throughout Europe they created a climate of peace and stability that allowed merchants to trade at minimum risk and with comparative ease over greater distances than ever before. Europe began to bloom economically as a result, for their military and commercial activities had stimulated a climate of unprecedented commercial confidence and economic growth that strengthened the power of the merchant class and ultimately led to the development of capitalism. This era of stability and growth arose as a direct result of the application by the Templars of a bizarre mix of their military skills and sacred gnosis.

One of their stated objectives was to protect pilgrims *en route* to the Holy Land and this soon expanded into providing transport and shelter for all devout pilgrims, whether they journeyed to Jerusalem, Rome, Chartres, Mont St Michel, Rocamadour or Compostela. They were the first effective and commercial 'travel agents' in the world. The Benedictine tract, the *Codex Callextinus*, which is still extant, describes the precise route from any part of Europe to the shrine of St James at Compostela. It gives instructions on how to avoid thieves, bandits and dishonest innkeepers *en route*, and lists the appropriate hymns and prayers for the pilgrimage. The Knights acted as bankers to the pilgrims themselves, the rest houses, the monasteries and the cathedrals visited.[22] The pilgrimage to Compostela was, in religious terms at least, second only in importance to that to Jerusalem, and far more important than any pilgrimage to Rome. In straight commercial terms it was the most important single enterprise in Europe.

The pilgrimage to the shrine of St James of Compostela was known to the public as the Shell Pilgrimage. To the mystics and hidden gnostics, the Knights Templar and their heirs however, it was called either the Alchemist's Pilgrimage or the Pilgrimage of Initiation – an outward form of an inner, mystical journey along the path of learning.[23] Why was this journey undertaken not to Rome, easily accessible and eternally associated with both St Peter and St Paul, but to a small, obscure and relatively inaccessible corner of north-west Spain? To a city associated with James the Great, son of Zebedee, and James the Less, also known as James the Just, the brother of Jesus and the first leader of the Church in Jerusalem after the crucifixion.

The Templars, being true gnostics, in complete contrast to the Roman Church of which they were supposedly part, did not concern themselves with the salvation of individual souls, but with the spiritual and material transformation of entire communities and nations. Their ultimate objective was to restore true gnostic monotheism to the world, uniting Christianity, Judaism and Islam.[24]

Unlike many of their fellow crusaders, the Templars had a great respect for the culture of Islam. Most crusaders were an unprincipled and ill-disciplined horde of looters, landless nobility, robber barons, criminals, debtors, penitents, adventurers and intolerant fanatics invading a culture far superior to their own. At the fall of Jerusalem, the crusading armies butchered everyone in sight, be they Christian, Jew or Muslim; 25 per cent of the citizens slaughtered were Christian residents of the Holy City.[25] Chivalry was an alien concept that the Knights Templar acquired from the 'heathen' Saracens and brought back to Europe. The telescope, the principle of stellar navigation, the financial instrument known as the 'note of hand',[26] considerable advances in both medicine and surgery, mouth-to-mouth resuscitation and free access to the world of knowledge and ideas were among the benefits brought westwards by these Knights of the Holy Grail.

Many Church historians, from the time of the suppression of the Order to the present day, have slandered the Templar Knights, describing them as illiterate. These so-called illiterates used a highly sophisticated secret alphabet to encode their records, invented the earliest form of credit card and were the originator of the banker's cheque or banker's draft. The Templars used 'notes of hand' long before the Lombard bankers, who are often wrongly given the credit for this innovation.[27]

Contrary to public belief, the Knights Templar had not taken vows of poverty like many other Orders, but had sworn to hold all their property in common. They used their communal wealth wisely, building up their financial power base and then extending their activities into banking and power-broking on a massive scale. They lent vast sums to popes, princes, prelates, kings and merchants.

Within a short space of time the Templars were emulated in many countries by knightly orders of warrior monks who owed their allegiance to the king and not to the pope. One such Order, the Teutonic Knights, was actually founded by the Knights Templar. Principal among the others who modelled themselves on the Templars were the Spanish Orders of the Knights of Calatrava and the Knights of Alcantara.[28] Both were founded shortly after the Knights Templar, and St Bernard of Clairvaux is now known to have played some shadowy role in their foundation.

By the early fourteenth century, the power, wealth and influence of the Templars had aroused considerable jealousy and resentment among various heads of state and many members of the hierarchy. It had even been suggested that they amalgamate with the Knights Hospitallers, a move that both Orders resisted vigorously.

The Fall of the Templars

Philip le Bel (1268–1314), the king of France, was one monarch among many who was heavily in debt to the Order. He also had a further cause for resentment, for when a young man, his application to join it had been refused. During one period of civil unrest in his nearly bankrupt kingdom he sought refuge in the Paris Temple.[29] Bedazzled by the vast store of bullion he saw there, he resolved to find a way to acquire it and cancel his enormous debt to the knightly bankers. He soon found an opportunity to destroy the Order.

Plausible reasons for an investigation of any suspect individual or organization were not hard to find in that age of repression and injustice. The perfect means for this dubious enterprise had long been perfected; the dreaded Inquisition had honed its evil arts of torture, secret trial and condemnation during its sixty-year novitiate in the campaign against the Cathars.[30] Philip knew that there had been contact between the Templars and Islam, and links had also been proved between the Knights and the Cathars. Certain Knights who had been expelled from the Order were bribed or blackmailed into making accusations of heresy against their former brothers.

The French king prepared his case with secrecy and skill, and the death of the pope gave him the opportunity he was waiting for. On Friday 13 October 1307, Jacques de Molay, Grand Master of the Templars, and sixty of his senior Knights were arrested in Paris: simultaneously many thousands of other Templars were arrested throughout France.[31] A few escaped arrest and the remainder simply fled; an episode commemorated by the saying 'Friday the thirteenth, unlucky for some'.

Under the king's orders the Templar high command were tortured for several years. The financially astute monarch had the gall to charge the Order for their upkeep for the entire period of their imprisonment. The final barbaric act of this dreadful charade took place on the Ile des Javiaux, on 14 March 1314, when the elderly Grand Master, Jacques de Molay, and the Preceptor of Normandy, Geoffroi de Charney, were publicly burnt on a slow fire. Before his death de Molay is on record as prophesying the imminent demise of the king and the pope. Both died within the year.[32]

When the king's agents visited the Templar treasury immediately after the first arrests, their great treasure had vanished without trace, as had almost the entire Templar fleet. The king had been foiled. French Masonic ritual indicates that Scotland was designated as the place of refuge for the Templar treasures.[33]

One of the charges against the Templars was that of idolatry; the veneration or worship of an idol called Baphomet. Various translations have been offered for the name Baphomet; Idries Shah, author of *The Sufis*, claims that it is a corruption of the Arabic *abufihamet* (pronounced 'bufhimat') which translates as 'Father of Understanding'. Magnus Eliphas Levi, the mystical writer of the last century, proposed that it should be spelled in reverse as TEM. OHP. AB. This he construed as *Templi Hominum Pacis Omnium Abbas* or 'Father of the Temple of Universal Peace Among Men'.[34] Another legend equates Baphomet with the severed head of St John the Baptist who was venerated by the Knights Templar.[35] The Atbash cipher, an esoteric code used by the Essenes to disguise the meaning of their scriptures, was applied to the name Baphomet by the Dead Sea Scroll scholar Hugh Schonfield. The cipher produced the word 'Sophia', the spiritual principle of Wisdom which is usually associated with the ancient Greek or early Mesopotamian goddesses.[36] The Templar cult of the Black Madonna, black carvings or icons of the Madonna and Child, supports this concept.

At first glance this cult looks like a variation upon normal Catholic practice of the time. The reality is very different, however, especially when we take into account the influence of ancient Egyptian ideas on the Templars. In ancient Egyptian symbolism, the colour black indicates wisdom. In the cult of the Black Madonna the Templars were venerating the Mother of Wisdom, the ancient goddess Sophia embodied in the form of the goddess Isis with the Horus child. This pagan concept was disguised as the Christian Madonna and Child.

When drawing up the rule for the Templars in 1128, St Bernard of Clairvaux laid down a specific requirement on all the Knights to make 'obedience to Bethany and the house of Mary and Martha'.[37] Many scholars now believe that the great Notre-Dame cathedrals built by the Templars and Cistercians were dedicated not to Mary the mother of Jesus as the Church teaches, but to 'Our Lady' Mary Magdelene and the son of Jesus instead. In esoteric tradition, Mary Magdelene is described as 'the symbol of divine wisdom'. According to the Nazorean tradition, the Magdelene was to be depicted garbed in black like the priestesses of Isis, surmounted by Sophia's crown of stars. Her infant child wears the golden crown of royalty.

Reactions to the suppression of the Templars varied from country to country. German Knights of the Order either joined the Hospitallers or the Teutonic Knights. One leading Scottish Templar, William St Clair of Roslin, the great-great-grandfather of the founder of Rosslyn Chapel, was killed in Lithuania fighting for the Teutonic Knights. In Portugal the Templars were not suppressed, but changed their name to the Knights of Christ and carried on under royal patronage.[38] Many years later the explorer Vasco de Gama became a member and Prince Henry the Navigator was a Grand Master of the renamed Order.[39] The Archbishop of Compostela made a vain plea for clemency for the brave knights by writing to the pope begging that the Templars be spared as they were needed for the Reconquista, the fight against the Moors to recapture Spain for the Catholic monarchy.[40]

This pressing need for military skills, discipline and dedication to the Christian reconquest of Spain was fulfilled in a simple way. Ex-Templars were encouraged to join similar military Orders which differed only in that they owed their allegiance to the Spanish crown rather than the pope. One Order, that of St James of the Sword, or the Knights of Santiago, was actually affiliated to the Knights Hospitallers to ensure its survival. They too became immensely powerful and controlled more than 200 commandaries throughout Spain by the end of the fifteenth century. Thus Templar influence continued in mainland Europe. In France and England some Templars joined the Knights Hospitallers, but most simply seemed to vanish.[41]

People condemned for heresy in medieval Europe shared a similar fate to the alleged dissidents condemned in Soviet Russia during the Stalinist era. The victims became 'non-persons'; their records were destroyed and all traces of them and their beliefs were completely erased. The only records remaining intact are those of the persecutor, Holy Mother the Church. Thus getting to grips with the reality that lies behind the romantic legends surrounding the warrior knights is extremely difficult. The French local archives disclose many details of their land dealings, while other documents revealing some of their history do surface from time to time.

Fortunately one perceptive and courageous man, Earl William St Clair of Roslin, attempted to counteract the repressive attitude of the Church and celebrate the vibrant truth of Templar beliefs. He realized that books, authors and even readers could be burnt for heresy, and so created a permanent and fireproof library of arcane and gnostic instruction. The architect, builder and patron of Rosslyn Chapel, he created a storehouse of secret coded Templar information, a superb legacy to all who seek spiritual enlightenment: Rosslyn Chapel is a veritable, three-dimensional 'teaching board' of gnostic, late medieval initiation.

Rosslyn Chapel, important though it is as a testament to Templar beliefs, is the last and most important ecclesiastical building erected as a result of the application of the principles of sacred geometry by the noble Knights and their associates. Most of the buildings in the apocalyptic configuration in stone were financed, built or heavily influenced by these Knights of the Holy Grail.

9

The Rise of the Gothic

The single most influential force that helped to create, shape and sustain Western European culture in the medieval period was, undoubtedly, Christianity; not the diverse array of sects and denominations we know so well today, but Christianity of a particularly monolithic and dogmatic variety, namely the Roman Catholic Church.

Yet even this form of Christianity was not the seamless society it appeared to be. We have seen how the Church created an intolerant, persecuting society. As the ecclesiastical hierarchy became ever more venomous, those of conflicting beliefs, independent mind and all who followed the ancient paths to spiritual wisdom had to go underground in order to survive. Christianity therefore had two very different aspects: the exoteric and visible façade of power, strength and unity, given tangible form in the Basilica of St Peter in Rome, and the esoteric, hidden, phenomenally creative yet heretical stream represented by Rosslyn Chapel in Scotland. The Basilica of St Peter which stood in Rome at the time of the Knights Templar was the one built by Constantine during the fourth century, on the alleged site of St Peter's tomb. The present basilica of the same name was built during the sixteenth and seventeenth centuries and contains magnificent works of art contributed by Bramante, Michelangelo, Maderno and Bernini, amongst others.

Under the apparently unified façade of medieval society, the two opposing streams of spiritual influence at work in Europe were the Church and that formed by a variety of gnostics and mystics. Outwardly successful, rich, powerful and repressive, the Church used the doctrine of personal salvation allied to fear of eternal hell-fire and damnation to achieve total domination over its flock. The gnostics and mystics, however, used the fruits of their spiritual insight for the direct and immediate benefit of the community in which they moved. European culture as we know it grew out of this conflict. Who was closer to the true teachings of Jesus, the Church or the gnostics? Perhaps the words of Jesus himself could assist us:

> Beware of false prophets, which come to you in sheep's cloth-ing, but inwardly they are ravening wolves. Ye shall know them by their fruits. Do men gather grapes of thorns, or figs of this-tles? Even so every good tree bringeth forth good fruit; but a corrupt tree bringeth forth evil fruit . . . Every tree that bringeth not forth good fruit is hewn down, and cast into the fire. Wherefore by their fruits ye shall know them.[1]

One of the 'fruits' by which we may know them can be found in the sudden outburst of cathedral building in the twelfth century; those majestic and powerful 'Prayers in Stone' that still adorn the European landscape. To ascertain what provoked this enormous expenditure of resources at this particular time, or from where the new technology, engineering and architectural skills that spawned the Rise of the Gothic came, we have to turn to one of the Church's traditional enemies, gnosticism, and examine the actions of some of the orders who had been influenced by it.

The Craftmasons

Initiatory Orders existed among the craftsmen who built the great cathedrals, and these craft guilds were known in England

as the Craftmasons. In France there were at least three such
fraternities: The Children of Father Soubise, The Children of
Master Jacques and The Children of Solomon. Their spiritual
heirs are now known as Les Compagnons des Devoirs du Tour
de France. All observed a moral tradition of chivalry within
their craft and a submission to work that must be done. All
'shared the same bread' and, according to Raoul Vergez, a
companion-carpenter of the Duties who rebuilt most of the
church spires in Brittany and Normandy after the Second World
War[2], they were men 'who knew how to use a pair of
compasses'.[3] Sharing the same bread is said to form a community or fraternity; by contrast, those who know how to use a pair
of compasses in masonry are those who have been granted
insight into the secret laws, knowledge and harmony of 'sacred
geometry'. It is that qualification that admits them to the status
of 'Mason'. The importance of this skill is remarked upon by the
English author Ian Dunlop when he said 'It is not uncommon
in medieval illumination to find God the Father represented as
the "elegans architectus" holding a large pair of compasses.'[4]

The initiated Masons of the craft were described as a hierarchy of three ascending degrees; apprentice, companion, and
attained-companion or master. As an outward expression of
their divinely inspired duties, these enlightened craftsmen
refused to bear arms or build fortresses or prisons. Apprentices
learnt their trade moving from yard to yard in the course of a
'tour de France', receiving instruction from 'compagnons'; they
later underwent initiation by their masters in secret conclaves
known as 'cayennes'.

The three fraternities, which later merged into one single
association had, at first, different duties and utilized different
techniques. Found in the very heart of the Benedictine monastic

system were the Children of Father Soubise who mostly built in the Romanesque style. Their 'signatures', or masonic marks, differ widely from those of the builders of Gothic, even when their work is contemporary. The Children of Master Jacques, known also as the 'Compagnons Passants du Devoir', were supposedly founded by Master Jacques, the son of Jacquin, a master-Craftmason who, as legend recalls, was created master after journeys in Greece, Egypt and Jerusalem. The same legends explain that it was he who made the two pillars of the Temple of Solomon: Boaz, and the one that is actually called Jacquin. It is possible that the medieval Children of Master Jacques were the successors to the ancient Celtic builders who signed their work with an oakleaf.

From the perspective of our investigations into the great Gothic cathedrals, the third brotherhood, the Children of Solomon, is the most important. They are credited with the building of Chartres Cathedral and most of the other Gothic Notre-Dames, such as those at Rheims and Amiens. Many of the churches and cathedrals they constructed bear their signature, the 'chrisme à l'epée' – a Celtic cross enclosed within a circle.

The Children of Solomon were instructed in sacred geometry by Cistercian monks. They were named after King Solomon who, according to the Old Testament, commissioned the Temple in Jerusalem and buried the Ark of the Covenant within it. Another branch of the Compagnonnage operated in Provence and built many of the Templar churches in the South of France. These were the 'Compagnonnage Tuscana' who traced their mysteries back to Egypt and biblical Israel via their Roman and Greek roots. They were part of a collegia of constructors known as 'Les Tignarii', founded by Numa Pompilius.[5]

The exact relationship between the Children of Solomon and the Order of the Templars is not clear. Were the craftsmen an integral part of the Order, affiliated to it, or just associated with it by usage? The Templars certainly gave a rule to this branch of the Compagnonnage with the agreement of Bernard of Clairvaux in March 1145, which laid down rules for living, working and honourable conduct for all the craft initiates involved in the construction of churches. The rule was prefaced by the words:

> We the Knights of Christ and of the Temple follow the destiny that prepares us to die for Christ. We have the wish to give this rule of living, of work and of honour to the constructors of churches so that Christianity can spread throughout the earth not so that our name should be remembered, Oh Lord, but that Your Name should live.[6]

It would therefore seem highly probable that this Order of Craftmasons was affiliated in some way to the Templars. In the eyes of the establishment at least, they were obviously viewed as close allies of the Order. The Children of Solomon were certainly under the protection of the Templars. They were granted great privileges, including freedom from all taxes and protection against legal action by the constructors of other buildings. It is also indicative of their status, *vis-à-vis* the Knights Templar, that at the time of the suppression of the Order, the Children of Solomon lost the privileges and immunities granted to Masons.

There is no doubt at all about the involvement of both the Knights Templar and the Children of Solomon in that fantastic era of cathedral construction so aptly called the Rise of the Gothic. The architectural historian Fred Gettings described this:

The Knights Templar who were founded ostensibly to protect the pilgrimage routes to the Holy Land, were almost openly involved in financing and lending moral support to the building of Cathedrals throughout Europe.[7]

The mysterious early twentieth-century Master, Fulcanelli, and his biographer Kenneth Rayner Johnson, both believed that Gothic architecture, which arose from Templar knowledge of sacred geometry, was also a three-dimensional code which passed its hidden message in an architectural form of 'la langue verte' – the green language, or the language of initiation. Fulcanelli and Rayner Johnson were not alone in this belief; at the end of the nineteenth century J F Colfs wrote that 'The language of stones spoken by this new art [Gothic architecture], is at the same time clear and sublime, speaking alike to the humblest and to the most cultured heart.'[8]

La langue verte originated from the understandable desire of the masters of their craft to disguise their real subjects of conversation from casual eavesdroppers. By this simple means, heretics were able to communicate with each other using a verbal code, without jeopardizing their freedom or their lives. This was a useful defence against persecution and became not only the language of the initiates but also of all the poor and oppressed. It was the direct medieval ancestor of cockney rhyming slang and the 'hip-talk' or 'rap' of the American inner-city ghettos,[9] so demonstrating how the language of any oppressed group becomes separatist in opposition to the dominant culture of the time.

Sacred geometry, in this context, is an art form encompassing the skills of engineering, building and design, which its practitioners claim was handed down from master to novice in an unbroken chain from the earliest times until the fall of Jerusalem in 70 AD. This chain of communication preserved and passed on the secret knowledge required for the construction of sacred buildings by the ancient Egyptian civilizations and the biblical Israelites. After the fall of Jerusalem, the knowledge was lost until the Knights Templar discovered documentation about it during their excavations under the Temple Mount in the twelfth century.

This tangible legacy of the Templars can still be seen in the flowering of artistic and religious expression that gave us the medieval cathedrals. Templar influence on the building of the Gothic cathedrals was noted by two early twentieth-century mystical writers:

> The building of cathedrals was part of a colossal and cleverly devised plan which permitted the existence of entirely free philosophical and psychological schools in the rude, absurd, cruel, superstitious, bigoted and scholastic Middle Ages. These schools have left us an immense heritage, almost all of which we have already wasted without understanding its meaning and value.[10]

Fulcanelli confirmed this in his work *Le Mystère des Cathédrales*, in which he described how a church or a cathedral was not merely a place of worship for the faithful, orthodox believers and a sanctuary for the sick and deprived, but also a place of commercial activity, public theatre and secular beliefs:

> The gothic cathedral, that sanctuary of the Tradition, Science and Art, should not be regarded as a work dedicated solely to the glory of Christianity, but rather as a vast concretion of

ideas, of tendencies, of popular beliefs; a perfect whole to which we can refer without fear, whenever we would penetrate the religious, secular, philosophic or social thoughts of our ancestors.[11]

He also described these buildings as a sort of philosophical 'stock exchange' where lingering pockets of arcana, with roots in pre-Christian systems, were flouted under the noses of an un-suspecting clergy.[12] Rosslyn Chapel was the culmination of this trend, being dedicated to a combination of gnostic Templar symbolism, punctuated by a comprehensive series of references to pre-Christian beliefs.[13]

The Hidden Hand of History

Despite their clandestine nature, 'schools of initiation' exerted a profound influence upon the development of European life. Behind the official view of the historical process there is always the so-called 'hidden hand' of history which is recorded in the secret traditions handed down over the centuries by folklore, poetry, esoteric schools and secret societies such as the Masons. Esoteric centres of belief, such as the Chartres mystery school, the Knights Templar and the Compagnonnage, exerted con-siderable influence in the world of mainstream Christianity. Another, far more ancient spiritual stream from a very differ-ent religious and cultural base also contributed significantly to the events we have described: the Sufis, nominally of Islam. Both the Cistercian and early Templar burial practice of inter-ring the corpse face down and coffinless as a final act of humility replicates that of this Eastern brotherhood of initiates.

The English poet Robert Graves, a mythologist of international repute, claimed that what we now call Freemasonry began as a Sufi society which first reached England in the reign of King Athelstan (924–939) and was introduced into Scotland in the guise of a craft guild. He not only describes the Sufic origins of the Craftmasons but also the part played by the Templars and the transformation of the guilds into Freemasonry. He traces their origins back to at least the second millennium BC and tells how their hidden wisdom was passed through the generations, from master to pupil.[14] The role of the Sufi masters in the building of Solomon's Temple is a key point. One of their founders, el Khidir, was known as 'the verdant one' – green is held to be the colour of illumination. They probably gained their ancient knowledge from either Babylon or Egypt, or perhaps the era the Pyramid Texts describe as 'the first time'.

Their teaching reached its zenith in Europe with the Sufi mystery schools of Spain in the ninth century, from where it slowly began to permeate into Christian Europe along with a Christianized version of the kabbala, a process which gathered great momentum with the formation of the Templar Order. The Templars were also on a path to spiritual enlightenment and used their insights for the benefit of the society in which they moved. Thus by the end of the twelfth century a wide variety of gnostic streams had begun to coalesce in secret and exert a subtle yet profound influence over the cultural developments in Western Europe. As well as the Sufi input Jewish kabbalistic thoughts and their Christian derivatives added to the dualistic philosophy of gnosticism, a combination which built upon the foundations that had long been established as an underground stream in Christian thinking.

That foundation itself was derived from at least three separate sources: Greek Hermetic thought which passed into Christian development through Dionysius the Areopagite; the influence of the Celtic Church which had always been closer to the mystical teaching of Jesus than its Roman rival; and the all-pervasive dualistic mysticism that flowed down through the ages through the Revelation of St John. We also have to consider the influence of the various heretical and mystical cults that were clearly founded on the basis of the True Teaching of Jesus, such as the Bogomils and their spiritual heirs, the Cathars.

All forms of gnosis were founded on dualism: for example, gnosis and ignorance, good and evil, life and death, spirit and matter, light and dark, the Alpha and the Omega. This is also found in the Revelation of St John with Christ and the Anti-Christ, and the Virgin and the Whore of Babylon. Yet because of the Church's horror of gnosticism with the exception of the dualistic imagery that occurs within the Revelation, most forms of dualistic symbolism were either anathema to the Church, or at best, highly suspect as manifestations of gnostic, heretical teaching and therefore liable to investigation.

Some aspects of dualism could be presented in an acceptable form. The role of the Templars, for example, was dualistic for they were both warriors, men of war, and monks, followers of the 'Prince of Peace'. They derived their wealth from their power base in Europe which then allowed them to operate in the Orient. Their symbolism is a graphic expression of their dualism: the black-and-white of their battle standard the Beausseante; the Templar seal of two brothers on one horse; the two knights behind the escarboucle seen in the doors of Rheims, Chartres and Amiens Cathedrals. Even their terrestrial domains were 'twinned' and this, like the symbolism of the two brothers, is believed to represent Castor and Pollux, possibly the Holy Twins, and often the two-faced god Janus. The Abraxus, which was the seal of the Grand Master of the Templar Order, was pure gnostic symbolism of such a nature that it is incapable of being described as orthodox. They also used the ancient symbol of the serpent who eats his own tail.

The Hidden Symbolism of Medieval Art

Sculpture was the major art form, other than architecture, used by the Compagnonnage in France and the various Masonic guilds and brotherhoods in Scotland and England to display their unequivocal gnostic beliefs. We have mentioned the mysterious abundance of Green Men found among the carvings at Rosslyn, and these are also found in large numbers at Chartres and to a lesser degree in most of the Gothic churches and cathedrals of the Templar era. The beliefs that sustained the creation of so many representations of the Green Man pervaded most of European life. They too refer us back directly to the Babylonian deities of Ishtar and Tammuz, which becomes clear when we study British folk tradition:

> . . . the May Queen followed in a cart, or chariot, drawn by young men and women. Her partner or 'consort', the Green Man, descendant of Dumuzi, Tammuz and Attis, also called 'the Green One', was clothed in leaves. In some parts of Europe the couple were 'married'. So May Day celebrated the sacred marriage and the ritual of the regeneration of life . . . The face of the Green Man gazes out from the midst of carved foliage on Gothic cathedral screens, pulpits, vaulted naves and

choir stalls . . . invoking that more ancient knowledge of the relationship of the goddess to her son, incarnate through him as the life of the earth.[15]

The association of the Green Man and the Masons was delineated further by another modern author:

> Even if one were to regard him at the lowest level, as a mascot of the Masons, his presence in so many regions and over so long a period indicates that he had a particular meaning for them. Did he sum up for them the energy they had to transform, the energy of both living nature and of the past stored in the collective unconsciousness? Did he, at the same time, express the spirit of inspiration, the genius hidden in created things?[16]

It is not only through the carvings of the Green Man that we can discern the importance to medieval man of this ancient gnostic stream; the same connection can often be found through other forms of artwork. In Rosslyn Chapel there are stained-glass windows dedicated to the Saints Michael, Longinus, Mauritius and George. What is St George, the patron saint of England, doing in a patently nationalistic Scottish chapel? Historical records reveal that the mythical personage we now call St George was reputed to be an Armenian. According to Pope Gelasius (494 AD), he 'was a Saint, venerated by man, but whose acts were known only to God'. Closer examination of the legends link his origins to St Michael and give us a basis upon which we can cast new light on his esoteric importance. The earliest known mythological personage on whom St George is held to be based is Tammuz, who provides one of the clues to the seemingly bizarre connections between the Sufis and their apparent enemies the Templars. Most modern authorities now believe that el Khidir, Tammuz and St George are the same person portrayed in a varying mythological guise.

Tammuz is variously described as the spouse, son or brother of the goddess Ishtar and is known as the Lord of Life and Death, a title which has deep Masonic overtones, and yet one which predates the reputed history of the Masonic movement by several millennia. One account tells that when Adam was sent to the Gates of Heaven, Tammuz offered him the bread and water of eternal life which Adam refused, thus losing his immortality. It is interesting to note that at Rosslyn Chapel St George is depicted as standing upon a rose-coloured board decorated with roses or rosettes, a symbolic reference to the goddess Ishtar. In contrast, Saints Longinus and Mauritius are shown standing on a chess board, the so-called 'checker-board of Joy' which represents both the Templar battle flag, the Beausseante, and the mystical 'hopscotch' symbol of the pilgrimage of initiation. Here it is depicted exactly as it is used in Masonic lodges; as part of the floor design upon which people stand for ceremonies and rituals.

Repression and Survival

With the crusade against the Cathars, the founding of the Inquisition, the suppression of the Templars and the withdrawal of immunities from the Children of Solomon, the initiatory Orders had to disappear from sight once more. We mentioned earlier that the majority of the Knights Templar simply seemed to have vanished, but in fact they fled to Lombardy, Scotland,

Portugal and the Baltic states. John Robinson, a writer with a special interest in medieval Britain and the Crusades, describes in his book *Born in Blood* how the fleeing knights were assisted to safe havens by the lodges of the Craftmasons. Were these particular lodges the Children of Master Jacques, or the Compagnons Passants? In Portugal the refugees joined the Order of the Knights of Christ; in the Baltic states they joined the Teutonic Knights; in Lombardy, aided by the Cathars who had preceded them, they used their skills to strengthen the emergent banking system; but in Scotland the story was very different.

The Knights Templar who reached Scotland fought as allies of Robert the Bruce and gained royal protection.[17] According to one of his descendants, 432 Templar knights, including Sir Henry St Clair, Baron of Roslin, and his sons William and Henry, took part in the charge at the battle of Bannockburn in 1314, which routed the English and preserved an independent Scotland for the king.[18] William's burial stone now rests within Rosslyn Chapel. Warned to go into hiding by the king, after an inconclusive trial on charges of heresy where the verdict was the equivocal Scottish one of 'not proven', the persecuted knights devoted themselves to the foundation of two important branches of the underground gnostic streams – Freemasonry and Rosicrucianism.

Earl William St Clair, the builder of Rosslyn Chapel, was appointed hereditary Grand Master of the guild of Craftmasons in Scotland for reasons that are far from clear. Nonetheless, the Hereditary Grand Mastership of the Masonic guilds remained in the St Clair family until St Andrew's Day in 1736 when the then Hereditary Grand Master, yet another Sir William St Clair of Roslin, resigned his Hereditary Patronage and Protectorship of the Masonic Craft to effect the erection of The Grand Lodge of Ancient, Free and Accepted Masons of Scotland.[19] He immediately became the first elected Grand Master in which position he served with distinction. With a family history so intimately linked with the higher echelons of the Templar Order from its conception, it is not surprising that Rosslyn Chapel would be built as a hymn to Templar ideals and as a source of coded teaching for Rosicrucianism and Freemasonry.

Their artwork has provided us with a vast library of arcane knowledge and signposts to the pathway of enlightenment. Rosslyn Chapel is not the only three-dimensional teaching board of gnosticism left in Europe, but it is the most important. All the sacred places of the apocalyptic configuration in stone were used, in secret, by the spiritual heirs to the gnostic groups in the centuries of repression that were to come.

PART III

⚜

The Pilgrimage of Initiation

Medieval feudal Europe was imperfect, unjust and élitist, yet it was a system founded on the conception that in order to survive it must serve all men whatever their rank, while each individual served almighty God and the Church who was God's representative on Earth. Tensions between the Church and the gnostics punctuated the calm of this apparently stable society with episodes of brutality and violence, of which the crusade against the Cathars in the Languedoc was the worst. However, the brief flowering of the Cathar society showed that change was not only possible but also highly desirable. According to C S Lewis, had it not been for the persecution of the Cathars, the culture of the Languedoc would have spawned a Renaissance nearly two centuries before that in Italy.

The hidden streams of spirituality did, however, exert an enormous influence on those who brought about the Italian Renaissance and the Protestant Reformation. This relatively small group of intellectual and spiritual giants created an intellectual climate within which science, democracy and intellectual freedom could flourish.

Nearly all the major intellectual figures of the period – including many of the founding fathers of modern science down to Newton's day – were deeply invested in . . . esoteric traditions, as if they believed there might lay hidden in these buried sources, secrets of human nature and the universe that were nowhere else to be found.[1]

The seminal thinkers, artists and philosophers of this period were all members of one or another of the spiritual organizations which were the heirs of the Knights Templar. Throughout the Middle Ages, the hidden streams of gnosticism had continued to secretly irrigate the spiritual desert of the times.

The Italian Renaissance was not merely a highly productive period of artistic creativity but the tangible consequence of a watershed in the evolution of consciousness that Trevor Ravenscroft believed had been foreseen by Earl William St Clair. This sudden flow of changed perceptions, thought and action, in religion, science, politics and man's basic conception of himself, turned into a flood of intellectual endeavour which burst upon the world like a tidal wave, sweeping aside old ideas and fertilizing the mind of the 'new scientific man' with conceptions that have affected the evolving world from that time to the present.

Very many of the advances in European culture derived largely from the gnostics who operated at horrendous risk because of the repressive attitude of the Church. Wider literacy, the concepts of freedom, democracy, philosophical and political advance and the very birth of modern science all spring mainly from the gnostic tradition.

It is not difficult to see why this period marks a critical turning point in the history of Western thought. Suddenly a flat, unmoving Earth, supposedly the very centre of the universe, became merely one planet among others, all revolving around the Sun in accordance with natural laws. Galileo's invention of the thermometer instigated the 'pointer reading age', and the conviction that mathematical concepts could be applied to natural events swept theology from its central position in European thought. The new world conception of Copernicus with its dynamic and heliocentric description of the solar system, together with Kepplar's laws, created both a pathway and a foundation for Newtonian physics.

> The medieval outlook changed radically in the sixteenth and seventeenth centuries. The notion of an organic, living, and spiritual universe was replaced by that of the world as a machine, and the world-machine became the dominant metaphor of the modern era. This development was brought about by revolutionary changes in physics and astronomy, culminating in the achievements of Copernicus, Galileo, and Newton. The science of the seventeenth century was based on a new method of inquiry, advocated forcefully by Francis Bacon, which involved the mathematical description of nature and the analytic method of reasoning conceived by the genius of Descartes. Acknowledging the crucial role of science in bringing about these far-reaching changes, historians have called the sixteenth and seventeenth centuries the Age of the Scientific Revolution.[2]

The Age of Discovery was about to commence and the new world would soon make its mark on European consciousness and trade. Later the Royal Society would be founded in England and Francis Bacon would proclaim that the world of the senses alone can provide us with realities – the realities of the empirical method.[3]

Prior to and throughout this formative era the hidden streams exerted their influence upon individuals who, at first glance, seem unlikely prospects for their attention. Luther, the prime mover of the Reformation, acknowledged that the mystics, especially the heretic Meister Eckhart, had influenced him profoundly. Sandro Philpepi, better known today as Botticelli, was a hermeticist and a pupil of Veruccio, a Master who also instructed Leonardo Da Vinci. Leonardo's historical reputation as an esotericist is well attested; he is described by some as a Rosicrucian, and by contemporary Catholics as 'of an heretical cast of mind'. Robert Fludd of England, the author of one of the most comprehensive compilations of ancient hermetic philosophy ever written, was reputedly a Rosicrucian, although this seems unlikely. He was, nonetheless, fulsome in his praise of them, and yet was one of the principal scholars responsible for the translation of what was later called *The Authorized Version of the Bible*. The priest, alchemist and author Johann Valentin Andrea was indeed a Rosicrucian of note and was, almost certainly, the author of the *Rosicrucian Manifestos* which gained wide circulation in Europe in the mid-seventeenth century.

The reaction of the Church to this explosion of creativity and scientific curiosity was predictable; a brutal but ultimately ineffective wave of censorship and torture was instigated in a vain attempt to put a stop to all advances in knowledge and freedom.

One important question remains: how did the gnostics achieve enlightenment in the medieval era of repression? For attain it they did, and in significant numbers if contemporaneous accounts of their influence are to be believed. The hidden heirs to the Knights Templar devised a method to pass on their sacred knowledge; a system that eventually developed into Freemasonry, Rosicrucianism and the Invisible College, which later transmuted itself into the Royal Society in England: the pilgrimage of initiation.

10

Rosslyn Chapel and
Spiritual Fulfilment

Rosslyn Chapel is the natural starting point in any rational search for clues to the methods of initiation used in the late medieval era. Created as a superbly carved reliquary for the Grail, which in itself is nothing less than an allegorical description of the path to enlightenment, it is also the ultimate pinnacle of the pilgrimage of initiation which was sacred to the memory and beliefs of the Knights Templar[1], and tradition tells us that their heirs used a hidden room under the chapel as an initiation chamber. The paucity of archival records of Templar beliefs makes the task of interpreting their romantic legends realistically extremely difficult.

It has long been recognized that the chapel was a site of special veneration and pilgrimage. Folklore recounts how pilgrims in their thousands travelled there after completing the arduous trek to the shrine of St James of Compostela. Tim had suggested in an earlier work that this may have been because of some relic kept at Rosslyn, a Black Madonna perhaps[2], though other authors do not agree with him; in *The Hiram Key* this possibility was dismissed.[3] The association of the Templars with the Black Madonna, however, is a matter of recorded fact. Ean Begg's book, *The Cult of the Black Madonna*, is perhaps the best-known exposition of this strange cult.

In describing their research into ancient Israel for *The Hiram Key* the authors did not mention the esoteric significance of the name of Israel itself. It is held to stand for ISis RA and ELohim, thus recording the three divine Egyptian and Canaanite roots of Hebraic gnosticism; the very foundation for the hidden streams which pervade and illuminate Judaeo-Christian spirituality. But why did such knowledge have to remain hidden?

The medieval Christian Church was the most intolerant and repressive authority that Europe has ever experienced. After the suppression of the Templar Order, their spiritual heirs had once again to disguise their initiatory processes under the cloak of acceptable Christian ritual and practice. What better than for its novices to make a series of ostensibly devout Christian pilgrimages to the cathedrals built on the seven sacred sites of the prophetic configuration?

Trevor Ravenscroft had often suggested that even before the advent of Christianity, Celtic pilgrims who worshipped the Earth goddess journeyed from Iberia to Scotland via the seven planetary oracles, associating the alignment of the spirit senses within themselves to the corresponding alignment of the Earth chakras.[4] The sequence of the sites corresponds to that of the planets in our solar system; the Moon, Mercury, Venus, the Sun, Mars, Jupiter and Saturn. There was no arbitrary choice involved in which seven cathedrals were an integral part of this apocalyptic configuration in stone.

Bounded by the pillars at either end, the seven sacred sites lie under the beneficent royal arch of the Milky Way. Trevor was convinced that this powerful configuration is not static; he believed that just as subliminal energies stream up and down through the chakras within the human body, so similar forces, the Wouivre, surge northwards and southwards along this great alignment of cathedrals. Dowsers have discovered that powerful lines of energy intersect at each of the sites along this route.

There was a complex web of inter-connecting routes to Compostela from all over Europe. The pilgrimage began to gain immense popularity during the reign of Charlemagne

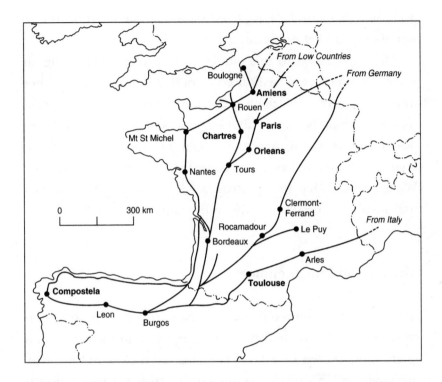

Far from being on one route, most of the seven sites of the configuration were on different routes to Compostela.

(768–814 AD), but the main guide for the intending pilgrims was published in the twelfth century as the Codex Callextinus. Included on the various itineraries were Amiens, St Denis in Montmartre, Notre-Dame de Paris, Chartres, Orléans, Tours, Poitiers, Le Puy and Toulouse.

Most of the seven sites of the configuration were on different routes to Compostela. Trevor Ravenscroft was convinced that insightful pilgrims journeyed from Compostela to Rosslyn, calling at each of the sites in turn. We have learnt since his death that his perceptions have almost invariably proved to be uncannily accurate. So, could he have been right in some mysterious way, and if he was what did it signify?

One of the keys to this puzzle proved to lie in applying an understanding of the Druidic concept that the seven sacred sites were the earthly equivalent of the seven chakras or energy centres in human beings. This idea that there are seven Earth power points arcing across Western Europe from northern Spain to Scotland has been confirmed from other sources.[5] What relevance has that to Rosslyn Chapel, other than the fact that Rosslyn is the seventh site in the alignment?

The Path to Enlightenment

Attaining enlightenment in the Western esoteric tradition involved a form of ritualized mysticism wherein the novice was taught and guided by a Master. These seven chakras were ritually awakened in a predetermined order, from the base upwards to the crown. When the powers of spirit and matter combined, the seven chakras acted as a single channel. This energetic power followed a winding path as it moved between the centres. In Eastern schools of philosophy it is described as the raising of the serpent known as the Kundalini, which then moves through the other chakras as the student ascends to the higher levels of awareness. It is not surprising that the esoteric symbol associated with the Wouivre, the telluric force recognized by the Druids and the Templars, is the serpent. The specific order of the awakening of energy centres from the base to the crown explains why, in the pilgrimage of initiation, the ritual order of progress is a complete reversal of the normal, orthodox pilgrimage to Compostela.

As each chakra is energetically opened the student, spiritually speaking, makes progress. Thus the pilgrimage is not simply one journey encompassing each of the seven sites, but a series of journeys made in a predetermined order, starting with the Druidic Moon oracle at Compostela, representing the base chakra, then moving northwards to each site in the alignment in turn before culminating at Rosslyn, representing the crown chakra. Each stage is only accomplished after an appropriate period of intense and spiritual preparation.

The novice making an initiatory pilgrimage to the shrine of St James by one of the routes laid down in the Codex Callextinus had demonstrated sufficient dedication and humility to qualify for the sublime gift of illumination. The achievement of this stage revealed a twofold quality of humility and obedience. The first was outwardly to the diktat of Holy Mother the Church; the second, and hidden form, was to his teacher and, through him, to his ultimate master, Almighty God.

First-degree initiation was the result that flowed spiritually from the awakening of the base chakra that connects us with the earth and physical reality; according to tradition it can only be opened after the attainment of true humility, for this is the chakra that literally keeps us rooted. In the human body it controls the base of the spine, and is closely linked with the adrenals, and therefore represents that most basic of all instincts, survival. The first degree, the Raven, symbolized the messenger of the gods. It was thus that the new candidate achieved, through inner toil, the first stage of soul conversion through which he gained the capacity to receive messages from spirits in the divine world. The Raven also represented the messenger of the mystery cults who had learned to express the visual in images which could be understood at different levels by both the outside world and by the initiated.

When the novice had progressed thus far along his chosen spiritual path, he was open to receive the messenger of the mystery cults. He would then be instructed to make the pilgrimage from Compostela to Toulouse, to the church built on the site of the Mercury oracle. Mercury was simply the Latinization of the Greek god Hermes, the winged messenger of the gods. At Toulouse he would be introduced to the mysteries of the second degree with the opening of the sacral or abdominal chakra, which lies between the base and solar plexus centres and works closely with them. The second degree is known as that of the Occultist and is symbolized by the Peacock, whose many-splendoured plumage represents the student's new powers of moral imagination. This was known to have been gained when he discovered his own inner space and could retire into the hidden isolation of his own spirit. He had become the Hidden One, or Occultist, who could now communicate directly with Hermes Trismegistus, the thrice-blessed one of the Greek mysteries whose bust adorns the eastern wall of Rosslyn Chapel.

The Knight was the symbol of the third and warrior degree and knighthood was bestowed for the attainment of it. When the aspirant had gained sufficient inner strength and moral courage to represent the good against the evil in the world, he was named the Warrior. The legendary Knights of the Round Table of King Arthur were initiates at this level, as were the Knights Templar who were able to represent the sword of justice in the barbaric medieval world. The fulfilment of this degree led to the awakening of the third chakra, said to be the storehouse of prana, the universal life-force. When fear and anxiety register here, thought becomes action. Many people see another linkage with the adrenals because of the fight-or-flight syndrome brought about by the action of adrenaline. This degree was achieved by entry into the mysteries of the Venus oracle at the sublime Cathedral of Orléans.

When suitably qualified candidates were prepared for further advancement along their chosen spiritual path they would visit the site of the heart chakra and undergo their initiation in the mystical underground chamber of la Vierge de Sous-Terre in the crypt of Chartres Cathedral, the ancient site of the Sun oracle. There they were accorded the degree of the Lion. The Swan was the sacred symbol of this, the fourth degree, because the swansong represented the death of self and the inner realization of the divine within the human breast. The fourth degree was only awarded when the aspirant had gained control of his subjective processes so that no unconscious prejudice could rule his actions. At this level of spiritual development the divine element within him had become so strong that he could look into the core of his own being and shrink from no toil which duty demanded of him.

This degree was mirrored by the awakening of the heart chakra, often called the Abode of Mercy, which is linked to the region of the thymus gland above the heart. This centre represents the union between the physical and spiritual aspects of the personality. It controls the individual's emotions and how they relate to others and to nature. Most importantly it is the spiritual centre controlling the sublime gifts of love and compassion. The colour traditionally attributed to this chakra is green, the colour of initiation and rebirth.

The first four degrees, the Raven, the Occultist, the Warrior, and the Lion, all represent the spiritual transformation of toil; the fifth and sixth degrees were gained through the spiritualization of

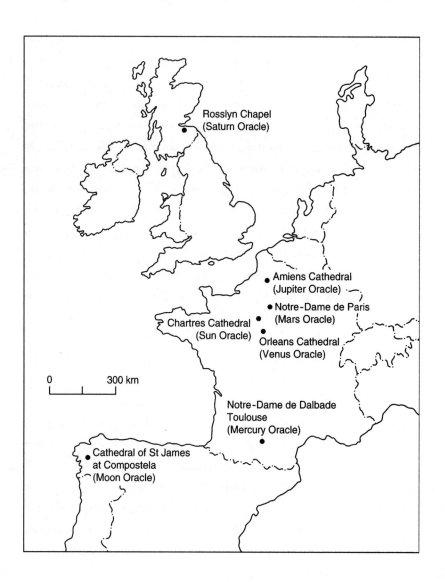

The builders of these great cathedrals deliberately erected them on Druidic sites, dedicated to the planetary oracles.

suffering. Induction into the fifth degree was performed in the chamber under Notre-Dame de Paris, the site of the Druidic oracle of Mars, and in Grail symbolism was depicted by the Pelican, the bird which wounds its own breast to feed its young. Such an initiate lived for the perpetuation of his own people, being granted their name – for instance, the Persian, the Egyptian, the Greek, or the Israelite – and dedicated his life to their service. He now worked within a conscious unity of the folk-spirit of his people, that is, he could suffer the responsibility of speaking for his own karmic community. The fifth centre is the throat chakra, and is the first of the higher ones. It is associated with communication and demands that a distinction be made between purposeful words and thought, and those which arc idle and meaningless noise. It is the centre of both speech and inner hearing, and is connected with the power of sound.

The brow chakra, known to many as the third eye, or eye of the mind, is connected with the pituitary gland. Clairvoyance is specifically connected with this centre, which relates to the right side of the brain and to the spiritual faculties of insight and intuition; it brings a direct 'knowing'. It is responsible for the balance and harmony of the energy system. When this chakra was awakened the, by now, highly qualified aspirant would be instructed in the sublime mysteries of the Jupiter oracle and gain advancement to the sixth and penultimate degree, denoted by the Eagle. This took place in the glorious confines of the Cathedral of Amiens, where he acquired the capacity to move and communicate in the spiritual world and gained a true insight into the secrets of space; he could expand his consciousness between Earth and Sun within the streaming of time.

All who were privileged enough to undertake this pilgrimage would have been spiritually gifted men, and those who rose to attain any of the higher degrees of initiation would have been men of exceptional talent, humility and dedication. There were only twenty-four men of supreme talent in the influential early Renaissance Order of the Golden Fleece, of which Earl William St Clair was a member. Was this chivalric Order the outward face of the Rex Deus families who claimed descent from the twenty-four High Priests of the Jerusalem Temple? Or was this perhaps the overt face of that secretive, select few who had finally achieved the highest order of them all: the Kings of the Grail?

The Crown was the royal symbol of the King of the Grail. To him was revealed an understanding of all the laws at work within human destiny. The holder of the seventh degree was given the name of 'the Father' because the initiate knew the secrets of time and had gained a true understanding of the working of the primal karma out of which the father-God was functioning.

This degree gave an insight into the spiritualization of death, which may have explained the ancient Knights Templar's well-deserved reputation for being fearless in battle. It was attained with the culmination of the spiritual journey at the opening of the crown chakra, which is mystically united with the pineal gland; known to the devotees of the Greek mysteries as the Seat of the Soul – the seat of consciousness and the doorway to the creator. Even the supreme rationalist Descartes claimed that the pineal linked body and soul. This chakra is sometimes regarded as a unique centre of consciousness and therefore separate from the other six. Its opening is essential for attaining complete attunement in the processes of both healing and meditation. The full flowering of the crown chakra occurs when the head of the serpent-like kundalini reaches it, for which the psychological keyword is Awakening.

The enlightenment which flows from the opening of the crown chakra is the supreme and total fulfilment of the Grail search, and was awarded at the seventh site, Rosslyn Chapel, the ancient and revered site of the Saturn oracle itself. The initiation ceremony for this degree took place in the hidden chamber under the chapel which was deliberately created by Earl William St Clair as the focal point for every known path of initiation. Rosslyn Chapel – the Omphalos or spiritual umbilicus of the world.

Other Pilgrims

There is evidence confirming this concept of the pilgrimage of initiation in scriptural sources and elsewhere. Biblical mention of the ravens who fed Elijah are held to mark the beginning of his path of initiation. The events at Serepha where he heals the son of the widow show him to be a Hidden One who has achieved the second degree. On Mount Carmel he defends the knowledge of the spirit, and as a Warrior represents the good in the fight against evil. On Horeb, when he perceives Jehovah within his own soul, he achieves the fourth degree, that of the Lion. His later achievement of the final three degrees was revealed to Elisha, who inherited his mantle on the occasion of Elijah's assumption into heaven, when his pupil saw the fiery chariot of the sun hero drawn by horses across the heavens. Elisha describes the vision in these words: 'My Father, my Father, the chariot of Israel and the horses thereof.'[6] In a single magnificent flight of imagination, Elisha describes the genius of Israel, the spirit of the sun-hero and the sphere of the Father.

One modern pilgrim recounts how, as she rested in the shade of Leon Cathedral, another pilgrim limped his way towards her and greeted her. She asked if he was a 'Peregrino a Santiago?' His response was strange indeed:

> No! I walk the Camiño de las Estrellas, the Milky Way, not the Camiño de Santiago. The Milky Way is the true and ancient path of spiritual death and rebirth. The Camiño was just a Christian attempt to camouflage the true way.[7]

The ancient centre of spiritual death and rebirth was of course the Moon oracle. He went on to describe the true way as one that led along a path under the vault of the Milky Way in the heavens and passed through churches marked by certain carvings of mystical birds and animals. The symbols of the seven degrees of initiation perhaps? He explained that:

> The ancients left carvings on the churches, but it is hard to read them because the initiation rites were secret and carried on by word of mouth, and that he and others were trying to reconstruct them.[8]

The pilgrim was a little confused by this encounter, for she was travelling the Camiño out of intellectual curiosity seeking data for her doctoral thesis in anthropology and not out of Christian faith. Yet eventually even she was to admit that she was not simply on a physical journey to Compostela but was treading a powerful and pervasive esoteric pathway: week after week along the route she was being spiritually transformed and both her sense of perspective and her values were undergoing a dramatic change. She stated in her essay 'Perhaps those who travel the

Camiño are impacted with faint echoes of ancient worship, faint images of archetypical power.' Her final sentence closely identified her with our own quest: 'I do not know what road I travel, except that there are many hidden beneath the one – and, perhaps beneath the many is the One.'[9]

Other 'enlightened' modern pilgrims have travelled the same path. In 1991, Trevor's ex-wife, Shirley Griffin, rode on horseback from Compostela along the same route through Toulouse, Orléans, Chartres, Paris and Amiens to Rosslyn in an arduous and profoundly moving re-creation of Trevor's original idea.[10] The very first time Tim went to Rosslyn, the scallop shell that Shirley had brought there from Compostela lay in a place of honour on one of the altars in the Lady Chapel.

As to the belief that there are Earth chakras of similar nature to the human spiritual centres, there are several well-respected theories, for example:

There seem to be strong parallels between energy in the body and energy in the landscape and . . . If the earth is a living being its energy flows and sacred centres correspond to the meridians and acupuncture points in the human body . . . Some have taken the parallels between the human body and the Earth much further and have postulated 'chakra' points on the Earth's surface which have specific effects in landscape terms appropriate to the nature of the corresponding chakra. The heart chakra, for example, has been seen in terms of a river curving around a conical hill with a church. They are often referred to as 'landscape temples'.

Various axes have been suggested incorporating the seven chakras. One is supposed to run from France up to Scotland.[11]

The crypt at Chartres Cathedral was used as an initiation chamber. Did similar chambers exist under the other six buildings of the alignment? The Druids were of an oral culture, so while there is little doubt about their use of the sites, there is no proof that they used them as planetary oracles. However, there is evidence of their use as sites of temples dedicated to the various planets during the Gallo-Roman era.

This evidence provides a context within which the esoteric carvings in Rosslyn and elsewhere may be better understood, and begins to explain many other of the enigmas that abound in that mystical place. In investigating these controversial and heretical matters it would be wise to remember that:

> There is a principle
> which is a bar against all information,
> which is proof against all arguments
> and which cannot fail to keep a man
> in everlasting ignorance
> – that principle is
> 'contempt prior to investigation'.[12]

This is vital caution to any scholar who carries within them the prejudice of scientific training or Cartesian logic and who is investigating the shadowy world of supersensible reality.

Spiritual power, like earth energies, may be beyond rational understanding, but it can be demonstrated, experienced and used. Let us all try and access this divine gift with humility and use its insights to get closer to the ultimate and eternal truth – spiritual reality itself.

11

Our Own Pilgrimage

The limping pilgrim's account of the Camiño de las Estrellas provided an uncanny confirmation of the results of our own researches, and we decided it was time to experience this sacred journey for ourselves. There was one essential difference between us and our gnostic ancestors for, despite following our own spiritual path, we had no hierophant to guide us. Nonetheless we were encouraged by the words of the nineteenth-century transcendentalist writer, Thoreau: 'Live your beliefs and you will change the world.' By experiencing the benefits of this pilgrimage we believed that we would be granted the insights that would help us in our quest. And so we began the long journey starting at Europe's base chakra at Compostela and on up through the buildings of the apocalyptic configuration in France before crossing the channel and travelling north to the crown chakra at Rosslyn.

And I said to the man who stood at the gate of the year:
'Give me a light that I might travel safely into the unknown.'
And he replied:
'Go out into the darkness
And put your hand
Into the hand of God.
That to you shall be better than light and
Safer than a known way.'[1]

St James de Compostela

Archaeologists have discovered that there was a significant town at Compostela during the Roman occupation. The interior of the Cathedral of St James has been thoroughly excavated, disclosing the remains of numerous pre-Christian burials under the nave and vestiges of Roman buildings, probably a temple, under the south transept.[2] These temple remains abut directly upon the foundations of the ninth-century Christian basilica, adding credence to Trevor's theory of Druidic, Roman and eventual Christian use of the same sacred site. Altar slabs dedicated to pagan deities previously venerated here had their original pre-Christian inscriptions erased before being incorporated into the so-called Apostle's Altar.[3]

The supposed tomb of the Apostle James was discovered between 813 and 818 AD but, ironically, the earliest account of Christian pilgrims to Compostela comes from the Muslim writer, Ibd Dihya, who noted that there were pilgrims visiting the tomb of St James as early as 844 AD. Louis VII of France, St Francis of Assisi, King Robert the Bruce of Scotland and Earl William St Clair all figure in the impressive list of those who made the arduous pilgrimage in medieval times. The prosperous medieval city of Compostela which grew up around the shrine was sustained by the countless generations of devout travellers.

The cathedral is a glorious example of Romanesque architecture whose vast interior is preserved in its almost original condition. Soft light floods the nave, emphasizing its size and grandeur, while in the galleries and lateral aisles the light and atmosphere is more subdued, as though the architects shared the meditative attitude of the pilgrims.

The figures of the great initiates Melchizedek, Abraham, David and Moses decorate the south door and the façade adjoining it. Many of the pillars of this doorway are also hauntingly familiar in style, being of a serpentine form. However, from our point of view it is the interior and its iconography, allied to the feeling of spirituality and vibrant energy, that is most significant.

The spiritual impact is overwhelming as soon as one enters the heavy main doors that divide the ornate Baroque granite exterior from the medieval carvings of the arches of the Pórtico de la Gloria. This superb *tour de force* by the medieval genius, Master Mateo, has been described as 'the finest monument of medieval sculpture' and, according to Street[4], 'one of the glories of Christian art'. It has also been described as 'resembling a giant triptych in which religious feeling is expressed as ingeniously and sublimely as the artistic ideal of the time was capable of'.

The central column is of finely carved marble, crowned by a capital that rests just above the seated figure of the Apostle St James who grips the top of a tau-shaped staff with his left hand, while in his right he holds a tablet inscribed with the Latin inscription *Misil me Dominus* – the Lord sent me. The central pillar is a symbolic reference to the genealogy of Jesus, a three-dimensional representation of the Tree of Jesse with David and Solomon discernible among the branches. The Tree of Jesse commences with Jesse, the father of King David, and is represented in Church iconography in sculpture, paintings, manuscript illuminations and stained glass. One of the oldest stained-glass windows in Chartres Cathedral which survived the destruction of the earlier building is a vivid depiction of this family tree. At Rosslyn Chapel, the Tree of Jesse is carved on a lintel by the Master Mason's pillar.

At Compostela, the majority of pilgrims place their fingers in five well-worn hollows visible at shoulder height in the leafy ornamentation around the shaft of the Tree of Jesse. Immediately behind the base of this column there is a sculpture of Master Mateo kneeling and facing the High Altar as if he was perpetually offering his great devotional work to Almighty God himself. Devout pilgrims knock their heads against the sculptured head of Mateo as if to receive a share of his wisdom and talents. For this reason the sculpture bears the Galician name *O sancto dos croques*; 'croques' means to 'bang one's head'.[5]

On passing through the arches of Mateo's masterpiece, one's eyes are immediately drawn to the imposing and over-ornate Baroque decoration of the main altar. This lies directly beneath a representation of the all-seeing eye of God embossed centrally in an equilateral triangle on the underside of the canopy that covers the whole area. Immediately below the altar is the Romanesque crypt containing the Apostle's sepulchre.

One of the two surviving original copies of the Codex Callextinus, the *Liber Sancti Jacobi* or Book of St James, is housed in the cathedral archives. In the Chapel of the Relics there is one artefact in particular which is of overwhelming significance: a jewelled and gilt reliquary in the form of an ornate silver bust with an enamelled face, containing the head of St James the Less, the brother of the Lord and the first Bishop of Jerusalem, James the Just, for whose sake, according to Jesus, 'the heaven and the earth came into existence'.[6] The cathedral guidebook seems to have slipped up, theologically speaking, by describing this reliquary as:

The most important silver bust is that of St James the Lesser. The cranium of this saint, the younger brother of St James the

Greater, was brought from Jerusalem to Braga in the 12th century.

Here James the Less is described as the *brother* of James the Great. The New Testament – an authority even the Catholic hierarchy cannot refute – describes James the Less as 'the Lord's brother'.[7] Thus literature published by the Church, backed up by the New Testament, reinforces our earlier deduction about the relationship between Jesus, James the Great and James the Less: Mary was the mother of the sons of Zebedee.

Heresy from Holy Mother the Church? Unlikely though it may seem, this is the inescapable conclusion arising from the cumulative effect of these statements. Yet only recently pope John Paul II declared as an absolute and infallible truth that Mary the Mother of God had but one child, Jesus. Now either the infallible pope has erred, or the New Testament, the inerrant word of God, has got it wrong.

This reliquary and its contents are considered only second in importance to the remains of St James the Great. Legend tells how the cranium of St James the Less was brought from Jerusalem to Braga in Spain in the twelfth century. The skull is pierced in the area of the temple in the same manner as the skull of St John the Baptist which is preserved in Amiens Cathedral.

The Lower Church, which was known in medieval times as the Crypt or the Old Cathedral, dates from the late eleventh or early twelfth century and is dedicated to James the Less. In the crypt are statues of both King David and King Solomon and three thick pillars, one decorated with a figure of St James the Just. Little did we know that when we claimed that under the guise of the official pilgrimage there may well lie another, we were describing a physical as well as a spiritual reality. When

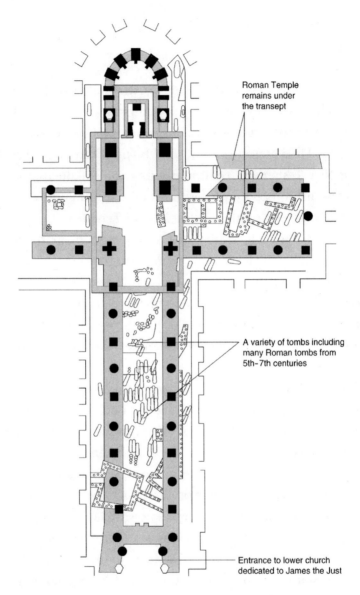

Roman Temple
remains under
the transept

A variety of tombs including
many Roman tombs from
5th–7th centuries

Entrance to lower church
dedicated to James the Just

Ground plan of St James of Compostela. The interior of the cathedral has been thoroughly excavated, disclosing numerous pre-Christian burials under the nave as well as vestiges of a Roman building, probably a temple, under the south transept.

8 Ruined Templar church
at Balantradoch

9 Engrailed cross of the St Clair
family showing the Templar cross
at the junction, Rosslyn Chapel

10 (left) The Apprentice Pillar, Rosslyn Chapel

11 (below) Green Man carving, Rosslyn Chapel

12 (above) Carving of the
head of the 'murdered
apprentice', Rosslyn
Chapel

13 (left) Central rose,
Retro Choir, with Madonna
and Child, Rosslyn Chapel

14 Lintel at Rosslyn Chapel referring to the book of Esdas and to Zerubabel's temple in Jerusalem

15 Carving of Ladislaus Leslyn and the future Queen Margaret of Scotland carrying the Holy Rood, Rosslyn Chapel

Catholic pilgrims were travelling to the main cathedral above to venerate St James the Great, Santiago Matamoros (St James the Moor Slayer), heretical pilgrims in the underground church immediately beneath their feet were paying their respects to that vitally important figure in gnostic belief, James the Just. As above, so below. High above the cathedral itself, over the triumphal arch which crowns the roof, is a bell arch crowned by the Agnus Dei, an item of church symbolism so intimately entwined with the heretical order of the Grail Knights that it is known to this day as the Templar Seal.

The Agnus Dei depicts a lamb, sometimes shown as jumping, in front of which is a croix patté, or Templar Cross, and a flag. It was used, among many other designs, as one of the seals for Templar documents, and is one of the symbols indicating Templar influence in a medieval building. These include carvings of a five-pointed star; the two brothers on one horse; the Agnus Dei; a stylized representation of the head of Christ such as that represented in the Shroud of Turin or in the Veil of Veronica known as the Mandylion; a dove in flight carrying an olive branch; and finally a form of oriental cross known as the Floriated Cross.[8] It must be remembered that all these signs are also part of orthodox symbolism, and so it is unsafe to attribute Templar influence unless four or more occur close together in the same building. Rosslyn Chapel contains examples of all of them.

Blanche Mertz has described the telluric powers of the cathedral, and suggests that the energy patterns reflect the watercourses that lie under it:

These water inflows are made conspicuous in the paving of the side corridors . . . by 14 wide inlays of black marble. During the decade of the 1960s there were large excavations under the cathedral of Santiago de Compostela, and what did they find? These old inflow channels had been dug by human hands . . . today, at Compostela the channels are dry! . . . as a consequence of these works executed between 1948 and 1968 . . . the subterranean water passages, programmed by the constructors, were cut.

It is often said that there are no more miracles at Santiago de Compostela.[9]

The fact that these watercourses had been 'dug by human hands' implies that their layout was a conscious and deliberate act, designed to imbue the site with a powerful energy, or to enhance already existing telluric forces. This is a vivid example of the skills and insight of the enlightened master craftsmen who laid the foundations of this spectacular shrine, and gives physical form to the allegorical concept of 'the hidden streams of spirituality'.

As pilgrims to the Cathedral of St James we too followed tradition and placed our fingers in the five well-worn hollows on the Tree of Jesse, the centrepiece of the Pórtico de la Gloria. I was overwhelmed with emotion, and experienced a buzzing in my fingers and a tendency to sway, accompanied by a feeling of light-headedness. Tim has never claimed to have any particular gifts in detecting telluric energies and, having read Blanche Mertz's comments about the diminished powers at Compostela as a result of the watercourses drying up, was distinctly surprised. To complete the ritual, he walked slowly to the other side of the pillar and made obeisance to the carving of Master Mateo.

Marilyn also experienced a feeling of considerable power, her notes recording that 'On first entering it my fingers began to tingle, a sign that I am picking up the telluric energy at a site.

I also felt a tightness in my chest and, initially, an increase in my heart rate. Visually, the immense size of the building was the first thing I became aware of, both from outside and on entering it. There is a feeling of solidity to it. The most striking feature is the main altar, with the figure of St James and the Eye of God looking down from above him.' If, as Blanche Mertz suggests, the telluric powers *have* diminished as a result of twentieth-century work, how much power was accessible in this shrine during the era of the pilgrimage of initiation?

We spent some time in quiet contemplation in the Lower Church. Undisturbed by the crowds who thronged the main cathedral above, we meditated and remembered the mysterious history of James the Just. It was here that the gnostics, gathered for initiation, would have experienced the awakening of their base chakra, so enabling all centres to synthesize increasingly higher energies. When this chakra was open and functioning the pilgrim began to experience the mystical interconnectedness of all things. He or she consciously became an integral part of nature, had a sense of belonging and felt grounded. This process was often accompanied by a strong emotional response.[10]

True spiritual experience is often only fully appreciated long after the event. Thus it was some time later that we began to wonder if the strong emotions we had felt in the cathedral at Compostela were indicative of some form of spiritual awakening within ourselves.

En Route to Toulouse

When we left Compostela we drove diametrically across Spain towards the southern edge of the Pyrenees *en route* to the medieval heart of the great modern city of Toulouse. We were to continue our pilgrimage by locating the site of the Mercury oracle. During that long drive we began to review some of the beliefs connected with Mercury, otherwise known as Hermes, the messenger of the gods.

Hermes is a god with many titles. To some he is 'the master of secrecy' and is equated with the prophet Moses, with Christ himself and with St John the Divine. The medieval Sufi Master Suhrawardi claimed that the sages of most religions in the ancient world had all preached the same doctrine. Originally it had been revealed by the gods themselves to Hermes; and in the Egyptian tradition, from which sprang Judaism and later Christianity, this divine teaching had been transmitted to mankind through the words of the Moon god Thoth, the god of knowledge. To the philosophers of ancient Greece, Thoth and Hermes were the same entity in differing mythological guise.

Suhrawardi also identified Hermes with the prophet Idris (mentioned in the Koran) and the prophet Enoch in the Bible. Hermes is also linked indirectly with the Druids, for one of the teachers of Pythagoras was the Druid Abaris. We mentioned earlier that Diogenes Laertes equated the Druids with the Magi. Pythagoras, initiated into the Hermetic mysteries and the teachings of the Magi is, through his teacher, linked to the Druids and the Kibeiri. Therefore the basic teachings of all of these strands must have been compatible. At the very least, Hermes in his various guises pervades them all as well as those of Egypt and the early Israelites. With the Enochian identification, the links between the messenger of the gods and Judaism are made even more explicit.

At Rosslyn Chapel, the winged helmet of Hermes 'the divine messenger' occupies an important position, just to the left of centre on the exterior face of the east wall.[11] Why is it that the pagan Hermes faces the source of light and energy that is then transmitted through him into the hearts and minds of all who enter this holy place?

To many classicists, Hermes is called the transmitter of light; he does this by veiling it, as secrets cannot be kept in the light or else they are soon revealed; the invisible only becomes visible through concealment. There is a bizarre justification for this recounted in the Gospel according to St Matthew:

> The light of the body is the eye;
> if therefore thine eye be single,
> thy whole body shall be full of light.[12]

The curious phrase 'if therefore thine eye be single' refers to the opening of the third eye, and the words 'thy whole body shall be full of light' describes the fruits of initiation and the state of illumination.

Suhrawardi was known in his own time as 'the sheik al-Ishraq' or the 'Master of Illumination'. Like the ancient Greeks and some later Christian mystics, he experienced God in terms of light. In Arabic, Ishraq is the first light of dawn that issues from the East; it is also the term for enlightenment; Jesus Christ is described as the Light of the World; Earl William St Clair of Roslin was renowned as 'one of the illuminati'. Is not the result of receiving the divine message from Hermes precisely that – enlightenment? The whole thrust of the complex, hidden message of Rosslyn is a celebration of this heretical process.

On our arrival in Toulouse we began our search for the Temple of Mercury. Acting on information supplied by Pat Sibille, we went to the pedestrian entrance of the car park in the

Place Esquirol, where there is a large mosaic mural, displaying the archaeological discoveries made as the car park was being built. Finds from different eras were depicted in contrasting colours against a background of a modern street plan of the district. Stretching from where we stood at the entrance, to the Place de la Trinité and beyond, was the emblem of a Roman temple – the Temple of Mercury! We now had to find the relevant church and trace the historical and esoteric linkages to the Druids and the Templars.

Standing beside the fountain in the Place de la Trinité we began to search in the narrow streets that radiate from this tiny square. Long before we could see the church itself, Marilyn could sense l'église de Notre-Dame la Dalbade.

Archival records disclose that the first church here was erected in 541, and was rebuilt at least once prior to the erection of the present place of worship. The church constructed between 1180 and 1200 interested us most, as it was the first Gothic building in the district, which was built on this site to replace the earlier Romanesque edifice. Both the old church and its Gothic replacement were dedicated to Notre-Dame la Dalbade – Our Lady in White. Not only did the date of construction place this building firmly in the Templar era, but its Gothic style, its grandeur and its dedication linked it to the white-robed Knights of the Grail. The guidebook to the present church recounts how, on 27 February 1442, a fire in this ancient quarter of Toulouse destroyed the Gothic church, many nearby houses and claimed many lives. It tells how the present building, built on the foundations of its Gothic predecessor, was consecrated on 1 November 1455.

As soon as we walked through the doors we realized that we had entered a church of stunning simplicity and harmony. The vault rises above a clerestory supported by a colonnade of perfectly proportioned pillars, each one adorned with the heraldic symbol of the croix patté, the distinctive splayed, eight-pointed cross of the Knights Templar. The church stands near the Hotel des Chevaliers which, according to the local archives, was once the property of the Knights Hospitallers, the Order who had inherited the vast bulk of Templar property in France. After our return to England we discovered evidence of a grant by Raymond Rater of Toulouse, of land, houses and the church Notre-Dame la Dalbade to the Templar Order in a charter dated between 1128 and 1132, so this indeed was the church we had sought.[13]

It was Marilyn's natural dowsing abilities that had led us to this site with comparative ease. In her notes recorded after three visits there she wrote: 'I felt the customary tingle in my finger-tips before the church even came into view. This happened on all three occasions, even when approaching from different directions. On entering the church itself the feeling intensified. On our first visit, which took place in the early evening, I was aware of feeling "drunk" as I walked down the centre towards the altar. As the church was empty I was able to spend some time just standing at what I felt was the most powerful point, absorb-ing the atmosphere. The power seemed to be more concentrated just in front of the altar in the centre of the aisle. When I encounter a force as powerful as the one I felt here I also tend to sway on my feet, which certainly happened on this occasion. I had a strong impression of cloaked figures from sometime in the past, possibly Druids, but this may have been my own fanciful imagination.

'On our third visit the initial tingling sensations were en-hanced by the same feelings of tightness in my chest accompanied by the increased heart rate that I had experienced at Compostela. Again I also felt drunk. We sat in meditation, during which I experienced some very odd and inexplicable sensations. The church was very quiet, so meditating was not difficult. I became aware that my hands no longer felt as if they were "mine"; they felt completely detached from my arms. I then started to feel as if they were like two round balls which were growing. This continued until it felt as if I had two large footballs on the ends of my arms. At this point I finished my meditation, but it was some time before I felt as if my hands were really mine again. In astrological terms, my ruling planet is Mercury. Could this be why I had such a mysterious experience on the site of the Mercury oracle?'

We meditated sitting as close as possible to the power point that Marilyn had discovered during our first visit. She was seeking confirmation of our direction, as Tim simply prayed for knowledge of God's will for us and the power to carry that out.

In the Druidic view of the seven sites as chakras, the site of the Mercury oracle was the earthly equivalent to the sacral chakra in the human body. When this centre is awakened it is usually accompanied by an increased activity in the dream life and an enhanced awareness of unconscious needs. Opening this chakra generally heightens sensitivity and specifically sharpens the psychic senses.[14] Is this why Marilyn saw cloaked, Druidic figures during her period of contemplation? Were our prayerful requests for a firm sense of direction and the knowledge of God's will for us and the power to carry that out, all part of an expression of our unconscious needs? After this quiet, but productive time, we left Toulouse and made our way northwards towards the city of Joan of Arc and its cathedral.

The Venus Oracle

Before the Roman invasion, Carnutum, or Chartres, and Cenabum, otherwise known as Genabum, now Orléans, were the principal towns of the tribal lands of the Carnutes. Both were Druidic centres and each had its own oracle dedicated to a different planet, with that of the Venus oracle dedicated to light and the morning star at Cenabum. The Roman conquerors under Caesar divided this tribal state into two: Civitas Carnutum, which developed into the present city of Chartres, and Civitas Aurelianorum, which corresponded roughly with the ninth-century county of Orléans.

The Cathedral of Orléans, built on the site of the Venus oracle of the Druids, has been substantially altered since its original construction. The exterior is truly magnificent in its own right, and Marilyn's description of it conveys something of its true atmosphere: 'My first impression was of a strikingly attractive building, with towers and an exterior which made me think of lacework. The interior is very light, both in the feeling of the architecture and the actual visibility. On our first visit I had a strong sense of feeling welcome.'

Marilyn's description is apt, for the west frontage contains the most impressive and delicate stonework that we saw in the entire configuration. Although much of it is of a later date than the other great cathedrals we visited, it is visually stunning and has more in common with the designs one finds in cake decoration than with medieval architecture. St John the Baptist, so revered by the Templars, is commemorated by a superb life-size statue in the ambulatory and is depicted in the baptizing position, with a scallop shell in his hand, thus linking the pilgrimage to Compostela with the Johannite heresy. This was an expression of gnostic belief that held John the Baptist in particularly high regard. From such evidence that still exists, it is plain that the Knights Templar were adherents of this heresy or one of its many variants.

The exact whereabouts of the Druidic site in Orléans are un-known. However, Roman temple remains have been excavated and preserved by the north side of the present cathedral. It is obvious from their size and shape that the cathedral stands, to a large degree, on the site of this pagan temple. Vestiges of an ear-lier Christian church can be seen in the crypt, which indicates that this site too has been continually used for worship since the earliest times, the structures and practices of one belief system simply being overlaid on the remnants of its predecessors. Just as in Compostela, where stones originally dedicated to a pagan deity were used to construct a Christian altar, in the crypt of Orléans on the Merovingian floor is a font created from ancient stones that were carved in honour of the goddess Venus, and which were found on this site. It is reasonable to assume that the Roman temple remains that abut against the foundations of the present cathedral are the ruins of a temple dedicated to Venus.

There is a strange and fascinating legend about the Cathedral of Orléans that tends to show divine approval of the work of the gnostic craftsmen who created this glorious place. The legend recounts how, at the service held to conse-crate the building, the bishop became too ill to function, and before the assembled clergy could devise an alternative way to continue with the service Almighty God took a hand. The glow-ing finger of God reached down from the clouds and gently touched each part of the cathedral as an act of truly 'divine' consecration.[15] To this day there are no consecration marks on the cathedral which, according to the beliefs current at that time, is supremely logical. How could mere man commemorate what God himself had done?

The medieval city that developed from Celtic and Gallo-Roman origins stood on one of the major routes from Paris to Compostela; pilgrims passed through Orléans and on via Tours, Poitiers, Bordeaux and Roncesvalles into Spain. In a small back street near the river there is an old, rather decrepit building called La Maison de la Coquille which was probably a hospice for the pilgrims. In the gardens of the Hotel de Ville near the cathedral stand the remains of the Chapelle St Jacques which were moved here some time ago. Thus Orléans meets all our criteria: it has a continuous history as a sacred site from the time of the Druids up to and including the present; it is adorned with symbolism that places it firmly in the context of the esoteric stream of spirituality which gave rise to Gothic architecture and all that it stood for; and there are many well-authenticated connections to the pilgrimage route to Compostela.

When we revisited the cathedral as we re-created the pilgrimage of initiation, it seemed much darker and less welcoming than before. Someone was playing very sonorous organ music, more like a dirge than something to celebrate and praise God; workmen were banging and clattering in the choir, which is supposedly reserved for quiet prayer. Meditating was almost impossible and although we persevered it appeared to be of no avail. It felt as if a dark force was trying to discourage us from continuing with our pilgrimage.

It is no coincidence that the solar plexus chakra, represented by the Venus oracle at Orléans, is intimately related to the personal will. The will, in this context, is described as a powerful force for good or evil that can be used to overcome serious problems or thwart or subvert the will of others. The awakening of this centre represents an important staging post on the path of becoming. When faced with difficult challenges, the rightful use of power and responsibility under will leads to a growing sense of self and a heightened ability to overcome all obstacles.[16] The achievement of long-term goals is accomplished by exercising the will. So it is not surprising that the events within Orléans Cathedral only made us more determined to carry on with our quest.

12

The Cathedrals of Chartres, Paris and Amiens

Situated at the very heart of the apocalyptic and prophetic configuration in stone, and built upon the sacred mound of the Carnutii, is Chartres Cathedral, the home of the medieval mystery school, and the mystical centre so beloved of the hidden streams of spirituality. This glorious monument to man's devotion to God dominates the surrounding area and the entire European Christian experience. Even Napoleon was so impressed that he said 'Chartres is no place for an atheist!'

Chartres marks the pivotal time that separates the Dark Ages from the early roots of the Renaissance, for it was from the time of Bernardus of Chartres and Abelard of Paris that one can date the first important breaching of the dam of ecclesiastically enforced ignorance. It was here that the philosophers of classical Greece were reinstated in the mainstream of European Christian philosophy.[1] Bernardus said of them:

> If we can see further than they could, it is not because of the strength of our own vision, it is because we are raised up by them and borne at a prodigious height. We are dwarves mounted on the shoulders of giants.

It was the Platonic masters of Chartres who conceived the true meaning of the prophetic alignment of seven cathedrals that lie between the two Pillars of Wisdom and Strength at Cintra and Rosslyn.[2]

Chartres is more than a mere cathedral; it is a superb restatement of the essential truths that lead man closer to God.

Each pilgrim who is drawn here will leave spiritually uplifted and transformed. This is the true measure of the enduring magic of the Cathedral of Chartres, known as the 'Golden Book' in which inspired sages have inscribed their wisdom as a lasting legacy to all who seek spiritual truth.[3] This was recognized by Vincent de Beauvais who claimed that 'Man can compass his salvation by means of knowledge.'

The west front, the remnant of Fulbertus' eleventh-century cathedral, houses the three main doors. In the centre is the main ceremonial door described by Charpentier as the door of Mystical Faith.[4] Above it, in the tympanum, is the figure of Christ in Glory, with his hand raised in blessing. On the right is the Gate of Birth crowned by a statue of Mary, the Christian incarnation of the Divine Mother, enthroned with the infant Jesus on her lap in manner reminiscent of the Black Virgin.[5] Around her, lying within the curves of the arch, are representations of the seven liberal arts and the sages who brought them back into European consciousness: dialectics was brought by Aristotle; rhetoric – Cicero; geometry – Euclid; arithmetic – Boethius; astronomy – Ptolemy; grammar – Donatus; music – Pythagoras. The door on the left is known as the Gate of the Ages with the Ascension of Christ carved in the tympanum above it. On the columns of this portico are figures said to represent the kings and queens of Judah, while above them are thirty-eight scenes from the life of Mary and Jesus. There is also a figure of Jesus on a pier of the central door of the south entrance and another in the tympanum of the door on the right, between Mary and John; he is again depicted between two angels at the door on the left, the Knights' door; there are other scenes from his life at the north door, but nowhere a Christ crucified. There is not one single depiction of the crucifixion that

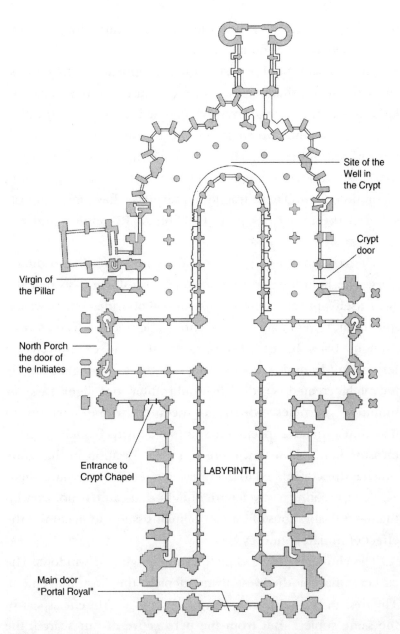

Ground plan of Notre-Dame de Chartres – the 'Golden Book' in which inspired sages inscribed their wisdom as a lasting legacy to all who seek spiritual truth

dates from the twelfth century in the entire cathedral,[6] a deliberate reflection of Templar belief.

The interior of this vast cathedral appears at first to be clothed in deep shadows. As our eyes adjusted to the change in light we stood as though transfixed. The interior glowed with a bluish opalescence which seemed to transfuse the massive pillars with vibrant energy. The vast array of medieval stained-glass windows transform the natural daylight into a shimmering haze of subtle colour. These fragile masterpieces have miraculously survived the ravages of time, the French Revolution and two world wars.

The stained glass of Chartres does not react like ordinary glass. The light seems to miraculously transform it so that the glass itself appears a luminous source of iridescent, jewelled splendour. It was made using scientific knowledge – true gnosis – brought back by the Templars from their excavations in Jerusalem.[7] Esoteric scholars claim that this form of glass was deliberately created so that it would filter out light rays, or luminous particles, which are deemed to be harmful to mankind's innate capacity for spiritual activity. Blanche Mertz's measurements show that there is a neutralization in that zone which is directly related to the filtering effects of the stained-glass windows, creating a wavelength of light that can harmonize with the natural vibrations of human cellular tissue and maximize the effect of initiatory energy.[8]

The climax is provided by the three huge rose windows. The earliest, that in the west front, depicts the Last Judgement. The rose in the south transept represents a different aspect of the same subject. But from the perspective of our search, the north rose window and the lancets that lie beneath it are the most important of all. As in all the other rosaces, direct homage is paid to alchemy. Below the rose in the central lancet we see St Anne, the mother of the Virgin; the other lancets on either side are a glowing litany of initiates. Melchizedek, the King of Righteousness, whose teaching inspired the Kibeiri and their spiritual heirs the Druids and the Essenes; beside him is Aaron, the brother of Moses, also a priest of the Egyptian Temple mysteries. To the right of St Anne is King David, and finally King Solomon, the builder of the first Temple in Jerusalem; the priest-king who was 'wiser than Moses and full of the wisdom of Egypt'.

It was at Chartres that the Church adopted the veneration of the fire-blackened, Druidic figurine Virgini Pariturae in the guise of the Black Madonna.[9] A medieval replica of the Druidic figure is found in the crypt, which the official guide states categorically was used as an initiation chamber. Also in the crypt is a deep well which sinks to the water table 123 feet (37 metres) below the floor of the choir. The main vault of the cathedral rises approximately the same distance above floor level[10]: 'as above, so below'. Mertz claims that the water sources here, like those in Compostela, have an intimate and causal relationship with the detectable telluric powers.

She describes an arrangement of fourteen fan-like streams of such regularity that they must be man-made. She also states that these fourteen streams are symbolized by the seven doves depicted around the Black Virgin, as each of these doves has two beaks. The Black Madonna, Notre-Dame de Sous-Terre, Our Lady Under the Earth, also known as the Virgin of the Druids, takes the place of honour on the altar in the underground chapel in the crypt. Mertz goes on to suggest that this mystical power point in Chartres is heightened by a large loop in the underground river and then strengthened by the fan-like convergence of the underground watercourses.[11]

There is another Black Madonna in the main body of the cathedral, the Virgin of the Pillar, which dates from the fifteenth century and is an object of immense veneration. She is clothed traditionally in heavy, ornate robes formally shaped in a triangle.[12] Immediately in front of the statue there is a tangible level of energy which is so intense that some find it almost intolerable; Marilyn felt emotionally drained by it; others describe the feelings as those of nervous excitement; some, approaching on foot, seem to visibly shudder. This is a point of God-given power where the vibration is especially low and induces a fainting, falling feeling which is comparable to going momentarily into a deathlike state; a point of transition where one is hurled against the very threshold of the spiritual world.

Earlier we referred to the Wouivre, the Druidic name for the numerous and various currents in the Earth. In the mound of Chartres there is one that is especially sacred, the Spiritus Mundi, that is capable of awakening man to the spiritual life. This has been recognized since Druidic times when the mound was known as the Hill of the Strong or the Hill of the Initiates.[13] This current, symbolized by the pillar on which the Virgin stands, is so sacred that no material influence may be allowed to trouble or destroy it; the sacred mound from which it arises must not be polluted in any way. Thus Chartres is the only cathedral in France wherein no king, cardinal or bishop is interred. The hill remains undefiled; *virgo intacta.*

The choir itself, with its boundaries so carefully delineated by later master craftsmen, is also believed to provide a vault of protection for those learned men who sought enlightenment and holiness. This complete and total transformation of man allied with a spiritual intelligence cannot develop in man just anywhere. Blanche Mertz claims that:

> . . . in the centre of the choir where fourteen subterranean
> watercourses curiously converge there is a precise point
> equidistant between the top of the gothic vault and the
> underground water which gives the individual an impression of
> weightlessness.[14]

The Earth gave Chartres a unique gift: the capacity to raise man
to a point of etheric enhancement, to a true State of Grace. This
was recognized and enhanced by the craftsmen who created
this magnificent cathedral.

The innate character and nature of this ancient sacred site
is commemorated by the figures flanking the entrance to the
north door, the Door of the Initiates. On the left is a carving of
Melchizedek holding a chalice – the Grail from which the
stone protrudes; he is handing the cup to Abraham. Next
comes Moses from whom we received the two Tablets of the
Law, which some claim are, in reality, the pillars of the Temple,
Jacquin and Boaz. He carries in his arms a pillar with a capital,
with the Wouivre in the shape of a winged dragon entwined
around it.

The carving of the Ark of the Covenant on a column of the
south porch stimulated Trevor and Tim to write in the *The Mark
of the Beast*:

> The first Knights Templar were quartered in the former stables
> of King Solomon beside the site of the destroyed Temple. It was
> here that the Ark of the Covenant had been hidden from the
> Roman soldiers of Trajan. Hugo de Payne, a close friend and
> relative of Chrétien le Troyes, had been chosen to unearth the
> Ark and to bring it back to Europe where it was later hidden
> beneath the crypt of Chartres Cathedral.[15]

Christopher Knight and Robert Lomas have found evidence to support this; they believe that the Templars went to Jerusalem not only to retrieve the Ark, but also many scrolls which may replicate some of those found at Qumran early in the twentieth century. They suggest that these were hidden at Chartres, among other sites, and that after the suppression of the Knights Templar were moved *en masse* to Rosslyn, which they claim was deliberately constructed as an ornate repository for the most sacred documents in the world.[16]

So there is another significant link between two of the most important sites in the configuration: Chartres Cathedral and Rosslyn were built for the same fundamental purpose. Outwardly they are superb examples of beautifully decorated places of Christian worship; but behind the deliberate creation of their exterior symbolism and its esoteric message, they share another, deeper and more important secret purpose. They were both constructed as superbly carved reliquaries for some of the most important religious documents known to man.

One of the most intriguing esoteric symbols within Chartres Cathedral is the labyrinth, a circular design made of black-and-white flagstones, that occupies over one-third of the floor space of the nave. The guidebook would have us believe that travers-ing the labyrinth, in bare feet or on one's knees, was a form of penance associated with the reward of an indulgence, or a sub-stitute form of pilgrimage, reaching the centre being the equivalent of reaching the Holy City of Jerusalem. Neither of these explanations is particularly convincing, as several ne-olithic labyrinths of an identical pattern have been found. They were hardly created to gain an indulgence from the Christian hierarchy, much less act as a substitute for a pilgrim-age to the Holy City. Tim came across a far more plausible

The labyrinth at Chartres was intended to be taken according to a fixed ritual, as a rhythmic dance performed unshod.

explanation within hours of his first sight of the labyrinth of Chartres.

He had visited the cathedral with a friend, and spent that evening at a folk festival in a small Breton town. When the compère announced that it was time for 'the Dance' an odd assortment of musicians took the stage; one carried a medieval drum, another a snake charmer's flute, the third was equipped with the strangest set of bagpipes he had ever seen and, finally, there was a guitarist. The music was haunting, distinctly foreign, yet oddly familiar. It was pure North African, Arab music; slow, reedy, rhythmical and, quite literally, entrancing.

The mayor and his wife led the dance, standing with their arms linked closely so that their sides seemed to touch, moving in a shuffling, sideways, curving pattern. They were joined by others until the entire population of the village were in the line. Slowly a formal pattern was being created by the long weaving line of serious-faced dancers, replicating the exact pattern of the labyrinth. It dawned on Tim that what he was privileged to see was a derivation of a traditional dance of Islamic origin.

The labyrinth of Chartres was intended to be taken according to a fixed ritual, as a rhythmic dance, performed unshod so that the feet were in direct contact with the stone which acted like a medieval accumulator for the currents of the earth. In the Middle Ages the bishop led a ritual dance through the labyrinth at the equinoctial festivals, when the telluric current was pulsating strongly. It is believed that those who reached the centre in this manner and at these times were changed, having experienced an opening of the intuition to natural laws and divine harmonies.

There are at least two other places, apart from the choir itself, within the cathedral at which the detectable levels of energy are those of an initiation point. One lies at the junction of the transept and the nave, which is now inaccessible as a large, solid-silver altar has been placed there. The other lies almost vertically underneath it, in the crypt, which was where we wished to meditate as part of our re-creation of the pilgrimage of initiation. On a guided tour this is simply not possible. However, mass is said in the crypt at 11.30 each morning, so we decided to take advantage of this for our own purposes.

When Tim was a young boy, Holy Mother the Church was a past master of theatricality and the solemn, impressive ritual of the old Tridentine Mass had a truly universal appeal, an innate majesty and a sense of mystery which was incomparable. The priestly robes, the ritual, the liturgy with its sonorous Latin phraseology, the bells and incense all combined to focus the attention, bodily, mentally and spiritually, on the glory of God. Like so much else, it has been dramatically changed in the name of progress! The mass we attended in the crypt of Chartres Cathedral had somehow been stripped of all reverential atmosphere. This uninspiring service, while it obviously satisfied the needs of the small, devout congregation, did little to distract us from our personal meditations. It is perhaps ironic that we had to camouflage these under the cover of an apparent devotion to dogmatic Catholicism, but circumstances beyond our control had forced us to replicate the actions of the Chartres masters who ran the hidden mystery school under the guise of dogmatic Christianity.

According to tradition, the awakening of the heart chakra brings an increased ability to direct the life force, especially for healing. This concern and increased ability to act for others cannot be awakened until the aspirant has overcome all egotistical sense of self. It is the meeting place of the divine and the human, where the spiritual and the material are in harmony. When this centre is fully open, the candidate is empowered to act for the benefit of all humanity. The gnostics of old were distinguished from all others because they used their knowledge and insight on behalf of the communities within which they operated.

Having satisfactorily completed our own mystical devotions in the place so physically and spiritually close to the grotto sacred to the ancient Druids, it was time to leave for Notre-Dame de Paris.

Notre-Dame de Paris

The island in the Seine on which now stands the Cathedral of Notre-Dame de Paris formed the ever-expanding nucleus – the Ile de la Cité – of what was to become the present capital city of France. Sacred to the Celts, a complex web of religious influences came to bear on the Ile de la Cité before, during and after, the Roman occupation. Two thousand years ago, during the reign of the Emperor Tiberius, the Parisii river people worshipped both Jupiter and Mars on or near the site of the present cathedral. We also found a strange connection with Rosslyn; the arms of Paris consist of a quartered shield, with different decorative panels contained in each of the four segments which are separated by an heraldic device that was well known to both of us, the engrailed cross of the St Clairs. The St Clair family once saved Paris from besieging forces while supporting the Capetian dynasty's rise to power in France, and thereafter their family crest was incorporated into the heraldic arms of the city.

On the main façade of the great cathedral is a pier dividing the entrance bay, decorated with carvings representing the medieval sciences, including alchemy. Alchemy, the allegory representing the hidden paths of initiation, is depicted in a highly specific manner as a woman seated on a throne with her head touching the clouds. In her left hand is the sceptre of royal power, while her right supports two books, one open, the other closed. The open book represents the exoteric path, the closed one symbolizes the esoteric path to illumination. Between her knees with the upper portion resting against her breast is a ladder with eight rungs, the scala philosophorum.[17] According to Nicolas Valois: 'Patience is the Philosophers'

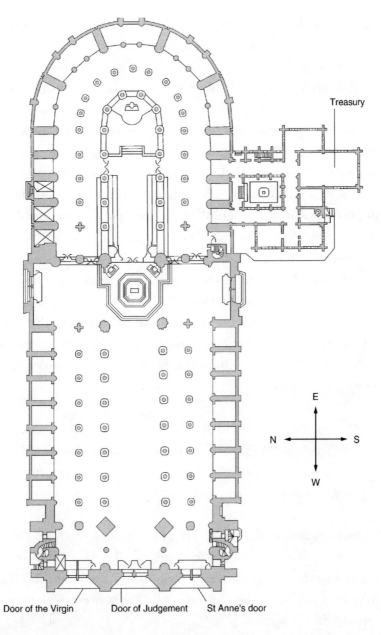

Treasury

E

N ← → S

W

Door of the Virgin   Door of Judgement   St Anne's door

Ground plan of Notre-Dame de Paris – not simply a temple of God but also a focus to the international tourist trade

ladder, and humility is the door to their garden; for whosoever will persevere without pride and without envy, on him God will show mercy.'[18]

Fulcanelli described this statue and its relationship to the cathedral as the title page to a book, the cathedral being the book which he describes as an occult Bible wrought in stone, which carries within its massive pages the hermetic secrets of 'the Great Work'. The Great Work is a euphemism for the alchemical process of transmuting the 'base metal' of imperfect man to the 'gold' of spiritual perfection and illumination; an allegory of initiation. For him the Virgin Mary to whom the cathedral is dedicated is, when stripped of the ill-fitting theological clothes of dogma, the Eternal Feminine; the personification of the principle of the Great Work itself. Christian dogma sometimes gets close to the eternal truth: it describes the Virgin as a 'vas spirituale' – the Vase containing the spirit of all things. One French eighteenth-century scholar, Etteila, wrote that:

> On a table breast high to the Magi were, on one side a book or a series of golden plates of the book of Toth, and on the other side a vase full of celestial liquid . . . the secret, the eternal mystery was therefore in that vase.[19]

Church texts describe the Virgin as the Seat of Wisdom, thereby consciously or unconsciously echoing the teachings of the hidden stream. This esoteric symbolism in the main portal is a preparation for entering one of the supreme alchemical temples in Europe.

One carving in the north portal is of particular relevance. On a cornice in the middle of the tympanum is a sarcophagus which figures in an episode of the life of Christ. On it are carved seven symbols representing the seven planetary metals: the Sun, gold; Mercury, quicksilver; Saturn, lead; Venus, copper; the Moon, silver; Jupiter, tin and Mars, iron. In describing this particular carving, Fulcanelli quotes the Master Jean d'Houry:

> Look at the sky and the spheres of the planets, you will see that Saturn is the highest of them all, succeeded by Jupiter and then by Mars, the Sun, Venus, Mercury and finally the Moon.[20]

Fulcanelli himself developed this further:

> Consider now that the virtues of the planets do not ascend, but descend. Experience itself teaches us that Mars can easily be converted into Venus, but not Venus into Mars – Venus being a lower sphere. Similarly Jupiter is easily transmuted into Mercury, because Jupiter is higher than Mercury . . . Saturn is the highest, the Moon the lowest. The Sun mixes with all of them but is never improved by the inferior ones. Further you will note that there is a great correspondence between Saturn and the Moon, with the Sun midway between them. There is also a correspondence between Mercury and Jupiter and between Mars and Venus. In the midst of all is the Sun.[21]

This grading of the planets according to alchemical precepts is a further explanation as to why the pilgrimage of initiation is a reverse process from Compostela, the Moon oracle, through Toulouse representing Mercury, Orléans, the Venus oracle, then on to the Sun oracle at Chartres, the Mars oracle at Paris, the Jupiter oracle at Amiens and finally to Rosslyn, the highest of them all, the Saturn oracle of awakening.

Acting on information supplied by Pat Sibille we discovered the links which completed the picture of continuous usage of the site. Excavations made under the choir in 1710 exposed five superbly carved blocks, now preserved in the Musée Cluny off the Boulevard St Michel, which are part of an incomplete column called the pillar of the Nautes, erected sometime in the 20s or 30s AD. It confirms that the Ile de la Cité was the Roman administrative centre of Paris. The prime relevance of this artefact lies in the representation of the gods carved upon it. The Parisii had erected a pillar primarily dedicated to the emperor and the god Jupiter, but which also contained carvings of other deities of importance to them. The faces of the blocks are decorated with carvings of Jupiter, Mercury, Castor and Pollux and above all, Mars. As Mars, Jupiter and Mercury were all Roman deities and important enough to the local people to be celebrated in this fashion, it must be assumed that there would be temples to them in the Romanized city of Lutetia (Paris). Corroborative evidence of the worship of Mars has been discovered and some fragments of high quality show the weapons of Mars as the god is being disarmed by little Cupids; another shows Mars, Vulcan and Venus. All were found on the Ile de la Cité. The final piece in this religious jigsaw puzzle is provided by Julius Caesar, who wrote about the ancient Gauls' worship of planetary deities:

> Among the gods they most worship Mercury . . . After him they set Apollo, Mars, Jupiter and Minerva . . . Mars controls wars. To Mars, when they have determined on a decisive battle, they dedicate, as a rule, whatever spoil they may take.[22]

Notre-Dame de Paris today is not simply a temple of God, but also a focus for the international tourist trade. We had to fight our way into the cathedral one mid-morning in early July. We struggled through the crowds, seeking a place to meditate which we found by the transept where there were several rows of seats behind a barrier which bore the message 'Reserved for quiet prayer' in several languages. Unfortunately, this area was being used as a short-cut by the tourists who were intent on seeing as much as they could and were completely oblivious of those who wished to worship. The situation was made worse by a priest who bellowed angrily over the tannoy for quiet in several languages. It is ironic that in a temple originally dedicated to Mars, the god of war, we had to virtually fight our way in and listen to a somewhat belligerent priest battling to make himself heard above the tumult.

But proof to us that this building is still a holy place was not long in coming. We each prayed and meditated and, despite the noise, the priest's protests and the pushing and shoving of the crowd, inner peace was attained with remarkable ease. Marilyn asked for some sign as to the direction we should take, and she was granted an answer that was clear and unequivocal: we were to continue.

This message was completely in keeping with the faculties and insights that were granted with the opening of the throat chakra, the centre of communication. Not only was the aspirant open to communication from the deity, but he was granted the ability to know the past, present and future as well as the capacity to withstand poisons, go without food and drink and achieve complete indestructibility. While these claims appeared to defy common sense, the pilgrimage along the spiritual path was the quest of the uncommon traveller.[23]

The Jupiter Oracle

Amiens Cathedral, the most sublime example of Gothic architecture, *l'église ogivale par excellence*, is the largest cathedral in
France, with a vault that soars heavenwards for 140 feet (42.5
metres). Set squarely in front of the central pillar of the main
door is a statue of Jesus known as the Beau Dieu of Amiens, depicted with his feet resting on a lion and a dragon;[24] so here, in
pride of place, is Jesus and the Wouivre. Immediately below this
example of initiatory symbolism lies another; a statue of the
supreme adept of the Old Testament, King Solomon. The walls
of the triple entrance are decorated with a profusion of quatre-
foils depicting alchemical symbolism, replicating the themes we
had already seen at Notre-Dame de Paris.[25]

The feeling of space and light that pervades the interior is
heightened by the simple, severe lines of arches surmounted by
the glorious vaulting which spreads its ribs as though Almighty
God himself supports the heavy stone roof with his fingers. Most
of the windows are clear or lightly coloured, adding to the all-
pervading sense of light. The rose window in the north transept
has an unusual and intriguing design based upon the five-
pointed star, the symbol that once decorated the Babylonian
Temples of Ishtar, the ancient Egyptian temples and tombs as
well as forming part of the insignia of the hidden streams of
spirituality that flowed on from the medieval period to our own
times; the roof of Rosslyn Chapel is adorned with a profusion of
five-pointed stars.

According to the mystical writer François Cali, if one passes
from Chartres to Amiens, an intriguing direction in the light of
the pilgrimage of initiation, one has made an almost impercep-
tible transition 'from the love of God to the love of Wisdom –

which is in order, number and harmony – which can be equated with God, but which need not be'. Order, number and harmony – all attributes of the gnosis rediscovered by the Templar Knights in their excavations in Jerusalem. This cathedral is a symphonic blend of space, stone and light, deliberately designed and constructed to celebrate the gnostic principle of Sophia or sacred wisdom and to house its most precious relic, the severed head of John the Baptist.

The guidebook recounts how the present cathedral was erected on the site of its predecessor, destroyed by fire in 1218, to provide a suitable resting place for this strange artefact, which was brought to Amiens from Constantinople by Walter de Sarton in 1206 and which has rested here ever since. This object of veneration is, according to Guy Jordan, the Provençal Templar scholar, nothing less than 'la vrai tête Baphometique Templière' – the true Baphometic head of the Templars. The head is mounted on a silver-gilt plate decorated with precious and semi-precious stones, a reproduction made in the nineteenth century to replace the original which was destroyed during the French Revolution. As evidence of the importance of the relic to the cathedral, the bulk of the outer wall of the choir is decorated with superbly sculpted scenes, in bas-relief, of the life and death of John the Baptist, including one where the top of his severed head is being pierced by a knife in a very similar manner to the piercing of the skull of James the Just at Compostela. The precise significance of this is not known, but its importance to the gnostic orders can be discerned in their burial practices. One old Templar church in Bargemon in Provence, which is now a museum, has preserved the crypt by the simple expedient of barring access to it. Part of the floor of the church has been replaced with a transparent perspex sheet which allows a clear view of the human remains beneath. A row of skulls and long bones lie in serried ranks, and the temple of each skull is pierced in the manner depicted in the carving at Amiens.

Some measure of the importance of John the Baptist to gnostics in general and the Templars in particular can be inferred from a passage in *The Gospel of Thomas* where Jesus is quoted as saying:

> Among those born of women, from Adam until John the Baptist, there is no one so superior to John the Baptist that his eyes should not be lowered [before him].[26]

The cathedral obviously exhibits more than enough esoteric symbolism to link it intimately with the Knights Templar and the Children of Solomon, but what of its Druidic connections? Archival and archaeological records of the use of this site from the Celtic era are non-existent, but Pat Sibille discovered evidence in the Amiens museum of the worship of Jupiter here during the Roman era.

On a plinth in a room in the lower basement of the museum stands an intricately carved pillar, dedicated to Jupiter, from the time of the Roman occupation. It had been discovered in the grounds of the present cathedral and was from a Roman temple that had previously occupied the site. We can assume with a fair degree of confidence that the Romans had simply taken over the sacred site and built their own temple there, and it is highly probable that the veneration of Jupiter on that site had long predated the coming of the Romans.

We meditated for about twenty minutes in the choir which, in complete contrast to the noisy hubbub of Notre-Dame de

Paris, was quiet and peaceful. It was at Amiens that the gnostics on the alchemical pilgrimage sought to awaken their brow chakra. The function of this spiritual centre within the human is the transcendence of consciousness and entry into the deep mysteries of total being. Apparently opposing factors are reconciled; both birth and death are seen to be mere transitions as the attention is directed towards the cosmic. The activities of this centre direct us to question the fundamentals of our human existence, the very meaning of life itself, the nature of consciousness and the mysteries of time and space.[27]

After our meditations we took a last look at the carvings and sculptures, stopping occasionally to take photographs. In the northern aisle are two immense serpentine pillars decorated with gold appliquéd leaves representing the pillars of Boaz and Jacquin, supporting a canopy over a larger than life-size statue of the Virgin. One large bas-relief sculpture of particular interest is to be found high on the south-western wall of the transept depicting, in glorious colour, pilgrims making their way to the shrine of St James of Compostela. The intricate detail of the folds of their cloaks, the colourful costumes, the facial expressions and, inevitably, the scallop shells they wore so proudly as badges of their devotion to the Apostle, are all superbly shown in this masterpiece of the medieval sculptor's art.

With a last glance at the Solomonic pillars flanking the statue of the Virgin in the north aisle by the choir, it was time to leave. Time to leave not merely this glorious building, but to leave France and return to Rosslyn. One thing was certain; whatever the outcome of our quest, we had been changed, or perhaps transformed, by the sacred nature of our journey.

13

The King of the Holy Grail

The apocalyptic configuration in stone forms an earthly pathway bounded at each end by a Solomonic pillar. One pillar stands in solitary splendour in the town square of Cintra in Portugal; the other is the world-famous Apprentice Pillar in Rosslyn Chapel. The Royal Arch across the heavens that unites them is the constellation of the Milky Way. In Celtic mythology the silvery constellation of the Milky Way was identified with Lug's Chain, often symbolized by the silvery smear of a snail's track, and also known as the Ashen Path, or the Track of Souls. Silver became the symbolic emblem of knowledge, and in the Dark Ages those who left bright 'tracks' behind them in the form of books were called the Snail Men. Not surprisingly, the Milky Way came to symbolize the attainment of great knowledge, the very quality celebrated in the name of Roslin, which translates from Scottish Gaelic as 'Ancient knowledge passed down the generations'.[1]

The Royal Arch of the Milky Way again demonstrates the ancient hermetic principle of 'as above, so below', for this starry pathway in the skies above northern Europe is mirrored on the Earth by the pilgrims' path, the Camiño de las Estrellas – the true and ancient path of spiritual death and rebirth.[2]

In *The Orion Mystery*, Robert Bauval recounts how one night in Egypt he awoke at about 3am and gazed up at the stars:

> High in the southern sky, arching over and almost marking for us the curve of the celestial equator, was a luminous band of light resplendent against the inky black of space. It was the Milky Way and it looked like a great river in the sky.[3]

Another scholar, Jane Sellars, found in the ancient Egyptian manuscript *The Book of Two Ways* that the topography of the roads to Rostau in the sky were replicated on water and land in the Two Kingdoms of Egypt. She suggested that the waters of the Nile were represented in the heavens by the constellation of the Milky Way; this is confirmed by the Egyptian Pyramid Texts which make it clear that the ancient Egyptians did make this link. Did the ancient Egyptians use the Nile as a pathway of initiation?

Peter Dawkins describes how the Two Kingdoms of Egypt were held to be a living temple built by the Spirit of God, where man could play his ritual part and reunite his spirit with the divine as the result of an alchemical process.[4] The Temple of God on the Earth, Egypt itself, was patterned on an eternal archetype of the supreme achievement of nature, namely *homo sapiens.* This geographical representation of the human archetype had a spine, a head in the north and a body in the south. Along the spine, represented by the River Nile, lay seven temples marking the great mystical centres which were the earthly equivalent to the seven major chakras in the human body.[5]

The root chakra was embodied on the Earth by the temple on the Island of Philae near the town of Elephantine. Some believe this to be the 'quarry' from which the stones were to be hewn in order to build the Temple of God on Earth. It was directly linked with the Earth Mother herself, Anna the Black Virgin.[6] Thebes was the site of the temple functioning as the sacral chakra,[7] the power centre of the body, generating the force that puts thoughts into action. In 1888, excavations at the Temple of Thebes revealed a statue of the god Kabeiros with a hammer in his hand. Many esoteric scholars believe that Kabeiros was worshipped by the ancient Egyptian-Hebraic sect of the Kibeiri, the precursors of the Therapeutae and the Essenes.

The Temple of Abydos was built on the site of the solar plexus chakra, the centre of transmutation where the energies of the lower body could be gathered up and transmuted into the higher self whose seat was the heart chakra.[8] This centre had two earthly forms, one at Hermopolis and the other at Akhetaton; dual centres of the Royal Self which acted jointly as the centre of inspiration, perfect love and life itself. Here all things were held to begin and end; it was the Alpha and the Omega, the centre of Truth and the Will of God.

The temple of the throat chakra was at Memphis, the centre of speech and spiritual creativity.[9] Here was born the Word of Love that inspired the initiate to hear God, talk to God and to know God. The brow chakra temple at Heliopolis represented the third eye, the eye of the mind where the voice of God was seen as a thought form. The final, or crown chakra had two temples, Behedet and Heliopolis, where the vision of absolute truth was completed.[10] This was the ultimate centre of illumination wherein was granted pure knowledge and an awareness of God that is beyond all understanding. Here the initiate was directly connected with the An, the Heavenly Father or the mind of God itself.

Peter Dawkins' account not only confirmed the basic principles of the pilgrimage of initiation, but provided further links that strengthened the derivation of much of medieval practice from its roots in ancient Egyptian belief and ritual. Firstly there is the veneration of the Black Virgin mentioned earlier in our search, with connections between medieval Knights Templar practices and Egyptian belief being reinforced, not only by the veneration of Isis, but also by the worship of the Earth Mother at the Temple at Philae.[11]

As we travelled the long road from Compostela to Rosslyn we had also puzzled over Cintra's role. If there were seven sacred sites in Europe which had in turn been used as Earth chakras, Druidic oracles, Roman temples and Christian churches, what was the purpose of an eighth site so far to the south in Portugal?[12] Using the evidence provided by Peter Dawkins, two possible solutions emerged.

In ancient Egypt, before being accepted as a candidate for initiation, the novice had to undergo a prolonged and demanding period of probation and preparation. Only when he had successfully passed the tests that demonstrated his purity, obedience, control over earthly desires and willpower, would he move on to the temple on the Island of Philae. This preparation took place at Buhen, on the Nile at Egypt's southern border.[13] This gave us an analogous position for Cintra which, like Buhen, lay far to the south of the other centres and, furthermore, was situated in the one mainland European country where the Knights Templar had been tried and found not guilty.[14] In Portugal the Order had continued with only its name being changed to the Knights of Christ.[15] The inclusion of Cintra also draws our attention to the magical number eight, a number of great importance to the ancient Egyptians and the Knights Templar. Including the preparatory Temple at Buhen, there are eight sacred sites in the Egyptian system. There are eight doors depicted in the allegorical symbolism of the Temple of Philae.[16] Eight occurs frequently in European esoteric symbolism, especially that associated with the Templars. There are eight steps on the scala philosophorum, or philosopher's ladder, depicted at Notre-Dame de Paris; there are eight points to the croix patté, the main badge of the Order; the octagon is the basis for much of the geometry used to construct the round Templar churches as well as playing a significant role in the sacred geometry of Gothic architecture.[17] Eight is also the symbolic number for resurrection, an important concept for initiation.

The Egyptian Pilgrimage of Initiation

During preparation at Buhen the novice learnt to control his physical appetites and underwent a prolonged period of purification. This was deemed to be one of the lesser mysteries, that of the Earth. Throughout all this time he was tested in his emotional responses, intelligence, willpower and obedience. When he manifested the required qualities he would undergo final preparation by being placed in a grotto in complete darkness.

At the Temple of Philae, his eyes were bandaged and he was led to the Gate of Man, where he was asked the password. He was questioned by a master and underwent trials to test his courage. He took his oath of fidelity with a sword at his throat, and only after that were the bandages removed. Before him lay a ladder of seven steps and an allegorical figure portraying eight doors. He ascended the ladder in the full knowledge that it was an allegory for the seven stages of alchemical transformation. He was then awarded the first degree, that of Pastophoris, taught the hand clasp and the password 'Amoun' – be discreet. Attaining this degree was held to represent the second of the lesser mysteries, that of Water. The knowledge associated with it was that of natural sciences, anatomy, healing, symbology and the common form of hieroglyphic writing.[18]

Mastery of the lesser mystery of the Air was attained at the Temple of Thebes. The candidate had to have undergone at least one year's apprenticeship and then be tested to verify that he had mastered the first degree. To prove that he had acquired control over earthly desires he had to resist the blandishments of Temple Virgins who first served him a delicious feast and then subjected him to sexual temptation. He was then questioned and, if his answers were satisfactory, baptized. Having manifested both wisdom and chastity he was accepted as a Necoris. After further trials he was given a caduceus, the insignia of the second degree which was also the symbolic staff carried by Mercury, the messenger of the gods. Here he was taught the word of that degree and given the sign, the arms crossed over the breast. The subjects studied in depth at this level included architecture, geometry, mathematics, and geographical and other measures of various kinds.[19]

At the Temple of Abydos the candidate was introduced to the last of the lesser mysteries, that of Fire. He entered an underground chamber by the Gate of Death and immediately discovered that he was surrounded by mummies, coffins and those who prepared the dead for their eternal journey. In the middle of the chamber was a sarcophagus, the coffin of Osiris, bearing traces of blood. He was told that Osiris had recently been assassinated and was questioned as to whether or not he had any part in the murder. On being offered a Golden Crown, the true aspirant refused it as a sign of his disdain for material power and wealth. In order to attain the Crown of Truth, he had to throw down the Golden Crown and trample it underfoot. At this, a priest cried 'Outrage, vengeance!' and, seizing an axe, struck him on the head. The 'dead' candidate was then wrapped in mummy bandages, laid in an open coffin and borne into the sanctuary of the Spirits. Later, in the Hall of Judgement, he was condemned to wander in the underground galleries. Here he was divested of his mortuary garments and received instruction on death and resurrection. He was then given the sign of this degree, a form of embrace, and the password. The knowledge associated with this degree was artistic, concerning drawing and painting. He was also taught the hierogrammatical alphabet, the history and geography of Egypt, the fundamentals of astronomy and the art of rhetoric.[20]

The candidates who acquired a satisfactory knowledge of the lesser mysteries, and practised the rites of the third degree satisfactorily for a minimum period of eighteen months, could then be selected for admission to the first of the greater, spiritual mysteries. This was the fourth degree, which was regarded as the Alpha and the Omega of the pathway to Truth and the Will of God. This opening up of the higher self, or transmutation, was celebrated with great solemnity and ritual at the dual centres of Hermopolis and Akhetaton. Armed with sword and shield the novice would be led through labyrinthine passages and subjected to attack by masked men carrying flaming torches and serpents. Overcome by these, he would be led, with eyes bandaged and a cord around his neck, into the hall of Maât. There he was raised extended (a term used by Freemasons today for a ritualized form of resurrection), his bandages were removed and he was introduced to the masters, who were attired in splendid robes and arrayed in order of rank. After an oration, he was ritually armed and presented to the pharaoh, who presided over the whole assembly. He then changed into robes more suited to his new status and had his name inscribed in the book of adepts. From this time on he had gained the privilege of communicating directly with the pharaoh and received material and spiritual nourishment from his court. This degree allowed access to the study of the secret language of Ammonitish and the sciences of the human soul in preparation for the final three degrees in which he would learn to use the Word with increasing power.[21]

Such was the importance of the attainment of the fourth degree that it brought with it the absolute right to demand entrance to the fifth at the Temple of Memphis. Here the candidate was led from one assembly to another where he watched others perform a drama which graphically portrayed the conquest of the 100-headed dragon, Typhon, by Horus. The learning that ensued after receiving this degree was in alchemy.[22]

Candidates for the sixth degree were led into the Temple of Heliopolis and down four steps to the Gate of Death before being rowed across a flooded crypt in the Barque of Caron and presented to the Assembly. After taking the oath of the degree he was instructed in the history and origin of the gods of Egypt. It was then explained to him that the entire pantheon of gods emanated from One God alone. After this he was led up into the great hall, entering it by the Gate of the Gods. He would then begin a long period of instruction, studying the esoteric history of Egypt, the world and the universe. His long-term aim in this degree was to perfect his knowledge of astronomy.[23]

Admission to the ultimate mysteries of Saphenath Pancah, revealed at the seventh and final degree, was granted at the twin temples of Behedet and Heliopolis which represented the dual attributes necessary for the awakening of the crown chakra. These were the ultimate centres of illumination into the pure knowledge of God that was held to be beyond all understanding. Attainment of this degree was far from automatic; the candidate had to be of such outstanding merit that he could be invited by the pharaoh with the full consent of the Inner Fraternity. There was a grand reception for the invited candidate, followed by a public procession, after which an assembly of the initiates was held during the hours of darkness in purpose-built houses called Maneras. Here the new member of the illuminati was given an ambrosial drink of the gods known as Omellas, and was told that he had finally arrived at the end of all proofs. He was invested with the insignia of the Ankh, dressed in a white striped robe and had his head shaved. The word of this degree was Adon. The most complete and detailed explanation of the supreme mysteries was then imparted to the new initiate, or prophet, whereby he gained both the right and the ability to read all the mystical books of Hermes and the scriptures of other nations to which he now had the Royal Key. The prophet was one who knew all the mysteries and had attained full illumination and union with the divine. His supreme prerogative was his entitlement to vote in the election of the pharaoh. It was also from the ranks of the prophets that all officers of the sacred society were appointed.[24]

The preparation for and the attainment of the seven degrees were all part of a continuous graded process leading to full illumination. The more we thought about these issues, the more obvious it became that the pilgrimage of initiation in the Western esoteric tradition had been founded on a far more ancient spiritual practice that had proved its worth throughout the history of the civilization of ancient Egypt. It is what lies behind the story we had first heard in Scotland, of pilgrims travelling from Compostela to Rosslyn to deposit their scallop shells. Thus Trevor's original theory that the seven sacred sites were all part of one mystical pilgrimage route was, in esoteric terms, fully justified.

Walter Johannes Stein had mentioned a similar idea in two of his works. The French mystical writer and restorer of medieval cathedrals, Emile Male, had specifically described one medieval pilgrimage route that linked Compostela with Edinburgh. Our seven sacred sites – one church, five great cathedrals and one Scottish chapel – all stand on this route. According to Male, the most creative and productive cultural life in the late medieval period flowed along this route in both directions.

Our discoveries along the route closely mirror the descriptions of its ancient Egyptian precursor. We began our pilgrimage at Compostela, the old Druidic Moon oracle; the centre of birth and death renowned for its female, quicksilver, generative energy whose symbolic colour is red. There, after viewing the jewelled reliquary containing the alleged head of James the Less, the brother of the Lord, we descended into the Lower Church dedicated to him. We reflected on the spiritual importance of James, otherwise known as James the Just or the Essene Teacher of Righteousness, as we began the meditative process that was to continue throughout our investigations. It was a moving experience to meditate and pray while retracing the footsteps of the Knights Templar, Gnostics, Freemasons and Rosicrucians who had risked their lives and their liberty for their beliefs. Perhaps this was particularly appropriate at the oracle of birth and death, for unless one is reborn of the true spirit of God there is no true religion, merely mindless conformity to empty ritual.

The Mercury oracle at the Church of the Dalbade in Toulouse is the centre for the spiritualization of the Earth. Mercury, or Hermes to give him his Greek name, is a spiritual alchemist. His Great Work is, like all alchemy, not in metals but in the souls of men. The way of attainment in alchemy is by means of the second birth, a concept well known to Jesus, as we read in the Gospel of John:

Jesus answered and said unto him, Verily, verily, I say unto thee, Except a man be born again, he cannot see the kingdom of God. Nicodemus saith unto him, How can a man be born when he is old? can he enter the second time into his mother's womb, and be born?[25]

Jesus was, of course, an initiate of the Nazorean sect of the Essenes. The second degree in the European pilgrimage of initiation was held at the Mercury oracle and his symbol of the caduceus was the sign of the same degree in the Egyptian tradition, which was a precursor of the Essene Way. An integral part of the repertoire of Hermes is the alchemical art of gathering, fixing and concentrating the Spiritus Mundi, the essential energy of spiritual awakening that, like the generative energy found at Thebes, transmutes thoughts into action. The symbolic coloration of this transforming energy is orange.

Introduction to the mysteries of the Venus oracle at Orléans was believed to release forces in the astral body which are related to the dragon that has now been tamed. The dragon is, of course, the symbol of Sophia, the goddess of Wisdom which, in esoteric lore, must always be tamed and never killed or destroyed. Like the process that took place at the Egyptian Temple of Abydos which empowered the energies of the lower body to be transmuted into the Higher Self, only those who have been purified can access the power of Venus and gain the capacity of unconditional love and service to mankind, the true function of the Higher Self. Yellow is the symbolic colour of the enobling energy of this oracle. To summarize the route so far, Cintra, Compostela, Toulouse and Orléans were the medieval equivalents to those in Egypt where the candidates were introduced to the lesser mysteries of earth, water, air and fire.

Green, traditionally the colour of initiation, is held to signify the energies released at the Sun oracle at Chartres, the centre dedicated above all to the love of God. The order of Melchizedek indicated that the New Tabernacle is the Tabernacle of the Sun and that the body of the New Adam was born of God by the power of the Sun. In Christian mythology St Michael is the Sun prince and, according to hermetic teaching, Christ, the Logos, descended from the Sun. Its energy is described as the male sulphur energy which is used to balance the female energy of the Moon oracle at Compostela.

Moving from Chartres to Paris, the candidate was initiated into the mysteries of the Mars oracle and gained the power to visualize the 'word in the air'. The soul of the universe, the world-soul, cannot be visible to our physical eyes or even be knowable through intellectual thinking. It is the bridge between the spiritual and the temporal worlds and imparts knowledge that is incommunicable through speech. The ability to visualize the word in the air is the capacity to communicate spiritually with the world-soul and, through it, directly to God.

Under the influence of Mars, the soul has refashioned the body to the form it will take in the next life. As the god of war and battles, Mars imparts the resilience and fortitude necessary to overcome the obstacles in life. Its strengthening energy is held to manifest with a blue coloration.

North of Paris, the sublime architecture of Amiens Cathedral welcomed us to the site of the ancient Druidic oracle of the Jupiter mysteries. Jupiter is the Latin name for the Father of Light and the Hebrew name for Jupiter was Zedek, the city-god of Salem revered by Melchizedek.[26] Jupiter is also described by Lewis Spence[27] as the father of the Kibeiri, a title usually reserved for Melchizedek. Are Jupiter and Melchizedek the same character in differing mythological guise? Whatever may be the truth of this, it was believed that thinking and thus meaningful life itself have their home at the Jupiter oracle; it is the centre of true knowledge. The art of Jupiter is rightful speech, for as Mars has formed the word in the air, Jupiter takes it and fills it with divine, spiritual life and vitalizes the form of the body prepared for the next life. Indigo is the colour of his life-enhancing, radiant energy.

Rosslyn Chapel is the seventh sacred site that lies within the mystical embrace of these two pillars that symbolize the Alpha and the Omega of an ancient pathway of initiation. This is the site revered by the Druids as the oracle of Saturn, the supreme Guardian of Secrets.

Rosslyn Chapel: the Supreme Centre of Initiation

High in the north clerestory wall of the chapel are three stained-glass windows installed by insightful Freemasons in the nineteenth century. The designs of two of them are particularly important in respect of the process of enlightenment at the site of the Saturn oracle, for they are pictures of two ancient Roman saints, Longinus and Mauritius. Longinus holds a long lance in his right hand, Mauritius a similar one in his left. These two symbolic lances are in fact one and the same. In a persistent esoteric legend, both saints are associated with the Spear of Destiny, the Holy Lance that is believed to be the one that Longinus used to pierce the side of Christ on the Cross. The legend recounts how, for that brief moment, Longinus held the destiny of the world in his hands. This strange story suggests that all those who possess this sacred relic also hold the destiny of the world in their hands, for good or evil.[28]

According to esoteric lore, the combination of Saturn and the lance reveal the divine calling; that when a man knowingly makes the lance part of himself and then consciously incorporates the strength of Saturn into himself as well, he becomes the Grail King.[29] Saturn ensouls the creation of the vitalized bodily form of the next life; his symbolic colour is violet. Yet Saturn, the guardian of the secrets, does not act alone. Just as there was a dual energy acting at the two centres of the crown chakra in Egypt, there are two forces operative at Rosslyn. Here Saturn is assisted by Mercury, the god who manifests light by veiling it. Somehow, the combination of the two powers behaves alchemically like a pure crystal prism that controls the process whereby all seven colours radiated by the energies of each of the seven oracles are collectively transmuted to form the radiant white light of true purity and illumination. Thus Rosslyn Chapel, built on a site of sacred significance since the Stone Age, once used by the Druids as the oracle of Saturn, was the supreme centre of initiation in pre-Renaissance Western Europe.

Earlier we asked why it might be that it is the pagan Hermes who faces the source of light and energy, that then seem to flow through him into the hearts and minds of all who enter this holy place? In the interior of the chapel, directly in line with the pagan bust, is a spot that Tim had long discerned as manifesting considerable power. The Tantric Buddhist initiate, Professor Thomas Lin Yun, on his first visit to Rosslyn in July 1994, declared that this precise spot was the most powerful teaching position in the entire building.[30] Tim was far from surprised, but only made the connection with the bust on the exterior wall at that time. Hermes, or Mercury to use his Latin name, is renowned as the trickster. His symbolic wand, the caduceus, is perhaps better known today as the emblem of the medical profession.

The caduceus consists of one staff with two serpents entwined about it, the whole being surmounted by a sun-disc. This is the ancient magical symbolism of energies operating in balance; the two serpents represent the solar and lunar energies which in the human body begin at the base chakra and terminate at the brow chakra. The caduceus is deeply symbolic of the positive and negative life-streams which, when perfectly balanced, produce light. In alchemy they are described as the male sulphur of the Sun and the female quicksilver of the Moon.[31] These two basic generative forces of the universe interact, and the resulting, compelling energy is the Spiritus Mundi. They are nothing less than the two transformative currents of cosmic life.

The double spiral of the caduceus is a truly ancient, yet magically prescient, symbol. It is an almost perfect representation of the model for DNA, the building block of all organic life; the vibrant, biological equivalent of the 'silicone chip', that programmes all development and evolution. Both the caduceus, with its four complete loops on either side of the staff, and the DNA spiral, represent the number eight which since ancient times has been held to symbolize eternal, spiral motion, the supreme signature of the universe. The Lord of the eighth was Melchizedek, the spiritual father of the Kibeiri, the sons of Zadok, the Essenes and the Druids.

Tradition declares that when the dead body of Hermes Trismegistus was found at Hebron by the initiate Isarim, Hermes was holding an emerald tablet. Inscribed upon it were a few brief sentences which encapsulate the very essence of Hermetic wisdom:

> What is below is like that which is above, and what is above is similar to that which is below to accomplish the wonders of one thing.
>
> As all things were produced by the mediation of one being, so all things were produced from this one by adaptation.
>
> Its father is the sun; its mother is the moon.
>
> It is the cause of all perfection throughout the earth.
>
> Its power is perfect if it is changed into earth.
>
> Separate the earth from the fire, the subtile from the gross, acting prudently and with judgement.
>
> Ascend with the greatest sagacity from the earth to heaven and then descend again to earth, and unite together the power of things inferior and superior; thus you will possess the light of the whole world, and all obscurity will fly away from you.
>
> This thing has more fortitude than fortitude itself, because it will overcome every subtile thing and penetrate every solid thing.
>
> By it the world was formed.[32]

The alchemical ascension and transmutation of the human soul is an active evolution towards a conscious perfection. Through the process of initiation, whose early stages are symbolized by the mysteries of earth, water, air and fire, the natural soul is sufficiently transformed to attain knowledge of the spiritual mysteries. Therein it gains the blessed capacity to progress to the spiritual heights and eventually to union with the divine, which in the late medieval era and for some centuries afterwards, was attained by candidates of purity, humility and devotion within the confines of a little-known church 7 miles south of Edinburgh: Rosslyn Chapel.

14

The St Clairs of Roslin

Rosslyn Chapel is renowned for its carvings, with curious pilgrims flocking there in their thousands. Built on the site of the Druidic oracle dedicated to Saturn, the guardian of secrets, even the name Roslin itself echoes the all-pervading theme of secrecy, for its translation as 'ancient knowledge passed down the generations' comes from a time when ancient and heretical knowledge had to remain secret if one wished to survive. Is there any evidence in the history of the St Clair family to confirm the validity of this translation?

If the St Clair family were trusted by the Knights Templar to be the custodians of secret knowledge, then it is highly probable that they would have been guardians of some, or perhaps all, of the vanished Templar treasure; a hoard that would be worth millions of pounds today. Does the history of this aristocratic family disclose any evidence of great wealth or their involvement in a conspiracy that resulted in the foundation of the Templars? Were they, in fact, members of that group of families known as Rex Deus? Above all, what relevance does the power of Rosslyn and spiritual insight have to our quest?

As we have seen, French Masonic ritual indicates that Scotland was destined to be the repository of the Templar treasure. Almost immediately after the suppression of the Templars in Europe and the mysterious disappearance of their treasure from France, the fortunes of the St Clairs of Roslin, who were already wealthy, took a dramatic turn for the better. From then onwards, the Lords St Clair of Roslin were escorted by 400 mounted knights when they rode abroad, their ladies were attended by 80 ladies-in-waiting, and they were reputed to have dined off gold plate.[1] The wealth of the family continued to grow and posed severe problems in their relationship with their king. The solution to these difficulties is commemorated in the chapel by the Caithness memorial, which was erected in

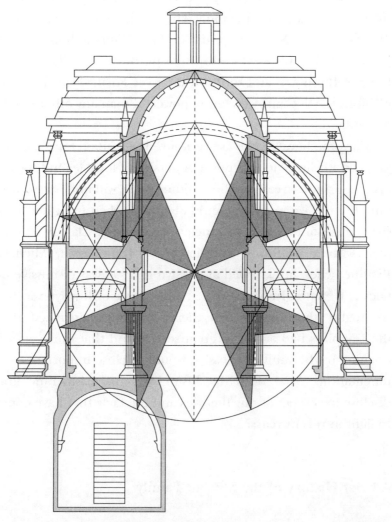

A cross-section of Rosslyn Chapel displaying the application of 'an insight into the laws and harmony of sacred geometry'

memory of George, the grandson of the chapel's founder and the last St Clair to be in sole possession of all their hereditary lands of Caithness, Sutherland, Fife and Roslin. At the king's request, George left his lands to be divided among his three older sons, thereby reducing the threat posed to the crown by such a rich and powerful family. This was the second major sub-division of the St Clair lands, as Earl William himself had previously split his estate into three portions; the Islands, and lands to the north and south of the river Forth. Prior to these divisions the St Clairs were more powerful than any other family in Scotland.

Many medieval castles are rumoured to contain buried treasure, and Roslin is no exception. A persistent local legend speaks of an enormous treasure whose hiding place will not be revealed until the day when a trumpet blast shall awaken from her long sleep 'a certain Lady of the ancient house of St Clair'.[2] Yet one man with a profound knowledge of Templarism, Michael Bentine, when interviewed at Rosslyn in 1994 was dismissive of tales of treasure. In his view the real treasure of Rosslyn was the spirituality that can be felt there.[3] He was convinced that the Templars had access to great secrets and that the eventual opening of the vaults of Rosslyn would disclose important doc-umentation. What does the history of this aristocratic line disclose in respect of our theories and the facts that have come to light in recent years?

A Brief History of the St Clair Family

The St Clairs of Roslin can trace an unbroken ancestry back to Røgnvald the Mighty, Earl of Möre, an area on the north-west coast of Norway near the present city of Trondheim.[4] It was Røgnvald's second son, Hrolf, or Rollo, who provides the direct biological link with the dynasty whose exploits form such an unbroken record of service, loyalty and courage that they became known to later generations as 'the Lordly line of the High St Clairs'.

Rollo invaded the north-west of what is now France and established his own personal fiefdom in Nuestria (Normandy). His hold on this new territory was legitimized by a treaty with King Charles the Simple of France, which was signed at the Castle of St Clair-sur-Epte in 912 AD. To further strengthen the ties that bound King Charles and his new ally and vassal, the king gave his daughter Gizelle as wife to Rollo, the first Duke of Normandy.[5]

The new duke, like all his ancestors, was warlike, prolific in breeding and, above all, shrewd in the way of the world. He extended his lands by conquest and his influence by alliance and marriage with the leading aristocratic families of the time, including those of Chaumont, Gisors, d'Evreaux and Blois, the family of the Counts of Champagne.[6] William the Conqueror, who seized the throne of England in 1066, was a direct descendant of Rollo, and many of the knights who accompanied him across the Channel were members of the wider St Clair family.

The first member of the family to come to Roslin, William the Seemly St Clair, came by a rather strange route, from Normandy via Hungary to Scotland, in 1057. He arrived there with the knight Bartholemew Ladislaus Leslyn as escort to Princess Margaret, who was to marry King Malcolm Canmore of Scotland.[7] As a mark of the king's appreciation, William was granted lands at Roslin and also became the queen's cup-bearer. This event is commemorated at Rosslyn Chapel by the carving on the south wall often referred to as 'two brothers on one horse'.[8] This shows the knight Leslyn, the ancestor of the Leslie family, on horseback with the future queen riding pillion. The queen is carrying a symbolic representation of the relic known as the Holy Rood of Scotland, which was part of her dowry. Thus the carving celebrates the arrival of the Holy Rood in Scotland, the first grant of land to the St Clairs by King Malcolm Canmore, and also provides an acceptable vehicle for the heretical Templar emblem of two brothers on one horse.

The first of the St Clairs to be born in Scotland, a certain Henri de St Clair, accompanied Godfroi de Bouillon to the Holy Land in 1096 and was present at the fall of Jerusalem.[9] He was accompanied by knights from eleven other leading Scottish aristocratic families. Representatives of all twelve families met regularly at Roslin prior to that crusade and for many centuries afterwards. The meetings originally took place at the castle and later, after 1490, at the chapel. They continued on a regular basis until the late eighteenth century, when all hopes of a Stuart restoration had died. The group included ancestors of the Stuarts, with whom the St Clairs made marital alliances: the Montgomerys, the Setons, the Douglases, the Dalhousies, the Ramsays, the Leslies, the Lindsays and the St Clairs. A group of families linked by marriage, blood and shared loyalties and beliefs who were involved with the Templars throughout their history, with the propagation of their traditions after the suppression, with early Freemasonry in Scotland and with support for the Stuart cause. Recent studies of the Rex Deus legend have suggested that the Stuarts were actually descended from leading families among the hierarchy in biblical Israel at the time of Jesus,[10] and even that the Stuart dynasty is still extant to this day.[11] It is reasonable, therefore, to presume that these beliefs in their biblical dynastic roots were shared by these twelve families who were so committed to both the Templars and the Stuarts.

Hidden 'Treasures'

The leading role played by the St Clairs in the preservation of Templar ideals through Freemasonry has already been mentioned. Two historical documents attest quite strongly to the preservation of secret knowledge within the family. One by Father Hay, the seventeenth-century St Clair historian, which Tim quoted in the *Illustrated Guide to Rosslyn*, reads as follows:

> About this time [1447] there was a fire in the square keep by occasion of which the occupants were forced to flee the building. The Prince's chaplain seeing this, and remembering all of his masters writings, passed to the head of the dungeon where they all were, and threw out four great trunks where they were. The news of the fire coming to the Prince through the lamentable cries of the ladies and gentlewomen, and the sight thereof coming to his view in the place where he stood upon Colledge Hill, he was sorry for nothing but the loss of his Charters and other writings; but when the chaplain who had saved himself by coming down the bell rope tied to a beam, declared how his Charters and Writts were all saved, he became cheerful and went to recomfort his Princess and the Ladys.[12]

It seems strange that Earl William was more concerned with the safety of his precious documents than with the welfare of his ladies. Chris Knight and Robert Lomas used this passage to support their thesis that Rosslyn Chapel had been built to house the sacred texts brought back from Templar excavations in Jerusalem.[13] This intriguing idea is further strengthened by the second document which dates from a later period. The National Library in Edinburgh contains a letter from Mary of Guise, the Queen Regent, writing in 1546 to Lord William St Clair of Roslin, in which she swears to be a 'true mistress' to him and protect him and his servants for the rest of her life in gratitude for being shown 'a great secret within Rosslyn'.[14] The general tone of the letter is bizarre; it is more like that of a subservient person to a superior lord than that of a sovereign to her vassal.

While we have no real knowledge as to the nature of this secret, it is reasonable to assume from the contents of Mary of Guise's letter that it is accessible from within the chapel. However, we do have more positive information as to what else might be contained within its vaults and hiding places. Predating this letter are two passages from the 'Acts of The Lords of Council in Public Affairs', which cast a puzzling light on the behaviour of the Lords of Roslin and which disclose that Rosslyn may well be the repository for some of the lost crown jewels and the Holy Rood of Scotland. Both passages are dated 21 March 1545.

> The lords ordain William St Clair of Roslin to produce within three days all jewels, vestments and ornaments of 'the abbay and place of Halyrudhous . . . put and ressavit within his place' so that the Cardinal and administrator may see them and that they may be 'usit in this solempnyt tyme now approchand, to the honour of god and halykirk and upoun the expens of the commendatar and administrator thai payand to the gentill men of the said place . . . the somme of xx lib. for thair labouris maid in keiping (tharof).[15]

The laird of Craigmillar protested by his procurator that he should be assoilzied in the matter against the laird of Roslin for detaining the Holyrood jewels.[16]

As far as can be established, the jewels and the Holy Rood entrusted to William St Clair were never recovered. Perhaps the disclosure of the great secret to Mary of Guise gave Lord William the means to silence his critics. Be that as it may, the whereabouts of both relic and jewels as well as the reasons for this act of apparent betrayal are mysteries which seem to defy explanation. Legend has it that they lie hidden somewhere in, or under, Rosslyn Chapel, guarded by the long-buried Lords of Roslin attired in their armour,[17] a strange burial tradition of the St Clairs that was immortalized by Sir Walter Scott:

> Seemed all on fire that chapel proud,
> Where Roslin's chiefs uncoffined lie;
> Each baron, for a sable shroud,
> Sheathed in his iron panoply . . .
> There are twenty of Roslin's barons bold
> Lie buried within that proud chapelle.[18]

All but one of the male members of the St Clair family were interred coffinless, beneath Rosslyn Chapel, encased in their armour, knightly and chivalrous unto death and beyond: Father Hay tells us that when the vaults were opened at the funeral of his stepfather, the body of yet another Sir William St Clair, buried on 3 September 1650 (the date of the battle of Dunbar) seemed to be entire.[19]

The possible implications of this, especially when one remembers that since that time the vaults have remained sealed and probably airless, are remarkable. Tim vividly remembers as a small child being taken to the vaults of St Michin's church in Dublin to shake hands with the mummified corpse of the first Norman invader of Ireland, Strongbow himself. It is highly likely that the conditions that obtain in the vaults of Rosslyn had the same effect on the corpses interred there.

Many of the problems of interpretation of the carvings at Rosslyn may be largely clarified if the vaults are opened, for they may contain the statues that once adorned the chapel walls. There is no sign of vandalism on any of the plinths where they rested; each one is clinically clean, as if the statuary had been re-moved with as much care as was originally lavished on their installation.[20] It seems hardly likely that they were destroyed on site by mobs of fanatical, iconoclastic Calvinists, despite the ru-mours and traditions that this was their fate. Some churches did receive advance warnings of the puritans' rampages and it is likely that Rosslyn was among them. Statuary from at least one other church, hidden for centuries, has recently been discovered at the bottom of a nearby lake. If a similar find were made at Rosslyn it could provide the essential key to the true import of the carvings.

Journey's End?

We puzzled over these problems when we reached Rosslyn at the end of our recreation of the pilgrimage of initiation. Whatever metaphors are used by different cultures to describe a pilgrim-age towards a fixed goal, certain descriptive terms are common to them all. There is a specific road to be followed for a great distance, which is described as being both difficult and demanding. The pilgrim is not merely undertaking a physical journey but is, at a far higher level, inwardly seeking his spiritual destiny. There is also the mystical effect of the sacred landscape itself to be considered, and in our case the landscape of Spain, the peace and tranquillity of rural France and the mystical air of Rosslyn all combined to have a transformative effect.

Early on in our travels we had developed the habit of travelling by small back roads and mountain tracks, as if we could not get close enough to nature itself. We had seen the seasons change from the deep snow in the mountains in spring, to the dry and arid plains in central Spain in early summer. We had luxuriated in lush valleys, marvelled at panoramic views, and sat quietly in fields listening to the wildlife. We had been part of it all and had experienced at some inexplicable level the interconnectedness of all things; a small part of God's creation, not its masters. Now we both knew, not in an intellectual sense but in an experiential one, something of why the medieval mystics wrote so much of nature; an experience we shared not only with them, but with the spiritually insightful initiates of all cultures. Let them speak for themselves:

> Every single creature is full of God and is a book about God.
> Every creature is a word of God.[21]

> What is the test that you have indeed undergone this holy birth?
> Listen carefully. If this birth has truly taken place within you,
> then . . . every single creature points you toward God and towards
> this birth.[22]
>
> *Meister Eckhart*

> The word is a living being, spirit, all verdant greening, all creativity.
> This word manifests itself in every creature.[23]

Glance at the sun. See the moon and the stars . . .
All nature is at the disposal of humankind.
We are to work with it.
For without it we cannot survive.[24]
Hildegarde von Bingen

The day of my spiritual awakening
was the day I saw
– and knew I saw –
All things in God
and God in all things.'[25]
Mechtilde of Magdeberg

All praise be yours, my Lord, through sister Earth, our mother,
who feeds us in her sovereignty and produces various fruits and
coloured flowers and herbs.[26]
St Francis of Assisi

This we know – the earth does not belong to man, man belongs to
the earth. All things are connected like the blood which unites one
family. Whatever befalls the earth befalls the sons of the earth. Man
did not weave the web of life, he is merely a strand in it. Whatever he
does to the web, he does to himself.[27]
Chief Seattle

All things are the work of the Great Spirit. We should all know that
he is within all things: the trees, the grasses, the rivers, the
mountains, and all four legged animals, and the winged people: and
even more important, we should understand that he is above all
these things and peoples.[28]
Black Elk

Tao is beyond words . . . and beyond things
. . . it is not expressed . . . either in word or in silence.
. . . Where there is no longer word or silence
. . . Tao is apprehended.[29]

Chuang Tzu

Every church and cathedral we had visited was decorated by beautifully carved depictions of nature, which arose from the consciousness of medieval man. Symbols of an earlier form of consciousness, that of prehistoric man, can be seen in the many neolithic sites we found. These are stark reminders that nature's abundance and fertility were always of prime importance to the spiritual life of mankind. We are no different today. For all our technological expertise and intellectually developed conscious-ness, we are still dependent on and in awe of nature. The prophets of biblical Israel experienced Almighty God both in nature and in the history of their people, and so had the me-dieval mystics, the masons and the gnostics. This particular form of insight is so all-pervading that the seven steps of initiation are sometimes described in terms of the natural kingdom. The Sufi Attar wrote a poem called *The Colloquy of the Birds*, which describes initiatory pilgrimage in just this manner.

Now we had returned to Rosslyn it was time to consider what we had discovered along the way. Our thoughts turned again to the question which had originally inspired us: 'Did an align-ment of some of these specially sited and uniquely constructed cathedrals hide a secret configuration built to represent the Earth as the Temple of God as it is described in the Revelation?' As we sifted through the evidence it became clear to us that we had indeed rediscovered this secret configuration, this ancient Temple of God.

We have established that the seven Christian buildings comprising the apocalyptic configuration in stone, the churches and cathedrals at Roslin, Amiens, Paris, Chartres, Orléans, Toulouse and Compostela, were all founded on Druidic sites dedicated to the planetary oracles. The buildings had all been erected by insightful master masons, and contained carvings and artwork of immense esoteric significance. They were not merely places of mainstream Christian worship, but also three-dimensional esoteric teaching boards of gnostic belief.

The use of these buildings as part of the pilgrimage of initiation is incontrovertible. When we related the medieval gnostic's pilgrimage of initiation to its ancient Egyptian predecessor, we found proof that the configuration was intended to be the representation of the Temple of God on Earth. The Knights Templar, in common with many other gnostic groups, derived their spiritual roots from the esoteric traditions of Egypt and biblical Israel. Peter Dawkins states unequivocally that in ancient Egypt the initiatory sites were erected on the Earth chakras and were held to be a living temple built by the Spirit of God, where mankind could reunite the human spirit with the divine as the result of an alchemical process. In the light of the history of gnosticism and Templar beliefs it is plain that the apocalyptic configuration in stone is a precise replication of just that principle.

But what of the second idea, that of the prophetic element of the alignment? We could not put aside the conviction that the actual geographical location of Rosslyn and the Apprentice Pillar was an integral part of some great unsolved mystery concerning both the symbolism of the Apocalypse and the exact date in which its most crucial events would take place.

The Oracle Speaks

Trevor had been convinced that when the relationship of the planets in the heavens represented that of the seven planetary oracles in our configuration, this would herald a time of cataclysmic change. We had to ascertain whether this replication was even possible. If it were to prove viable, then perhaps the chapel would disclose yet another secret, the date of apocalyptic change.

The positions of each of the seven major sites were plotted, and then mapped in order to see if they would marry up with the projected positions of the planets in the heavens.

The actual mapping was relatively simple, but assessing whether they matched the planetary alignments was far more complex. The many imperfect ways of trying to produce a viable map of the curved surface of the Earth on a flat piece of paper were dealt with by using a variety of projections. In each projection several maps were drawn in different scales. Then came the problems inherent in projecting a small part of the Earth's surface onto the great dome of the heavens. We used a print-out of the skyglobe computer programme and compared that to the wide range of maps we had produced. As we studied the immense variations in the relative positions of the planets, all of which move in different orbits through three dimensions, each according to its own timescale, we had serious doubts as to whether or not the theory could be accurately tested at all.

Surprisingly, we did find a date on which not only did the planets align themselves in the order of the sites, but when we compared the print-out to one of our large-scale maps covering a major proportion of the northern hemisphere, the replication was almost exact. The date of this alignment in the heavens is one that falls well within the lifetime of most of our readers.

That date is 28 July 2019.

The Apocalypse and the Aquarian Age

Many fundamentalist Christians, as well as a large proportion of the general public, believe that apocalyptic prophesies herald the end of the world. The visions conveyed by biblical sources, esoteric tradition and teachings from all the great religions tell a very different story. There is a startling similarity between the Essene, Christian and Hindu beliefs concerning the cataclysmic events usually associated with the apocalypse. These traumatic times are believed to herald not the end of civilization as we know it, but the dawn of a new era where life will be transformed into 'heaven on earth'.

The dualistic imagery of the Revelation of St John describes the catastrophes that will be followed by the creation of a 'New Jerusalem'. The Knights Templar and the hidden streams of spirituality carried this message down through the ages, as did popular tradition acting out its role as part of the 'hidden hand' of history. The result is that as we move into the twenty-first century, while many people are unfamiliar with the biblical idea of the New Jerusalem, they willingly accept the concept of the 'New Aquarian Age'.

It is widely recognized that we live in a transitional period between two astrological eras. We are leaving the Age of Pisces, a 2000-year period characterized by failure, brutal intolerance, changeability and despondency. For the last forty years we have been in transition, moving into the Age of Aquarius. According to astrologers, under the influence of this sign there will be a strong emphasis on science used not for its own sake, but in the service of humanity. It is believed to be a time of growing international co-operation and possible world government when mankind can apply warm-hearted generosity to practical ends. It is also predicted that there will be a reconciliation between science and the ageless stream of truths that run through man's unconscious. According to *The New Compleat Astrologer* the Age of Aquarius will be exciting, stimulating and at times dangerous.

Ever since the social activism of the 1960s and the 'consciousness revolution' of the early 1970s, we have been moving towards a transformation of society which flows from an individual and spiritual form of internal transformation – change from the inside out. This process can provide the means to achieve the more harmonious way of life prophesied for the new age. A new spiritual climate is emerging wherein the old gnosis is being used like a warrior's sword against the aggression of destructive technologies.

This change in consciousness is as startling as all those that preceded it. We live in an era characterized by a high moral idealism and a deep spiritual thirst. The great task that now confronts us is to seek a new ecology of the spirit.

The full richness of many religious cultures, the whole spectrum of worldwide mystical experience, has now become available to entire populations. Mystical literature abounds and courses offering instruction in a wide range of meditative and contemplative techniques are easily accessible. Holistic therapies such as reflexology, which dates back to ancient Egypt, and acupuncture, which was practised by the ancient Chinese, are gaining wide acceptance. All offer pathways that help people connect to new sources of spiritual change, personal transformation, integration, harmony and unity. A vast global constituency is arising formed of the spiritually aware among us who seek peace, non-violent change, justice and harmony. This is the audience to which Rosslyn will speak.

In a recent publication, *The Holy Land of Scotland*, the author, Barry Dunford quoted an article published earlier this century which stated:

> In many respects Scotland is a chosen land; there is a Greek tradition that Abaris was a Caledonian, and visited Greece in the days of her early mysteries, and brought to the Druids and others some knowledge of the Ancient Wisdom . . . Some of the sacred spots seem still to be *alive* with the spirit of the old gods and initiates . . . let Scotland prepare the way of the Lords of Wisdom.[30]

Scotland, the home of the St Clairs of Roslin, was the resting place chosen by the Templars as the repository of their treasure and their secrets. Rosslyn Chapel was built specifically as the memorial for the order, but it is far more than that. Encoded in its carvings are signposts to every effective spiritual path known at the time of its construction, that will be of vital importance in effecting the transformation of consciousness that is to bring about the new age. Trevor Ravenscroft perceived that Earl William St Clair had foreknowledge of our present scientific age with mankind gaining apparent mastery over nature. The earl knew that the day would come when the world would need the knowledge and spiritual insight preserved by the Knights Templar. Is this why the leader of the Black Tantric Buddhist sect described Rosslyn Chapel as a centre of world peace? This belief is further supported by the fact that there are two Tibetan Buddhist centres in Scotland, one in Eskdalemuir and one on

Holy Isle, off the island of Arran, which operates as an inter-faith centre for people from all faiths.

We believe that hidden within the fabric of the chapel are the scrolls discovered by the Templars during their excavations in Jerusalem, containing what HRH Prince Michael of Albany describes as 'the fruits of thousands of years of knowledge'. Along with these will be religious artefacts from the Temple in Jerusalem of incalculable value to historians, archaeologists and those of the Judaeo-Christian faiths. It is inevitable also that Earl William will have left his own personal message for posterity. Records disclose that the vaults contain the mortal remains of the Lordly line of the High St Clairs; a family so intimately en-twined with the Templars and their traditions of service to the communities in which they moved.

Templar teaching and tradition were about brotherhood, service, co-operation and the management of natural resources. They were devoted to the protection of others, particularly those more vulnerable than themselves. These are the very insights we need to act upon if we are to bring about a peaceful new age.

The evolution of consciousness and mind have given us the capacity to create great art, design wondrous buildings and com-pose great works of music, but it has also granted other, more dubious benefits such as weapons of mass destruction. We know we have the responsibility of choice; self-responsibility has to be the keynote of the Age of Aquarius. Earl William's legacy to us will enable mankind to live in growing harmony with our own species and with nature, and to fulfil our spiritual destiny.

Within the next two years, a leading American university will undertake ground scans of the vaults of Rosslyn Chapel and also examine the walls of the building. That investigation is the first step in the long process of revealing Earl William's bequest to our nation.

NOTES

Introduction

[1] *Proverbs from Hell*, William Blake.

[2] *Kritik der Hegelschen Rechtsphilosophie*, Introduction, Karl Marx.

[3] Michael Baigent, Richard Leigh & Henry Lincoln.

[4] Michael Baigent & Richard Leigh.

[5] Andrew Sinclair.

[6] Chris Knight & Robert Lomas.

[7] Originally published by Sphere Books, England, in 1990, later by Carol Publishing Co NY and now by Samuel Weiser Inc.

[8] *The Mark of the Beast*, Ravenscroft & Wallace-Murphy, p54.

[9] *The Temple and the Lodge*, Baigent & Leigh.

[10] *Sie Sullen Ihn Nicht Haben*, Johann Nestroy, 1850.

Part I

[1] *To Roslin From The Far West*, published by Johnstone Hunter & Co, Edinburgh 1872.

[2] *Castellated and Domestic Architecture of Scotland*, McGibbon & Ross.

[3] *Account of a Tour in Scotland*, 1677, Thomas Kirk.

Chapter 1

[1] *Ruined Castles of Mid-Lothian*, p132.

[2] *The Rosslyn Chapel Guidebook*, p11.

[3] *The Forgotten Monarchy of Scotland*, HRH Prince Michael of Albany, p102.

[4] *ibid*, p13.

[5] *The Mark of the Beast*, Trevor Ravenscroft & Tim Wallace-Murphy, p64.

[6] There is a document attesting this and signed by King James II kept in Freemasons Hall in Edinburgh.

[7] *Guild Laws, Forest Laws & the Lawis and Custumis of Ye Schippis*, which are among the collection of St Clair related mss in the Scottish National Library.

[8] *The Mark of the Beast*, Ravenscroft & Wallace-Murphy, p63.

[9] *The Templar Legacy and the Masonic Inheritance within Rosslyn Chapel* Tim Wallace-Murphy, p39.

[10] Rosslyn Chapel Guidebook, p27.

[11] *Diary of my Scottish Tour*, Dorothy Wordsworth.

[12] Article in *Interiors* magazine, 1982.

[13] Such as in *The Hiram Key*, Chris Knight & Robert Lomas.

[14] *The Encyclopedia of Mystical and Paranormal Experience*, Rosemary Ellen Guiley.

[15] *An Illustrated Guidebook to Rosslyn Chapel*, Tim Wallace-Murphy, p10.

[16] *The Second Messiah*, Knight & Lomas, p32.

[17] See *The Hiram Key*, Chris Knight & Robert Lomas, pp133–4.

[18] *The Mark of the Beast*, Ravenscroft & Wallace-Murphy, p65.

[19] *An Illustrated Guidebook to Rosslyn Chapel*, Tim Wallace-Murphy, p18.

[20] *Scotland – Historic and Romantic*, Maria Horner Lansdale, p121.

[21] *Moses*, Emile Bloch.

Chapter 2

[1] *The Mark of the Beast*, Ravenscroft & Wallace-Murphy, pp69–71.

[2] *The Templar Legacy and the Masonic Inheritance within Rosslyn Chapel*, Tim Wallace-Murphy, p24.

[3] *The Hiram Key*, Knight & Lomas.

[4] *The Templar Legacy and the Masonic Inheritance within Rosslyn Chapel*, Tim Wallace-Murphy, p25.

[5] *An Illustrated Guidebook to Rosslyn Chapel*, Tim Wallace-Murphy, p3.

[6] *Rosslyn – East Meets West*, a video produced for The Friends of Rosslyn by Niven Sinclair.

Part II

[1] *The Templar Legacy and the Masonic Inheritance within Rosslyn Chapel,* Tim Wallace-Murphy, pp31–2.

[2] *ibid* p9.

[3] *The Mark of the Beast,* Trevor Ravenscroft & Tim Wallace-Murphy, p49.

[4] *The Templar Legacy and the Masonic Inheritance within Rosslyn Chapel,* Tim Wallace-Murphy, p16.

[5] *The Mark of the Beast,* Trevor Ravenscroft & Tim Wallace-Murphy, p50.

Chapter 3

[1] 'The Ley Hunters', an article by Richard Leviton in *The Power of Place,* James Swan ed, p245ff.

[2] 'Befriending the Dragon' by Prof Thomas Lin Yun in *The Power of Place,* James Swan ed, p201ff.

[3] *A Test of Time,* David Rohl, p14.

[4] *Ancient Egyptian Religions,* Stephen Quirke, pp152–5.

[5] *Newgrange,* Michael J O'Kelly, p8.

[6] The alignment of the pyramids of Giza with the constellation of the Belt of Orion is the main theme of *The Orion Mystery* by Adrian Gilbert & Robert Bauval.

[7] *The Power of Myth,* Joseph Campbell & Bill Moyers, p163.

[8] *The Mark of the Beast,* Trevor Ravenscroft & Tim Wallace-Murphy, p43.

[9] *ibid* p44.

[10] *The Descent of Consciousness and the Breakdown of the Bicameral Mind,* Julian Jaynes, pp83–94.

Chapter 4

[1] *A History of Scotland,* J A Wylie.

[2] *Celt, Druid & Culdee,* Isabel Hill Elder, p20.

[3] Strabo *Geographica*, IV, 4, 197–8.

[4] *De Situ Orbis*, III, 2, 18 & 19.

[5] *Celtic Art*, J Romilly Allen, p136.

[6] Minutes of the Antiquarian Society 1762.

[7] *Celt, Druid & Culdee*, Isabel Hill Elder, pp26–7.

[8] The Abbé de Fontenu's *Mem de Litterature*, tome Vii, p126.

[9] *Roman Britain*, R C Collingwood, p76.

[10] *Celt, Druid & Culdee*, Isabel Hill Elder, p27.

[11] Strabo, I, IV, p197 & Mela Pomponius, III, 2, 18.

[12] *Celtic Researches*, Davies ed, pp172–82.

[13] *Early English History*, Yeatman, p9.

[14] *America BC*, Barry Fell.

[15] *Celt, Druid & Culdee*, Isabel Hill Elder, p53; *Traditional Annals of the Cymry*, p27, & H Sharon Turner's *History Anglo Saxon* Vol 1.

[16] *Celtic Lore*, Ward Rutherford.

[17] An essay by Godfrey Higgins, 'Moral Doctrines of the Druids', from *The Celtic Druids*, cited in *The Druid Source Book*, compiled by John Matthews.

[18] *Vitae*, Introduction I, 5.

[19] *Stonehenge*, Sir Norman Lockyer, published in 1906.

[20] *Celtic Researches*, Davies ed, pp171–182.

[21] *De Divinatione*, I, 41, T D Kendrick trans.

[22] *De Bello Gallico*, VI.

[23] *Histories*, V, 28 & 31, Kendrick trans.

[24] *Historia Naturalis*, XVI, 249.

[25] *Histories*.

[26] *De Situ Orbis*.

[27] Strabo I, IV, p197; Caesar Comm Lib V; Suetonius, V.

[28] *Celt, Druid & Culdee*, Isabel Hill Elder, p55.

[29] Cicero, *De Divinatione*, I, 41.

[30] *Triads of Dynvall Moelmund*, ap Walter p315 listed in Vol III of *Ancient Laws of Cumbria*.

[31] Diogenes Laertius *in proem*, pp5–6.

[32] *The Mark of the Beast*, Ravenscroft & Wallace-Murphy, pp69–70.

[33] *Works* XV, 9, pp4–8.

34 *Stromata.*

35 *De Bello Gallico.*

36 *A History of the English Church and People,* Bede p66.

37 *Trias Thermaturga,* p156b.

38 *Malmes, History of the Kings,* pp19–20.

Chapter 5

1 *The Mark of the Beast,* Ravenscroft & Wallace-Murphy, pp48–9.

2 *A History of Christianity,* Paul Johnson, pp45–52.

3 *The Templar Legacy and the Masonic Inheritance within Rosslyn Chapel,* Tim Wallace-Murphy, pp12–13.

4 *A History of Christianity,* Paul Johnson, p55.

5 *Jesus ou le Mortel Secret des Templiers,* Robert Ambelain, p106, citing Josephus *Antiquities of the Jews,* book XX ch9.

6 *James the Brother of Jesus,* Robert Eisenman, Introduction, pxxxii.

7 Epiphanius-Haeres lxxviii.

8 The Gospel according to St Mark, ch6, v3, the King James version.

9 The Gospel according to St Matthew, ch13, v55.

10 *Homilies Clementines.*

11 The Gospel according to St Matthew, ch27, v56.

12 From *The Gospel of Thomas* as translated in *The Nag Hammadi Library* (revised edition), James Robinson ed.

13 From the Epistle to the Galatians, ch2, v9.

14 *Jesus ou le Mortel Secret des Templiers,* Robert Ambelain, p95.

15 *Putting Away Childish Things,* Uta Ranke-Heinemann, p173.

16 From *The Gospel of Thomas* as recounted in *The Nag Hammadi Library,* James M Robinson ed.

17 The Acts of the Apostles, ch2, v22 KJV.

18 Paul's first Epistle to Timothy 1, vs15–17, NIV.

19 Paul's Epistle to Titus 2, v13, NIV.

20 *The Bloodline of the Holy Grail,* Laurence Gardner, p154.

21 *Ecclesiastical History III,* xxvii, LCL, p261.

22 *ibid* IV, xvii, LCL II, p53.

[23] *A History of Christianity*, Paul Johnson, pp3–4.

[24] The Acts of the Apostles, ch15, vs1–26.

[25] *A History of Christianity*, Paul Johnson, p41.

[26] See the account preserved in the *Pseudoclementine recognitions*, and the chapter entitled *The Attack by Paul on James and the Attack on Stephen* in *James the Brother of Jesus*, Robert Eisenman.

[27] The Acts of the Apostles, ch21, v33.

[28] *James the Brother of Jesus*, Robert Eisenman, pp349–50, 389, 412, 441, 656, 798–9.

[29] First epistle to the Corinthians, ch9, vs1–6, NIV.

[30] First epistle to Timothy, ch2, vs5 & 7.

[31] *The Bloodline of the Holy Grail*, Laurence Gardner, p154.

[32] Cited by Douglas Lockhart in *Jesus the Heretic*, p230.

[33] *ibid* pp229–230.

[34] Origen, vir ill 2, cited in *James the Brother of Jesus*, Robert Eisenman, p395.

Chapter 6

[1] The first report of this was by the Roman commentator Lactantius in *De mort pers*, 44 (on the manner of death of the persecutors).

[2] *A History of the Church*, Hubert Jedin ed, Vol I, pp413–4.

[3] *A History of Christianity*, Paul Johnson, p76, & *A History of Heresy*, David Christie-Murray, p1.

[4] *A History of the Church*, Hubert Jedin ed, v1, pp416.

[5] DE Trintate 7. 7. 10.

[6] *The Coming of the Cosmic Christ*, Matthew Fox, pp31–2.

[7] *A History of Christianity*, Paul Johnson, p77ff.

[8] *A History of Heresy*, David Christie-Murray, p1.

[9] *A History of Christianity*, Paul Johnson, p117.

[10] *ibid* pp116–17.

[11] Cardinal Ratzinger, 1990, cited in *The Dead Sea Scrolls Deception*, Michael Baigent & Richard Leigh, p191.

[12] *The Formation of a Persecuting Society*, R I Moore, p12.

13 *The Early Church*, H Chadwick, pp169–70.

14 *The Formation of a Persecuting Society*, R I Moore, p13.

15 *A History of Christianity*, Paul Johnson, p424.

16 *The Mark of the Beast*, Trevor Ravenscroft & Tim Wallace-Murphy, p79.

17 Declaration of the Council of Hagia Sophia.

18 The Gospel of St John, ch1, v21.

19 Origen, from Contra Celsum.

20 *The Supergods*, Maurice Cotterell, p143.

21 *A History of Christianity*, Paul Johnson, pp135–8.

22 *Putting Away Childish Things*, Uta Ranke-Heinemann, p278.

23 *The Templar Legacy and the Masonic Inheritance within Rosslyn Chapel*, Tim Wallace-Murphy, p12.

24 *ibid* p13.

25 *The Mark of the Beast*, Trevor Ravenscroft & Tim Wallace-Murphy, pp76–8.

26 *The Forgotten Monarchy of Scotland*, HRH Prince Michael of Albany, p30.

27 *ibid* p19.

28 *Celt, Druid & Culdee*, Isabel Hill Elder, pp131–2, 134.

29 See *The Holy Land of Scotland*, Barry Dunford.

30 *A History of the English Church and People*, Bede, pp187–93.

31 *Celt, Druid & Culdee*, Isabel Hill Elder, p128.

Chapter 7

1 *The Formation of a Persecuting Society*, R I Moore, p2.

2 *The Mark of the Beast*, Trevor Ravenscroft & Tim Wallace-Murphy, p124.

3 *ibid* pp106–8.

4 *ibid* p132.

5 *ibid* p125.

6 *The Coming of the Cosmic Christ*, Matthew Fox, p63.

7 *Original Blessing*, Matthew Fox, p75.

8 *The Coming of the Cosmic Christ*, Matthew Fox, p63.
9 *Original Blessing*, Matthew Fox, p75.
10 *The Mark of the Beast*, Trevor Ravenscroft & Tim Wallace-Murphy, p73.
11 Chartres Cathedral Guidebook.
12 *The Mark of the Beast*, Trevor Ravenscroft & Tim Wallace-Murphy, p75.
13 *An Illustrated Guidebook to Rosslyn Chapel*, Tim Wallace-Murphy, p33.
14 *The Mark of the Beast*, pp73, 76–7, also cited in *Trois Notres Dames de Chartres*.
15 *Trois Notres Dames de Chartres*.
16 *The Mark of the Beast*, Trevor Ravenscroft & Tim Wallace-Murphy, p75.
17 *Mirrors of Truth*, Frederic Lionel.

Chapter 8

1 *The Ninth Century*, Walter Johannes Stein.
2 *The Power of Myth*, Joseph Campbell & Bill Moyers, p199.
3 *ibid* p197.
4 *ibid* p200.
5 *The History of the Knights Templar*, Charles Addison, 1842, p5.
6 *The Holy Blood and the Holy Grail*, Baigent, Leigh & Lincoln, p61.
7 'Une Vie par reforme l'église', Michel Kluber, in the journal *Bernard de Clairvaux*, les editions de l'Argonante.
8 *Bernard de Clairvaux*, les editions de l'Argonante.
9 *Liber ad milites Templi: De laude novae militae*.
10 The Copper Scroll discovered at Qumran.
11 *The Sign and the Seal*, Graham Hancock, p363.
12 *The Mark of the Beast*, Ravenscroft & Wallace-Murphy, p52, and *The Hiram Key*, Lomas & Knight, p306.
13 *The Forgotten Monarchy of Scotland*, HRH Prince Michael of Albany, p61.
14 *The Holy Blood and the Holy Grail*, Baigent, Leigh & Lincoln, pp373&ff.

[15] *Histoire Généalogique de la Famille de St Clair*, L-A De Saint Clair, Paris 1905.

[16] *The Holy Blood and the Holy Grail*, Baigent, Leigh & Lincoln, p59.

[17] *The Trial of the Templars*, Malcolm Barber, p6.

[18] *The Holy Blood and the Holy Grail*, Baigent, Leigh & Lincoln, p61.

[19] *The Second Messiah*, Knight & Lomas, pp78&ff.

[20] *An Illustrated Guidebook to Rosslyn Chapel*, Tim Wallace-Murphy, p35.

[21] See *Les Sites Templiers de France*, éditions Ouest-France, for a fairly comprehensive list of most Templar sites so far identified in France.

[22] The original document can be found in the archives of St James of Compostela.

[23] *The Templar Legacy and the Masonic Inheritance within Rosslyn Chapel*, Tim Wallace-Murphy, p42.

[24] This is one of the main objectives ascribed to the Templars in *The Holy Blood and the Holy Grail*.

[25] See *The Chronicles of the Crusades*.

[26] *The Forgotten Monarchy of Scotland*, HRH Prince Michael of Albany, p118.

[27] Derived from conversations with Michael Bentine recorded in the video film, *Rosslyn – East Meets West*.

[28] *The Templar Legacy and the Masonic Inheritance within Rosslyn Chapel*, Tim Wallace-Murphy, p21.

[29] *The Mark of the Beast*, Ravenscroft & Wallace-Murphy, p52.

[30] *A History of Heresy*, David Christie-Murray, pp104–8.

[31] *The Trial of the Templars*, Malcolm Barber, p46.

[32] *The Mark of the Beast*, Ravenscroft & Wallace-Murphy, p53.

[33] *The Forgotten Monarchy of Scotland*, HRH Prince Michael of Albany, pp62–4.

[34] *The Templar Legacy and the Masonic Inheritance within Rosslyn Chapel*, Tim Wallace-Murphy.

[35] To judge the importance of John the Baptist to the Templars, see the allegation against the Templars and Freemasons by Pope Pius the ninth, which accuses the Order of belief in the Johannite heresy from the outset. Also Amiens Cathedral, financed by the Templars, was built to house the relic containing the head of the Baptist.

36 *The Cult of the Black Madonna*, Ean Begg, p103.
37 *The Sign and the Seal*, Graham Hancock, p334.
38 *Born in Blood*, John Robinson, p137.
39 *The Mark of the Beast*, Ravenscroft & Wallace-Murphy, p40.
40 *Born in Blood*, John Robinson, p137.
41 *ibid* pp164–6.

Chapter 9

1 The Gospel according to St Matthew, ch7, vs15–20.
2 *The Mysteries of Chartres Cathedral*, Louis Charpentier, p86.
3 *ibid* p145.
4 *The Cathedrals' Crusade*, Ian Dunlop, p6.
5 Information supplied by the Provençal Templar scholar, Guy Jordan.
6 *La règle de St Devoir de Dieu et de la Croissade.*
7 *The Secret Zodiac*, Fred Gettings.
8 *La filiation généalogique de toutes les Écoles Gothiques*, J F Colfs 1884.
9 *The Templar Legacy and the Masonic Inheritance within Rosslyn Chapel*, Tim Wallace-Murphy.
10 *A New Model of the Universe*, P D Ouspensky, p345, Arcana ed.
11 *Le Mystère des Cathedrales*, Fulcanelli, p36.
12 *ibid* pp39–41.
13 *An Illustrated Guidebook to Rosslyn Chapel*, Tim Wallace-Murphy, p24.
14 Robert Graves in his Introduction to the first English edition of *The Sufis*, Idries Shah.
15 *The Myth of the Goddess*, Baring & Cashford, pp411–12.
16 *The Rise of the Gothic*, William Anderson.
17 *The Forgotten Monarchy of Scotland*, HRH Prince Michael of Albany, pp64–5.
18 *ibid* p150.
19 *The Templar Legacy and the Masonic Inheritance within Rosslyn Chapel*, Tim Wallace-Murphy, p24.

Part III

[1] *Unfinished Animal,* Theodore Roszak, p9.

[2] *The Turning Point,* Fritjof Capra, p38.

[3] *The Mark of the Beast,* Ravenscroft & Wallace-Murphy, p55.

Chapter 10

[1] *The Templar Legacy and the Masonic Inheritance within Rosslyn Chapel,* Tim Wallace-Murphy.

[2] *An Illustrated Guidebook to Rosslyn Chapel,* Tim Wallace-Murphy, p21.

[3] *The Hiram Key,* Chris Knight & Robert Lomas, p314.

[4] *The Mark of the Beast,* Ravenscroft & Wallace-Murphy, pp69–70.

[5] *The Elements of Earth Mysteries,* Philip Heselton, p78.

[6] The second book of Kings, ch2, v12 (KJV).

[7] *Following the Milky Way: a pilgrimage across Spain,* Elyn Aviva, published by the Iowa State University.

[8] *ibid.*

[9] *ibid.*

[10] This particular pilgrimage on horseback was funded by a Churchill Scholarship.

[11] *The Elements of Earth Mysteries,* Philip Heselton (Element, 1991), p79.

[12] Herbert Spenser.

Chapter 11

[1] *The Desert,* M Louise Haskins.

[2] *The Guide Book to the Cathedral of Santiago de Compostela.*

[3] *ibid.*

[4] Cited in *The Guide Book of Santiago de Compostela.*

[5] *The Guide Book of Santiago de Compostela.*

[6] *The Gospel of Thomas* as translated in *The Nag Hammadi Library.*

[7] The Acts of the Apostles.

[8] Article entitled 'Les Templiers dans les Alpes-Maritimes', by J-A Durbec, *Nice Historique* Jan/Feb 1938, pp4–6.

[9] *Points of Cosmic Energy*, Blanche Mertz, p121.

[10] *Chakras for Beginners*, Naomi Ozaniec, pp6–7.

[11] *An Illustrated Guidebook to Rosslyn Chapel*, Tim Wallace-Murphy, p10.

[12] The Gospel according to St Matthew, ch6, v22.

[13] *The Templars*, Malcolm Barber.

[14] *Chakras for Beginners*, Naomi Ozaniec, p16.

[15] *The Guide Book to the Cathedral of Orléans*.

[16] *Chakras for Beginners*, Naomi Ozaniec, p25–26.

Chapter 12

[1] *The Mark of the Beast*, Ravenscroft & Wallace-Murphy, pp73–4.

[2] *ibid* p76.

[3] *The Mysteries of Chartres Cathedral*, Louis Charpentier, p81.

[4] *ibid*.

[5] *The Mark of the Beast*, Ravenscroft & Wallace-Murphy, p73.

[6] *The Mysteries of Chartres Cathedral*, Louis Charpentier, p165.

[7] *ibid* p139.

[8] *Points of Cosmic Energy*, Blanche Mertz, p105.

[9] *Les Trois Notre Dame de Chartres*, Y Delaporte, p11.

[10] *The Mysteries of Chartres Cathedral*, Louis Charpentier, p121.

[11] *Points of Cosmic Energy*, Blanche Mertz, pp110–11.

[12] *Les Trois Notre Dame de Chartres*, Y Delaporte, p33.

[13] *The Mysteries of Chartres Cathedral*, Louis Charpentier, p25.

[14] *Points of Cosmic Energy*, Blanche Mertz, p110.

[15] *The Mark of the Beast*, Ravenscroft & Wallace-Murphy, p52.

[16] This forms the main theme for *The Hiram Key* by Knight & Lomas.

[17] *Le Mystère des Cathédrales*, Fulcanelli, p70.

[18] *Les Oeuvres de Nicolas Grospony et Nicolas Valois*, Mss biblioth de l'Arsenale, no2516, p176.

[19] Etteila in *Le Dernier du Pauvre* from *Sept nuances de l'oeuvre philosophique*, (1786), p57.

[20] *Nouvelle Lumière Chymique, Traite du Mercure,* Jean d'Houry (1695), ch IX, p41.

[21] *Le Mystère des Cathedrales,* Fulcanelli, pp104–5.

[22] *De Bello Gallico.*

[23] *Chakras for Beginners,* Naomi Ozaniec, pp48–9.

[24] *The Cathedral of Amiens,* brief guide, p5.

[25] *Le Mystère des Cathedrales,* Fulcanelli, p123.

[26] *The Gospel of Thomas* as told in *The Nag Hammadi Library,* James M Robinson ed, p131.

[27] *Chakras for Beginners,* Naomi Ozaniec, pp57 & 60.

Chapter 13

[1] Tessa Ranford, cited by Chris Knight & Robert Lomas in *The Second Messiah,* p32.

[2] *Following the Milky Way: a pilgrimage across Spain,* Elyn Aviva, published by the Iowa State University.

[3] *The Orion Mystery,* Adrian Gilbert & Robert Bauval.

[4] *Arcadia,* Peter Dawkins, p39.

[5] *ibid* p39.

[6] *ibid* p40.

[7] *ibid* p40.

[8] *ibid* pp40–1.

[9] *ibid* pp40–1 & 44.

[10] *ibid* pp40–1 & 44.

[11] This gives further proof of the origins of the Templar cult of the Black Madonna, displays the roots of the veneration of the Virgin of the Apocalypse and reinforces the esoteric significance of Bernard of Clairvaux's sermons on the Song of Solomon.

[12] *The Mark of the Beast,* Ravenscroft & Wallace-Murphy, p68.

[13] *Arcadia,* Peter Dawkins, p41 & 58.

[14] *The Trial of the Templars,* Malcolm Barber, p213.

[15] *The Templar Legacy and the Masonic Inheritance within Rosslyn Chapel,* Tim Wallace-Murphy, p21.

[16] *Arcadia*, Peter Dawkins, p59.

[17] *Sur les Traces des Templiers dans le Var*, published by the Musée des Empreintes et Traditions des Maures et Provence, p50.

[18] *Arcadia*, Peter Dawkins, p59.

[19] *ibid* p59.

[20] *ibid* p60.

[21] *ibid* p61.

[22] *ibid* p61.

[23] *ibid* p61.

[24] *ibid* p62.

[25] *The Encyclopedia of the Occult*.

[26] *Hebrew Myths – The Book of Genesis*, Robert Graves.

[27] The historian of druidism and early religious beliefs.

[28] For further information see *The Spear of Destiny*, Trevor Ravenscroft.

[29] *The British*, Walter Johannes Stein.

[30] From a conversation at Rosslyn between Professor Thomas Lin Yun and Tim Wallace-Murphy.

[31] *Le Mystère des Cathedrales*, Fulcanelli.

[32] The Wordsworth *Dictionary of the Occult*, p50.

Chapter 14

[1] *Genealogie of the Saint Claires of Rosslyn*, Fr R A Hay, Edinburgh 1835.

[2] *An Illustrated Guidebook to Rosslyn Chapel*, Tim Wallace-Murphy.

[3] The video film, *Rosslyn – East Meets West*, produced by Niven Sinclair for the The Friends of Rosslyn.

[4] *Histoire Généalogique de la Famille de Saint Clair*, L-A de Saint Clair, Paris 1905.

[5] *ibid*.

[6] *ibid*.

[7] *The Templar Legacy and the Masonic Inheritance within Rosslyn Chapel*, Tim Wallace-Murphy, p25.

[8] *An Illustrated Guidebook to Rosslyn Chapel*, Tim Wallace-Murphy, p34.

9 *Histoire Généalogique de la Famille de Saint Clair*, L-A de Saint Clair, Paris 1905.

10 *The Bloodline of the Holy Grail*, Laurence Gardner.

11 *The Forgotten Monarchy of Scotland*, HRH Prince Michael of Albany.

12 *Genealogie of the Saint Claires of Rosslyn*, Fr R A Hay.

13 *The Hiram Key*, Knight & Lomas, p307.

14 Also cited by Fr Hay in *The Genealogie of the Saint Claires of Rosslyn*.

15 *Acts of The Lords Of Council In Public Affairs 1501–1554*, selections from the *Acta Domiorum Concili*, introductory to the Privy Council of Scotland, Robert Kerr Hannay ed, Edinburgh 1932, p540.

16 *ibid* p540.

17 *An Illustrated Guidebook to Rosslyn Chapel*, Tim Wallace-Murphy, p10.

18 'The Lay of the Last Minstrel', Sir Walter Scott.

19 *The Genealogie of the Saint Claires of Rosslyn*, Rev Fr Hay.

20 *An Illustrated Guidebook to Rosslyn Chapel*, Tim Wallace-Murphy, p21.

21 Meister Eckhart: the work of this important medieval mystic is available in a series of books entitled *Meditations with . . .* Published by Bear & Co in the USA, all available in the UK.

22 *ibid.*

23 Hildegarde von Bingen, much of whose work is also available in the *Meditations with* series mentioned above.

24 *ibid.*

25 Mechtilde of Magdeburg, also available in the *Meditations with* series.

26 *The Canticle to the Sun*, St Francis of Assisi.

27 Chief Seattle, cited by John M Rich in *Chief Seattle's Unanswered Challenge*.

28 Neihart, John G, *Black Elk Speaks*, Washington Square Press, 1959.

29 *The Way of Chuang Tzu*, Thomas Merton (James Legge trans), p152.

30 Theosophy in Scotland, August 1910.

SELECTED BIBLIOGRAPHY

Addison, Charles G, *The History of the Knights Templar*, Black Books, London, 1995

Albany, HRH Prince Michael of, *The Forgotten Monarchy of Scotland*, Element, Shaftesbury, 1998

Albright W F, *From the Stone Age to Christianity*, Doubleday, Baltimore, 1957

Allegro, John, *The Dead Sea Scrolls*, Penguin, London, 1964

Allen, Grant, *The Evolution of the Idea of God*, Watts & Co, London, 1931

Alvey, Ada, *In Search of St James*, Cornish, Cornwall, 1989

Ambelain, Robert, *Jesus ou le Mortel Secret des Templiers*, Editions Lafont, Paris, 1970

Anderson, William, *Green Man*, HarperCollins, London, 1991

Anderson, William, *The Rise of the Gothic*

Anon, *To Roslin From the Far West*, Edinburgh, 1872

Armstrong, Karen, *A History of God*, Mandarin, London, 1993

Ash, David and Hewitt, Peter, *The Science of the Gods*, Gateway Press, Bath, 1991

Ashe, Geoffrey, *The Virgin*, Paladin, St Albans, 1976

Aubarbier, Jean-Luc & Binet, Michel, *Les Sites Templier de France*, Ouest-France, Rennes 1995

Baigent, M & Leigh, R, *The Temple and the Lodge*, Corgi, London, 1992

Baigent, M & Leigh, R, *The Dead Sea Scrolls Deception*, Corgi, London, 1992

Baigent, M, Leigh, R & Lincoln, H, *The Messianic Legacy*, Jonathan Cape, London, 1986

Baigent, M, Leigh, R & Lincoln, H, *The Holy Blood and The Holy Grail*, Book Club Associates, 1982

Barber, Malcolm, *The Trial of the Templars*, Cambridge University Press, 1994

Barber, Malcolm, *The Templars*, Cambridge University Press

Baring, Anne & Cashford, Jules, *The Myth of the Goddess*, Arcana, London, 1993

Bartlett, Robert, *The Making of Europe*, Penguin, London, 1994

Bauval, R & Hancock, G, *Keeper of Genesis*, Heinemann, London, 1996

Bayley, Harold, *The Lost Language of Symbolism*, Carol & Co, NY, 1990

Bauval, Robert and Gilbert, Adrian, *The Orion Mystery*, Heinemann, London, 1994

Bede, *A History of the English Church and People*, Penguin, London

Begg, Ean, *The Cult of the Black Madonna*

Berman, R, *Vierge Noire – Vierge Initiatique*, Dervy, Paris, 1992

Berrisford-Ellis, Peter, *The Druids*, Constable, London, 1994

Blatch, Mervyn, *Cathedrals*, Blandford Press, Poole, 1980

Boch, Emile, *Moses*, Floris Books, Edinburgh, 1986

Bonvin, J, *Vierges Noires*, Dervy, Paris, 1988

Brandecourt, Jacques & Desobry, Jean, *Cathedral D'Amiens*, Lescuyer, Lyon

Brydon, R, *The Guilds, the Masons and the Rosy Cross*, Friends of Rosslyn, Edinburgh, 1994

Burman, Edward, *The Inquisition*, Aquarian Press, Wellingboro, 1984

Caesar, Julius, *The Gallic War and Other Writings*, Heron Press, 1969

Campbell, Joseph, *The Masks of God – Primitive Mythology*, Arkana, London, 1991

Campbell, Joseph, *The Masks of God – Occidental Mythology*, Arkana, London, 1991

Campbell, Joseph & Moyers, Bill, *The Power of Myth*, Doubleday, New York, 1988

Campos, José Guerra & Lafuente, Jesús Precedo, *Guide to the Cathedral of Santiago of Compostela*, Aldeasa, Spain, 1996

Cannon, Dolores, *Jesus and the Essenes*, Gateway Books, Bath, 1992

Capra, F, *The Tao of Physics*, Fontana, London, 1996

Capra, F, *The Turning Point*, Flamingo, London, 1983

Chadwick, H, *The Early Church*, Penguin, London, 1997

Charpentier, Louis, *Les Mystères Templiers*, Lafont, Paris, 1967

Charpentier, Louis, *The Mysteries of Chartres Cathedral*, RILKO, London, 1993

Christie-Murray, David, *A History of Heresy*, Oxford University Press, 1989

Collingwood, RC, *Roman Britain*

Cotterell, Maurice, *The Supergods*, Thorsons, London, 1997

Cotterell, M & Gilbert, A, *The Mayan Prophecies*, Element, Shaftesbury, 1995

Crossan, John Dominic, *Jesus–a Revolutionary Biography*, HarperCollins, San Francisco, 1994

Dawkins, Peter, *Arcadia*, The Francis Bacon Research Trust, England, 1988

Delaporte, Y, *Les Trois Notres Dames de la Cathédrale Chartres*, Editions Houvet, Chartres, 1965

de Saint Clair, L-A, *Histoire Généalogique de la Famille de St Clair*, Paris, 1905

Desgins, A, *L'Ordre de Templiers & La Chevalerie Maçonnique Templière*, Trédaniel, Paris, 1995

Doresse, J, *The Secret Books of the Egyptian Gnostics*, Librarie Plon, Paris, 1958

Dunford, Barry, *The Holy Land of Scotland*, Brigadoon Books, Aberfeldy, 1997

Dunlop, Ian, *The Cathedral Crusade*, Hamish Hamilton, London, 1982

Edwardes, Michael, *The Dark Side of History*, Granada, London, 1978

Eisenman, R and Wise, M, *The Dead Sea Scrolls Uncovered*, Element, Shaftesbury, 1992

Eisenman, R, *James the Brother of Jesus*, Faber & Faber, London, 1997

Elder, Isabel Hill, *Celt, Druid and Culdee*, Covenant Publishing, London, 1994

Ellis-Davidson, H R, *Gods and Myths of Northern Europe*, Penguin, London

Epstein, Isadore, *Judaism*, Penguin, London, 1964

Fleming, Ursula (ed), *Meister Eckhart*, Fount Paperbacks, London, 1988

Fortune, Dion, *Esoteric Orders and their Work*, Aquarian Press, Wellingboro, 1987

Foss, Michael, *Chivalry*, Michael Joseph Ltd, London, 1975

Fox, Matthew, *Original Blessing*, Bear & Co, Santa Fé, New Mexico, 1983

Fox, Matthew, *The Coming of the Cosmic Christ*, HarperCollins, San Francisco, 1988

Fox, Matthew, *Creation Spirituality*, HarperCollins, San Francisco, 1991

Fox, R L, *The Unauthorised Version*, Penguin, London, 1992

Fox, Robin Lane, *Pagans and Christians*, Penguin, London, 1988

Franke, Sylvia & Cawthorne, Thomas, *The Tree of Life and The Holy Grail*, Temple Lodge, London, 1996

Frazer, Sir James, *The Golden Bough*, Wordsworth Editions, Ware, 1993

Fulcanelli, *Le Mystère des Cathédrales*, Neville Spearman, Suffolk, 1977

Gardner, Laurence, *The Bloodline of the Holy Grail*, Element, Shaftesbury, 1997

Gattey, Charles Neilson, *Prophecy and Prediction in the Twentieth Century*, Aquarian Press, London, 1989

Gauthier, M, *Highways of the Faith*, Wellfleet, Secaucus, New Jersey, 1983

Gettings, Fred, *The Secret Zodiac*

Gimpell, Jean, *The Cathedral Builders*, Cresset, 1988

Godwin, Malcolm, *The Holy Grail*, Bloomsbury Publishing, London, 1994

Golb, Norman, *Who Wrote The Dead Sea Scrolls?*, Simon & Schuster, New York, 1996

Graffin, Robert, *L'Art Templier des Cathedrales*, Garnier, Chartres, 1993

Graves, Robert, *The White Goddess*, Faber & Faber, London, 1961

Graves, Robert, *Hebrew Myths – The Book of Genesis*

Gruber, Elmer, R and Kersten, Holger, *The Original Jesus*, Element, Shaftesbury, 1995

Hancock, Graham, *The Sign and the Seal*, Mandarin Paperbacks, London, 1993

Hassnain, Prof Fida, *A Search for the Historical Jesus*, Gateway Books, Bath, 1994

Hay, the Rev Fr, *The Genealogy of the Saint Claires of Rosslyn*, Maidment, Scotland, 1835

Heselton, Philip, *The Elements of Earth Mysteries*, Element Books, Shaftesbury, 1991

Jackson, J, *The Chivalry Of Scotland in the days of Robert the Bruce*, Edinburgh

Jaynes, Julian, *The Descent of Consciousness and the Breakdown of the Bicameral Mind*, Houghton, Mifflin Co, Boston, 1976

Jedin, Hubert (ed), *History of the Church – to Constantine*, Burns & Oates, Tunbridge Wells, 1989

Johnson, Paul, *A History of Christianity*, Penguin, London, 1978

Josephus, *Life, The Antiquities of the Jews & The Wars of the Jews*, Nimmo, Edinburgh, 1879

Kersten, Holger, *Jesus Lived in India*, Element Books, Shaftesbury, 1991
Kirk, Thomas, *Account of a Tour in Scotland*, 1677
Knight, Chris and Lomas, Robert, *The Hiram Key*, Century, London, 1996
Knight, Chris and Lomas, Robert, *The Second Messiah*, Century, London, 1997

Lacroix, P, *Military and Religious Life in the Middle Ages*, Chapman & Hall, 1874
Lamas, Manuel C, *Guide to Compostela*, Silex, Spain, 1996
Lancaster-Brown, Peter, *Megaliths, Myths And Men*, Bookclub Associates, 1977
Lionel, Frederic, *Mirrors of Truth*, Archedigm, Olney, 1991
Lockhart, Douglas, *Jesus the Heretic*, Element, Shaftesbury, 1997
Lockyer, Norman, *Stonehenge*, London, 1906
   The Lost Books of the Bible, Gramercy Books, New York, 1979

Mack, B, *The Lost Gospel – Q*, Element Books, Shaftesbury, 1993
Matthews, John (ed), *The Druid Source Book*, Blandford, London, 1996
Mertz, Blanche, *Points Of Cosmic Energy*, Daniel & Co, Saffron Walden, 1987
Mcgibbon & Ross, *Castellated and Domestic Architecture in Scotland*
Millar, Hamish & Broadhurst, Paul, *The Sun and The Serpent*, Pendragon Press, Cornwall, 1989
Miller, Malcolm, *Chartres Cathedral*, Pitkin Pictorials Ltd, Andover, 1992
Mitchell, Ann, *Cathedrals Of Europe*, Paul Hamlyn, Feltham, 1968
Mountfield, David, *Les Grandes Cathédrales*, PML, France, 1995
Moore, R I, *The Formation of a Persecuting Society*, Basil Blackwell, Oxford, 1990
Mullins, Edwin, *The Pilgrimage to Santiago*, Secker & Warburg, London, 1974

Neihart, John G, *Black Elk Speaks*, Washington Square Press, 1959
Nieuwbarn, M C, *Church Symbolism*, Sands & Co., London, 1910
Guide to *Notre Dame de Paris*, Association De Sulley, 1996

O'Kelly, Michael, *Newgrange*, Thames and Hudson, London, 1996

Ouspensky, P D, *A New Model for the Universe*, Arkana, London

Ozaniec, Naomi, *Chakras for Beginners*, Headway, London, 1997

Querido, Rene, *The Mystery of the Holy Grail*, Rudolf Steiner College, 1991

Quirke, Stephen, *Ancient Egyptian Religions*, British Museum, London, 1995

Ranke-Heinemann, Uta, *Putting Away Childish Things*, HarperCollins, New York, 1995

Ravenscroft, Trevor, *The Spear of Destiny*, Samuel Weiser Inc, York Beach, Maine, 1982

Ravenscroft, Trevor, *The Cup of Destiny*, Samuel Weiser Inc, York Beach, Maine, 1982

Ravenscroft, Trevor & Wallace-Murphy, Tim, *The Mark of the Beast*, Sphere Books, London, 1990

Richards, M C, *The Crossing Point*, Weslyan University Press, Middletown, Connecticut, 1973

Rigby, Greg, *On Earth As It Is In Heaven*, Rhaedus, Alet-les-Bains, 1996

Robinson, James M, *The Nag Hammadi Library*, HarperCollins, San Francisco, 1990

Robinson, John J, *Born in Blood*, Arrow, London, 1993

Rohl, David, *A Test of Time*, Century, London, 1995

Roszak, Theodore, *Where the Wasteland Ends*, Faber & Faber, London

Roszak, Theodore, *Unfinished Animal*, Faber & Faber, London, 1976

Runciman, Stephen, *A History of the Crusades*, (3 vols), Pelican, London, 1971

Rutherford, Ward, *Celtic Mythology*, Aquarian Press, London, 1987

Schonfield, Hugh, *The Essene Odyssey*, Element, Shaftesbury, 1993

Schonfield, Hugh, *The Passover Plot*, Element, Shaftesbury, 1985

Schonfield, Hugh, *The Pentecost Revolution*, Element, Shaftesbury, 1985

Schuré, Edouard, *The Great Initiates*, Harper & Row, San Francisco, 1961

Shah, Idries, *The Way of the Sufi*, Penguin, London, 1982

Shah, Idries, *The Sufis*, Octagon, London, 1996

Sinclair, Andrew, *The Sword and the Grail*, Century, London, 1992

Stein, Walter Johannes, *The British*

Stein, Walter Johannes, *The Ninth Century*, Temple Lodge Press, London, 1996

Stevenson, David, *The First Freemasons*, Aberdeen University Press, 1989

Stourm, *Notre Dame D'Amiens*, Hachette, 1960

Stoyanov, Yuri, *The Hidden Tradition in Europe*, Arkana, London, 1994

Swan, James A, *The Power of Place*, Quest Books, Wheaton, 1991

Thiering, Barbara, *Jesus the Man*, Corgi, London, 1992

The Tanakh, The Jewish Publication Society, Jerusalem

Thomas, Keith, *Religion and the Decline of Magic*, Penguin, London, 1991

Thompson, J, *The Illustrated Guide to Rosslyn Chapel & Castle, etc*, McNiven, Edinburgh, 1899

Trevor-Roper, Hugh, *The Rise of Christian Europe*, Thames & Hudson, London, 1965

Underhill, Evelyn, *Mysticism*, One World Publications, Oxford, 1993

Upton-Ward, G M, *The Rule of the Templars*, The Boydell Press, Suffolk, 1992

Villette, Jean, *Le Plan de la Cathédrale de Chartres*, Mayenne, Chartres, 1994

Waite, A E, *The Holy Kabbalah*, Oracle Press, Royston, 1996

Wallace-Murphy, T, *An Illustrated Guide Book To Rosslyn Chapel*, Friends of Rosslyn, Edinburgh, 1993

Wallace-Murphy, T, *The Templar Legacy and The Masonic Inheritance Within Rosslyn Chapel*, The Friends of Rosslyn, Edinburgh, 1994

Wilson, A N, *Jesus*, HarperCollins, London, 1993

Wilson, Colin, *The Occult*, Grafton, London, 1979

Wilson, E, *The Scrolls from the Dead Sea*, W H Allen & Co, London, 1955

Wilson, Ian, *Are these the Words of Jesus?*, Lennard Publishing, 1990

Wylie, J A, *A History of Scotland*

INDEX

Aaron 163
Abaris 44, 150, 212
Abelard of Paris 159
Abraham 62, 143, 165,
Abraxus, the 118
Abydos 182, 185, 190
Acts of John, The 90
Acts of the Apostles, The 60, 67, 68
Adam 62, 120
Agnus Dei, The 147
Ahuro Mazdao 36
Akhetaton, 182, 186
Alchemist's Pilgrimage, the 100, 179
Ambelain, Robert 55, 61,
Amiens 139, 177, 178
Amiens Cathedral 21, 111, 117, 129,
135, 176, 179, 191, 208
Ammianus Marcelinus 49
Andrea, Johann Valentin 126
Apollo 50, 174
Apprentice Pillar 13, 17–18, 208
Aristides 43, 56
Aristotle 44, 160
Ark of the Covenant, The 96, 111, 65–6
Artemis 49
Ashen Path, the 160
Astarte 76
Athelstan, Saxon King 116
Attar, the Sufi poet 207
Avebury 32, 48

Bacon, Francis 125
Baigent, Michael 98
Balantradoch xiii, 98
Balaton, Lake 42
Bannockburn 121
Baphomet 104, 177
Barnabas 61
Bauval, Robert 180
Beausseante, the 117, 120
Bede 78
Begg, Ean 127
Behedet 182, 187
Benedictines, the 25, 94, 110
Bentine, Michael 198

Bernard de Fontaines – Bernard of
Clairvaux, or St Bernard 94–8,
102, 105, 112
Bernardus 87, 159
Bernini 108
Black Elk 206
Black Madonna 17–18, 62, 105,
127, 163–4
Black Virgin 160, 181–2
Blake, William xi, 27
Blois, family of 199
Boaz 10, 110, 165, 179
Boethius 83, 160
Bogomils, the 117
Bonnie Prince Charlie 96
Book of Two Ways, The 181
Born in Blood 121
Botticelli, *see also* Philpepi,
Sandro 126
Bramante 108
Brehon Laws, the 41, 47
British Museum, the 40
Buhen 183–4
Bure-les-Templiers 99
Burgundy, Duke of 7, 94
Burns, Robert 5
Byron, Lord 5

Cali, Francois 176
Camiño de las Estrellas 138,
141, 180
Camiño de Santiago 138
Campbell, Professor Joseph 35,
36, 93
Cardinal Gray 23
Cardinal Ratzinger 73
Carnutes 155, 159
Carnutum 49, 155
Castor and Pollux 118, 174
Cathars 22, 28, 68, 81, 103, 117, 120,
121, 123
Cathedral of St James, *see also* St
James of Compostela, cathedral of
Celtic Church 38, 51, 77, 79–80,
83, 117

Celts 29, 38–52, 128, 170
Cenabum, *see also* Orleans 155
Cephas 61, 66
Chang-Tzu 207
Charlemagne 128
Charles the Bald 76
Charles the Simple, King of France 199
Charpentier, Louis 160
Chartres 13, 22, 45, 49, 87, 89, 100, 191
Chartres Cathedral 13, 22, 87, 111, 117–18, 129, 133, 139–40, 143, 159–60, 163, 165–6, 169, 176, 208
Chartres mystery school, the 22, 87, 89, 155, 159
Chartres, stained glass of 162
Children of Father Soubise, the 110–11
Children of Master Jacques, the 110–11, 121
Children of Solomon, the 110–12, 120, 178
Christ 53, 63–4, 66, 71–2, 95, 150–1, 160, 173
Cicero 45–6, 160
Cintra xi, 10, 159, 180, 183, 190
Cistercians, the 25, 94–5, 97–8, 105, 111, 115
Clement of Alexandria 50, 57, 59, 68, 90
Codex Callextinus, the 100, 129, 131–2, 144
Colfs, J F 113
College, The Invisible 126
Colloquy of the Birds, The 207
Columbus 19
Coming of the Cosmic Christ, The 71
Compagnonnage, the 95, 110–11, 115, 118
Compagnonnage Tuscana, the 111
Compagnons des Devoirs du Tour de France, les 110
Compagnons Passants 111, 121
Compostela 100, 128–31, 138–9, 141, 143–4, 148–9, 154–7, 163, 183, 188, 189
Compostela, Cathedral at, *see also* St James of Compostela, Cathedral of Confucius 100, 142, 173

Congregation of the Doctrine of the Faith 73, *see also* Inquisition, the
Constantine the Great 70–1, 108
Constantinople 177
Copernicus 125
Council of Hereford, the 79
Council of Nicea, the 90
Council of Troyes, the 97
Count of Champagne 94, 97–8, 199
Craftmasons, the 17, 25, 109–10, 121
Cuchullin 13
Culdee Church, *see* Celtic Church; Celtic Christianity
Cult of the Black Madonna, the 127
Cybele 13, 49, 89

d'Evreaux, family of 199
d'Houry, the Master Jean 173
da Vinci, Leonardo 27, 126
Dalai Lama, the 23
Dalhousies, the 200
David, King 62, 143, 145, 163
Dawkins, Peter 181–3, 208
de Beauvais, Vincent 160
de Bello Gallico 49
de Bouillon, Godfroi 200
de Chardin, Pierre Teilhard 37
de Charney, Geoffroi 104
de Gama, Vasco 106
de Molay, Jaques 103–4
de Montbard, Andre 94, 97–8
de Payne, Hughes 94–5, 97–8, 165
de Sarton, Walter 177
de Troyes, Chretien 92
Dead Sea Scrolls, the 65, 96
Demeter 13, 49, 89
Descartes 125, 136
Didymus Judas Thomas, *see* Thomas Didymus
Diodorus Siculus 45
Diogenes Laertius 42, 48, 150
Dionysius the Areopagite 117
Dionysos 36
Divitiacus 46
Donatus 160
Doncourt aux Templiers 99
Douglases, the 200

Druidism 46, 51, 79, 87–8, 130, 140, 142, 155–6, 164, 178, 183, 189, 191

Druids, the 41–51, 80, 150, 152–4, 157, 163, 169, 193, 194, 212

Drunmeton in Galatia 42

Dunford, Barry 212

Dunlop, Ian 110

Ebionites, the 61, 64–5, 67, 70

Edict of Milan, the 70–2

Edinburgh xii, xiv, 1, 189, 195

Egaria 36

Eisenman, Robert 55, 65

el Khidir 116, 120

Elephantine 181

Elijah 43, 75, 137

Elisha 137

Enoch 150

Epistle to the Corinthians 66

Epistle to Timothy 66

Epistles of St Paul 66–8, 80

Essenes 44, 56, 61–2, 90, 92, 104, 163, 181, 189–90, 194, 210

Etteila 172

Euclid 160

Eusabius 57, 64

Feng Shui 32

Fiskin, Judy 5, 7, 16–17

Floriated Cross, the 147

Fludd, Robert 126

Fox, Matthew 71

Freculpus 51

Freemasonry 13, 114, 121–2, 126, 200–1

Freemasonry, A New Encyclopedia of 79

Freemasons xii, 16–17, 21–2, 189

French Masonic ritual 104

Fulbertus 87, 160

Fulcanelli 113–14, 172–3

Fuller, Thomas 77

Gadarn Hysicion 42

Gaia 13, 49

Galatia 42, 44

Galileo 124–5

Gallician Church, the 79–80

Gettings, Fred 112

Giza, *see* Pyramids of Giza

Gnostics 70, 79–81, 86, 101, 107, 109, 141, 156, 179, 189, 207

Gnosticism 53–4, 107, 115–17, 124, 127, 177, 208

Goethe 27

Golden Book, the 160

Gospel according to St John 67–6, 89–90, 189

Gospel according to St Matthew 58–9, 67–8

Gospel according to St Mark 58–9, 67–8

Gospel of Love 68

Gospel of Mark, a secret apocraphal 68

Gospel of Thomas 59–60, 62, 93, 178

Grail, King of the 136, 193

Grail, the Holy, *see* Holy Grail

Graves, Robert 44, 115

Green, Mike xiv, 5, 19, 23

Gregory the Great 78

Griffin, Shirley 139

Guilliame of Tyre 94

Hay, Fr 201, 203

Heliopolis 182, 187

Henry II, King of England 79

Hermes 12, 132, 150–1, 188, 190, 193–4

Hermetic texts 34

Hermopolis 182, 186

Herod 57

Heroditus 46

Higgins, Godfrey 79

Hildegarde von Bingen 85, 206

Hiram Abif 13, 17

Hiram Key, The xi, 127

History of Heresy 72

History of the English Church and People, A 78

Holy Blood and the Holy Grail, The xi

Holy Grail,the 22, 80, 92–3, 101, 107, 136, 165

Holy Land of Scotland, The 212–13

Hopkins, Marilyn 23–4, 148, 152, 153–5, 164, 175

Horus 105

Howard, John Elliot 46
HRH Prince Michael of Albany 96, 213
Hrolf, *see* Rollo, first Duke of Normandy

Ibd Dihya 142
Idris 150
Illustrated Guide to Rosslyn, An 201
Imhotep 33
Inquisition, the 74, 81, 103, 120
Iraneus, Bishop of Lyon 64, 67
Ishtar 8, 12, 34, 88–89, 118, 120, 176
Isis 36, 62, 88–89, 105, 182
Issa 62
Ivry-le-Temple 99

Jacquin, *see* Joachin
James II, King 8
James the brother of Jesus, *see* James the Just
James the Great 57
James the Just 51, 55, 57–62, 64–70, 80, 89, 101, 145, 147, 149, 177, 189, *see also* St James the Less
James the Less 144, 181, *see also* James the Just
Janus 118
Jaynes, Julian 38
Jehovah 36
Jerusalem xiii, 10, 51, 55, 60, 65–6, 68–70, 77, 89, 94, 98, 100–1, 114, 162, 166, 177, 202, 210, 213
Jesus 14, 42, 51, 55–8, 61, 63–69, 71, 74, 78, 85, 88, 90–3, 96–7, 101, 105, 109, 117, 143–5, 151, 160, 176, 178, 189–90, 200
Joachin 10, 111, 165, 179
Joan of Arc 154
Johannite heresy 155
John the 'Disciple whom Jesus loved' 61
John the Baptist 56–7, 69, 145, 155–6, 177–8, *see also* St John the Baptist
John the son of Zebedee 59, 61
John Paul II 145
Johnson, Kenneth Rayner 113
Johnson, Paul 65

Jordan, Guy 177
Joseph, the father of Jesus 59, 65
Josephus 55, 69
Joses 58
Juda 58
Julian of Norwich 86
Julius Caesar 40, 45–6, 49–51, 155, 174
Jupiter 50, 170, 174, 178, 191–2
Jupiter Oracle 135, 173, 192

Kabbala 28, 83, 116
Kabeiros 181
Kepplar 125
Kerygmata Petrou 64, 67
Khammurabi 36
Kibeiri, the 44, 150, 163, 181, 191, 194
King Athelstan 116
Knight Gaudri of Touillon 95
Knight, Christopher 22, 166, 201
Knights Hospitaller 102, 105–6, 153
Knights of Alcantara 102
Knights of Calatrava 102
Knights of Christ 105, 121, 183
Knights of Santiago 106
Knights Templar xii–xiii, 1, 12, 15, 18, 22, 25, 62, 91–2, 94–108, 112–18, 120–2, 124, 126–8, 130, 136, 151, 153, 155–6, 162, 165–6, 177–8, 182–4, 196–8, 200–2, 208, 210, 212–13, *see also* Templar
Kundalini, the 130, 136

la langue verte 113
La Rochelle 99
Laertius 45
Laws, Brehon 42
Le Puy 129
le Troyes, Chretien 92
Leigh, Richard 98
Leon Cathedral 138
Leslies, the family of 200
Leslyn, Bartholemew Ladislaus 199–200
Levi, Magnus Eliphas 104
Lewis, C S 123
Liber Sancti Jacobi 144, see also *Codex Callextinus*

Lincoln, Henry 98
Lindsays, the family of 200
Lockyer, Sir Norman 43
Lomas, Robert 22, 166, 201
Louis VII of France 142
Lug's Chain 180
Luther, Martin 126

Maderno 108
Maeshowe 32
Magi, the 42, 50, 150, 172
Malcolm Canmore, King of Scotland
    199–200
Male, Emile 189
Mandylion, the 147
Mani 73
Manichaeism 73
Mark of the Beast, The xi–xiv, 24, 165
Mars 50, 170, 174–5, 192
Mars Oracle 135, 173, 191
Marx, Karl xi
Mary Magdelene 105
Mary of Guise 202–3
Mary the mother of Jesus 58–9, 61,
    65, 72, 88, 105, 145, 160, 172
Masada 40
Masonic Lodges 120
Masparo 34
Master Mason's pillar 143
Master Mateo 143–4, 148
Mechtild of Magdeberg 86, 206
Meister Eckhart 86, 126, 205
Melchizedek 43–4, 143, 163, 165,
    191, 194
Memphis 182, 187
Mercury Oracle 132, 150, 154,
    173, 189–90
Mercury 50, 150, 154, 174, 185, 189,
    see also Hermes
Mertz, Blanche 147–9, 162–4
Michaelangelo 27, 108
milice du Christ, la 94
Milky Way, the 10, 127, 138, 180
Milvian Bridge, battle of the 71
Minerva 50, 174
Mithras 76
Moissy-le-Temple 99
Mont St Michel 99
Montgomerys, the family of 200

Montségur 22
Moon Oracle 131, 138, 173, 189
Moses 28, 36, 43, 47, 61–2, 143, 150,
    163, 165
Moyers, Bill 34
Musée Cluny 174
Mystère des Cathédrales, Le 114

Nag Hammadi 60
Napoleon 159
Neifelheim, dragons of 17
Nestorians, the 83
New Compleat Astrologer, The 211
Newgrange 32
Newton, Sir Isaac 123, 125
Notre-Dame de Paris 21, 129, 135,
    139, 169, 174, 176, 178, 183
Notre-Dame la Dalbade 152, 189
Notre-Dame de Sous-Terre 88,
    133, 163
Numa Pompilius 36, 43, 111

ogham script 41
On the Consolation of Philosophy 83
Order of the Golden Fleece, the 71
Order of the Poor Knights of Christ
    and the Temple of Solomon, see
    Knights Templar
Origen 50, 69
Orion 35
Orion Mystery, The 180
Orleans 156–7, 190
Orleans Cathedral 21, 129, 133,
    155–7, 208
Osiris 34–6, 88, 185
Ovingdon skull, the 45

Parisii 170, 174
Pelagius 51
Philae 181–4
Philip le Bel 103–4
Philo of Byzantium 33
Philpepi, Sandro, see Botticelli
Phoenicians 40
Pilgrimage of Initiation 100–1, 126,
    176, 184, 204
pillar of the Nautes 174
Plato 43, 44
Pliny 46

Poitiers 129, 157
Polyhistor 50
Pomponius Mela 39, 46
Pórtico de la Gloria 143, 145
Posidonius 44
Prince Henry the Navigator 106
Priory of Sion 96–7
Priscillian of Avila 73
Ptolemy 160
Pyramid of Zoser 33
Pyramid Texts 33–5, 181
Pyramids of Egypt, the 33
Pyramids of Giza 32, 35
Pythagoras 43, 44, 50, 150, 160

Qumran 96, 166

Ramseys, the family of 200
Ravenscroft, Trevor xi–xiv, 7–8, 11,
    14, 24–5, 90, 124, 128–9, 139, 142,
    165, 188, 208, 212
Reformation, the 55, 123
Renaissance, the 123–4, 159
Revelation of St John, the xi, 80,
    89–92, 117, 207, 209
Rex Deus 97, 98, 136
Rheims 111, 117
Robert I, King of France 74
Robert the Bruce 121, 142
Robinson, John 121
Rocamadour 99
Røgnvald the Mighty, Earl of Möre 198
Rollo – first Duke of Normandy
    79, 199
Rosicrucian Manifestos 126
Rosicrucianism 13, 121–2, 126
Rosicrucians xii, 21–2, 126, 189
Roslin xiii, 1–2, 8, 13, 98, 180, 196,
    200, 208
Roslin Castle 5, 11, 198
Roslin Glen 41
Roslin Moor, battle of 6
Rosslyn Chapel xi–xiv, 1–2, 5–6,
    8–18, 20–4, 29, 31, 38, 54, 74, 87,
    94, 107–8, 115, 118–22, 127,
    129–32, 137, 139, 141, 143, 147,
    150, 159, 166, 170, 173, 176,
    179–80, 183, 188, 192–3, 195–6,
    199, 201, 203–5, 207–8, 212–13

Royal Society, the 27, 125–6
Rutherford, Ward 43

Santiago Matamoros 147
Saqqara 33
Saturn Oracle, the 137, 173,
    192–3, 196
scala philosophorum 170, 183
Schonfield, Hugh 104
Scott, Sir Walter 5, 203
Sefer-ha-Zohar 28
Seattle, Chief 206
Setons, the family of 200
Shah, Idries 104
Shakespeare 27
Shamash 36
Shell Pilgrimage 100
Shroud of Turin 147
Sibille, Pat 24, 151, 174, 178
Simon Peter 61
Sinclair, Niven xiv
Skara Brae 37
Skorzeny, Otto 22
Smith, Professor Morton 68
Socrates 43, 44
Solomon, King 43, 95, 111, 143,
    145, 163, 165, 176
Solomon's Temple 116
Sophia the goddess of Wisdom 88,
    104–5, 177, 190
Southerland, Douglas 11
Spear of Destiny, The xi–xii
Spence, Lewis 191
Spiritus Mundi 164, 190
St Anne 163
St Augustine of Hippo 71–3
St Bernard of Clairvaux, see Bernard
    de Fontain
St Clair of Roslin, Catherine de 94
St Clair Prince Henry 19
St Clair, Earl William 7–8, 12, 14, 19,
    22, 54, 74, 93, 107, 121, 124,
    136–7, 142, 151, 198, 201, 212–13
St, Clair family xiii–xiv, 5–8, 18–19
    97–8, 105, 121, 170, 196, 198,
    200–3, 212
St Clair, William the Seemly 79, 199
St Clair-sur-Epte xiii, 199
St David 80

St Denis in Montmatre 129
St Francis of Assisi 85, 142, 206
St George 119–20
St Gildas 50
St Gregory, the Bishop of Nyssa 75
St James of Compostela 18, 21, 127, 148, 179
St James of the Sword, *see* Knights of Santiago
St James the Great 101, 142, 144–5, 149
St James the Just, *see also* James the Just 144
St Jerome 59
St John the Baptist 75, 76, 104, 177
St John the Divine 89–90, 160
St Longinus 119–20, 192
St Mauritius 119–20, 192
St Michael 119, 191
St Patrick 79
St Paul 55, 62–4, 66, 68–9, 88, 101
St Peter 55, 61–3, 101, 108
St Thomas Aquinas 85
Stein, Dr Walter Johannes 90, 93, 188
Steiner, Rudolf 90
Stonehenge 32
Strabo 39
Stuart dynasty, the, 200
Sufis 28, 83, 115–16, 120, 150
Sufis, The 104
Suhrawardi 150–1
Sun Oracle, the 133, 173, 191
Sword and the Grail, The 2
Synod of Whitby 78–9

Tacitus 46
Tammuz 8, 12, 34, 88, 119–20
Tancred, Anthony 3, 4
Templand 99
Temple xiii, 99
Temple and the Lodge, The xii
Temple Bar 99
Temple in Jerusalem 97, 111, 136, 163
Temple Mount 96, 88, 114
Temple of Artemis at Ephesus 33
Temple of God on Earth 181, 207–8

Temple of Solomon 110, 116
Templecombe 99
Templehall 99
Templehof et Colmar 99
Templeton 99
Teutonic Knights 102, 105, 121
Thebes 181, 184, 190
Therapeutae 44, 181, *see also* Essenes
Thomas Didymus 14, 59–60
Thoth 12, 34, 150
Thupton Tushi 23
Tiberius 170
Toulouse 21, 129, 132, 15-142, 154, 189–90, 208
Tours 129, 157
Tree of Jesse 143–4, 148

Valois, Nicolas 170
Veil of Veronica 147
Venus 156, 174
Venus Oracle 133, 155, 157, 173
Vergez, Raol 110
Veruccio 126
Virgil 43
Virgin of the Pillar 164
Virgini Pariturae 49, 88
von Eschenbach, Wolfram 92

Waite, A E 79
William Rufus 79
William the Conqueror 76, 196
Wordsworth, Dorothy 5
Wordsworth, William 10
Wouivre 48, 128, 130, 164–5, 176
Wylie, Rev J A 42

Yeats, W B 27
Yggdrasil tree 17
Yun Lin, Professor Thomas 193

Zadok 194
Zadokites 44
Zebedee 59, 145
Zeus 33
Zimmer, Professor H 76
Zoroaster 27, 36
Zoser, *see* Pyramid of Zoser